THE EAST INDIAN PROBLEM IN TRINIDAD AND TOBAGO 1953-1962 TERROR AND RACE WAR IN GUYANA 1961-1964

DAURIUS FIGUEIRA

iUNIVERSE, INC.
NEW YORK   BLOOMINGTON

The East Indian Problem in Trinidad and Tobago 1953-1962
Terror and Race War in Guyana 1961-1964

iUniverse books may be ordered through booksellers or by contacting:

iUniverse
1663 Liberty Drive
Bloomington, IN 47403
www.iuniverse.com
1-800-Authors (1-800-288-4677)

Because of the dynamic nature of the Internet, any Web addresses or links contained in this book may have changed since publication and may no longer be valid.

ISBN: 978-1-4401-5996-1 (sc)
ISBN: 978-1-4401-5997-8 (ebk)

Printed in the United States of America

iUniverse rev. date: 7/16/2009

DEDICATION

This book is dedicated to: Surendranath Capildeo and Christine Thomas. Without their contribution to this project it would have never been realised. With thanks and gratitude.

CONTENTS

Introduction xi

Chapter 1   The Colonial Discourse of the East Indian Problem - Trinidad 1953-1962 1

Chapter 2   Flashpoints 1956-1962 52

Chapter 3   Machinations/Corruption .67

Chapter 4   Williams and the British: 1962 to 1971 78

Chapter 5   Terrorism and Race War: Guyana 1953-1964 126

Chapter 6   American Declassified Files 144

Chpater 7   The British Declassified Files 168

Bibliography 255

ACKNOWLEDGEMENTS

I must acknowledge the support of the following persons of vital importance to this project: Charmaine and Brendan, Dr. Hamid Ghany and the Research and Publications Committee of the UWI, St Augustine.

INTRODUCTION

This is the final instalment of a trilogy of works which started with: "Simbhoonath Capildeo: Lion of the Legislative Council Father of Hindu Nationalism in Trinidad and Tobago" and "Tubal Uriah Butler of Trinidad and Tobago Kwame Nkrumah of Ghana" followed. The trilogy deals with the formation of neo-colonial states through the eyes of politicians of Trinidad and Tobago, Ghana and Guyana and the imperialist agendas of the colonial Massa the British and the post World War 2 hegemon the United States of America.

This present volume deals specifically with the formation of the neo-colonial states of Trinidad and Tobago and Guyana with specific emphasis on race relations, the British colonial overlord, American hegemony and the politicians of Trinidad and Tobago and Guyana. The emphasis of this volume is on the declassified files of the British and Americans to unearth their covert and overt strategies towards the creation of neo-colonial states, Trinidad and Tobago and Guyana, subservient and pliant to their geo-political interests. What is unearthed in the process are the lies of Independence fed to us by the politicians of the 1960's that insist these independent states were in fact the creation of the maximum leaders of Dr. Eric Williams of Trinidad and Tobago and Linden Forbes Burnham of Guyana. What is revealed is the hand of the British and Americans in fashioning these states to serve their interests and the use of a racist agenda to serve their power relations. The race relations of Trinidad and Tobago and Guyana are then the product of the North Atlantic imperialist agenda. In addition race relations in Trinidad and Tobago and Guyana involve Indo and Afro Trinbagonians and Guyanese with the Indo Guyanese being the majority race in the 1960's in Guyana and the Afro Trinbagonians was the majority race in Trinidad and Tobago in the 1960's. In addition because of the impact of Indo Trinbagonians and Indo Guyanese on the politics of their respective colonies and the fear of Indo linkages between the Indo politicians of Trinidad and Tobago and

Guyana the British colonial overlord was ever conscious of events in both colonies impacting developments in both colonies. The British were seeking a politician in Trinidad and Tobago who would consign the Hindu political movement to the wilderness of Opposition politics and at the same time isolate and weaken Cheddi Jagan and the PPP locally and internationally. Dr. Eric Williams was that politician ably assisted by Bhadase Sagan Maharaj and Rudranath Capildeo.

In Trinidad and Tobago leading up to Independence in 1962 the British colonial overlord insisted and ensured that no Hindu dominated political party be part of the political elite chosen to pass the neo-colonial state to. British colonial strategy was then to consign the Hindu dominated political movement of Trinidad and Tobago to the Opposition benches. And Hindu political leaders with the exception of Simbhoonath Capildeo did all in their power to ensure the success of the British political strategy in the period 1953 to 1962. In Guyana leading up to Independence in 1966 the Americans were adamant that Guyana must not be granted Independence under the leadership of Dr. Cheddi Jagan and the People's Progressive Party (PPP). To achieve the political destruction of the PPP the Americans created the dictatorship of Linden Forbes Burnham and the People's National Congress (PNC) in 1964 and thereafter. A minority race, the Afro Guyanese, was then placed in dominance over a majority race, the Indo Guyanese, to serve US geo-political interests. And Indo political leaders of Guyana did all in their power to ensure the success of the US strategy from 1961 and onwards.

The trilogy then focuses on the nature of the neo-colonial politician their servility to North Atlantic interests and their abject failure to leads us out of bondage to the North Atlantic.

CHAPTER 1

THE COLONIAL DISCOURSE OF THE EAST INDIAN PROBLEM TRINIDAD 1953-1962

The declassified Colonial Office Files on Trinidad reveal the existence of a discourse of the East Indian problem in the politics and internal security of the colony of Trinidad from 1953 to formal independence in August 1962.

The declassified file CO 1031/127 contains the monthly political report in the hand of the Governor of the colony of Trinidad and Tobago addressed to Oliver Lyttelton, the then Colonial Secretary, for the month of April 1953. The report states:

> "11. There has been for some time a reasonable suspicion that the East Indian element in the colony has been organising themselves politically along racial lines and recent happenings have tended to confirm this suspicion. The Honourable Bhadase Sagan Maraj, Member for Tunapuna who is reputed to be wealthy and who is alleged to have gained such wealth by somewhat dubious means has in the past year succeeded in uniting the two main Hindu factions-the Sanatan Dharma and the Maha Sabha Associations."

> "when the latter gave notice of his dissolution motion, it became known that plans had been made for a political campaign aimed at securing at least 10 East Indian seats in the Legislative Council should the present Council be dissolved and a new General Election held. It was hoped that with the support of the Butler Party and several other independents in the new Council, the East Indian element would be assured of the political domination of the Colony."

> (CO 1031/127)

The East Indians of the colony have in 1953 appeared on the radar screen of the colonial overlord. Political action to galvanize the East Indian specifically the Hindu population of Trinidad is a threat because it is premised upon the desire, the drive for the East Indian dominance of the political system of the colony in 1953. The political praxis of Bhadase Maraj in 1953 then constitutes a clear and present danger to the colonial political agenda.

In the monthly political report for May 1953 the then Governor of the colony H. Rance states:

> "The latest reports indicate that the Hindu East Indian element led by the Honourable Bhadase Sagan Maraj has been working steadily through the United Sanatan Dharam Maha Sabha Association towards their goal of political control of the Colony."

> "The Sanatan Dharam Maha Sabha Association is well organised and well backed financially. It employs a solicitor, Simboonath Capildeo, as Secretary and he is reported to receive $400 per month as salary. He is the person most active in the Association and has his agents in each Indian community. There are at least five active members of the Caroni County Council who take instructions from him. The inner core of Pundits (priests) are also organised and confer from time to time. Much Indian nationalist propaganda and ideology are being disseminated by them in their daily contacts with East Indian communities for religious instruction. There are reasonable grounds for suspicion that the Commissioner for India, Shri Anand Mohan Sahay, despite his non-committal references in public speeches, is encouraging this aspect of Indian advancement on parallel lines behind the scenes. Sahay at the moment is not, on friendly terms with Bhadase Maraj."

(CO 1031/127)

The leaders of the Hindu drive for political hegemony are identified: Bhadase Maraj and Simbhoonath Capildeo moreover the Commissioner for India to the Colony is also implicated. The lesson of the extracts from the file is the depth of surveillance being carried out on the East Indian political movement. Surveillance demands and begets action on the part of the colonial officials both in Trinidad and Britain to ensure that the drive for political hegemony is never attained by the East Indians in Trinidad.

The report for June 1953 in the hand of the Governor's Deputy states:

> "There is no doubt about the motives of the Honourable Bhadase Sagan Maraj and the objects of the Sanatan Dharam Maha Sabha."

"It is also known that plans have been made for the establishment of an East Indian (Hindu) political organisation and for the inauguration of a political campaign in the event of a general election with a view to securing ten East Indian seats on the Legislative Council."

(CO 1031/127)

In 1953 the monthly political reports are indicating the threat perceived in a move to organise the East Indian community into a block vote to acquire at minimum ten seats in the legislative council at maximum control of the legislative council. What then do the colonial officials do to ensure that the Indian agenda is not realised? It must be noted that monthly political reports and monthly internal security reports from the colony of Trinidad are not action files. The actions enumerated in response to these secret reports are not declassified. The monthly political report for April 1953 numbered 29 in the internal numbering of the contents of CO 1031/127 has a folio comment by the Colonial Office official one Wallace which states:

"The signs of the increasing organisation of the East Indian community as a political force are disturbing."

(CO 1031/127)

In declassified secret file CO1031/1804 folio entry number 3 in the hand of the colonial office official Wallace states:

"These Political Report files should not be used for action. If action arises out of anything said in them, that action should be taken on a separate file dealing with the subject of the action."

(CO 1031/1804)

The monthly political report for the colony by Governor Rance to the Colonial Office reports on the East Indian political movement as follows in speaking of the praxis of Bhadase Maraj:

"What may be more serious is a suggestion which seems to be reasonably well founded that he will attempt to stage a strike throughout the Sugar Industry during March. If he felt strong enough to do this, it might be dangerous."

(CO 1031/1804)

Folio number 1 from Colonial Office official Robertson to Wallace and Sir Charles Jeffries states in response to this report on Bhadase Maraj as follows:

3

"To see (1). Para. 5 is probably the most important item in this report. If B.S. Maraj does succeed in calling an effective strike in the Sugar Industry we may be in for trouble."

(CO 1031/1804)

The monthly political report for January 1953 by Governor Rance to the Colonial Office on the praxis of Bhadase Maraj states as follows:

"In the last monthly report, it was stated that Bhadase Maraj might well attempt to stage a strike in the sugar areas in March. According to many informed circles he will not attempt such drastic action unless he knows in advance that he has the support of the majority of workers which still remains a doubtful proposition."

"15 Maraj's chances of a successful strike are somewhat reduced by the stand taken by Lionel Seukaran, rural sugar union leader who described Maraj's latest antics in the sugar belt as mere political stunt to secure the majority in the next Legislative Council elections."

(CO 1031/1804)

The folio response to the report, quoted above, by Robertson of the Colonial Office to Wallace and Jeffries states:

"To see (2). It appears from paras 14 and 15 that the threatened strike in the sugar industry is not now likely to come off."

(CO 1031/1804)

It is apparent from Rance's report that the colonial overlords were seeking Indo-Trinbagonian politicians opposed to Maraj's agenda to blunt, even defeat Maraj's drive for political power in the twin island colony in the early 1950's. The record would show that Seukaran and Mitra Sinanan were viewed as two such Indo- Trinbagonian politicians of use to the colonial anti-Maraj agenda.

In the report for February 1954 Governor Rance not only reports on the political activities of Bhadase Maraj but for the first time concerted alarm bells are sounded on the activities of the Commissioner of India to the twin island colony. The activities of the Commissioner of India are reported as follows:

"The 15th February edition of the 'Indian News Bulletin' issued by the Commissioner of India for the West Indies and printed in Trinidad contains a number of reports of speeches condemning colonialism in no uncertain terms and depicting it as 'something

4

which is bad for those who are governed and those who govern....
a constant danger to world peace ... something which encourages
racial conflict'."

"According to reliable information at least 1,000 copies of this
bulletin are distributed fortnightly, and it is easy to imagine the
harm that this type of literature must do amongst semi-educated
East Indians who comprise one-third of the population of this
Colony. As previously reported the establishment of the post
of Commissioner for India in these parts does not appear to be
altogether a blessing."

(CO 1031/1804)

The folio entry with reference to the report as above states:

"we can't very well object to reprints of Mr. Nehru's speeches,
and the Indian Commissioner's speech in San Fernando was
unobjectionable. But I think we have strong grounds for taking
umbrage against the supplement to Bulletin iv. ii, I should
be grateful if this be re-circulated to me (with the Indian
Commissioner file) for further action."

(CO 1031/1804)

The writer of the folio entry remains unidentified. The discourse of the
coolie problem is clearly articulated in the governor's report to the colonial
office on the activities of the Commissioner for India in the colony of Trinidad
and Tobago. One third of the population of the colony are semi-educated
coolies who can be stimulated to anti-colonial actions by the Commissioner
for India.

The monthly political report for March 1954 by the governor of the
colony to the colonial office on the activities of Bhadase Maraj states:

"This was a good month for the party whose main activities were
still conducted behind the scenes."

"18. He was well received, and it has been observed that these
meetings are becoming increasingly popular. He is also, of course,
operating through the Hindu Maha Sabha of which he is the
President General and there is no doubt that in his bid for East
Indian domination he is slowly poisoning the mind of the East
Indians, not only against the British, but also against all West
Indians who do not belong to the East Indian race."

(CO 1031/1804)

"Unfortunately in March the Press gave considerable publicity to the activities of the Party, including the development of the Hindu Maha Sabha School building programme."

"19. Meanwhile further reports of corruption were received against

the Honourable B.S. Maraj, and the latest was in connection with the election of officers for the St. George County Council. According to reliable information received from two independent sources, the Honourable B.S. Maraj is alleged to have paid out the sum of $200 in order to influence the election of the chairman. The matter is under police investigation."

(CO 1031/1804)

The then governor of the colony was insisting that B.S. Maraj in fact constituted an effective and concerted threat to the colonial order in the early 1950's. The said report for March 1954 contained a report on the activities of the Maha Sabha for the month as follows:

"20. A specially chartered plane conveying 24 East Indian delegates from British Guiana arrived in the colony towards the end of the

month. According to reliable information this visit was instigated by the Honourable Bhadase Sagan Maraj, President General of the Trinidad Branch, and the object of which was to merge the Associations of the two colonies into a single powerful unit and thus assist him in furthering his plans for East Indian domination, not only in Trinidad, but on a regional basis."

(CO 1031/1804)

Bhadase Maraj's political vision is then the most concerted threat to the Colonial agenda as he strives for Indian hegemony in Trinidad and British Guiana. A series of questions flow out of this position such as: where does Cheddi Jagan fit into the vision of Bhadase Maraj? What is Maraj's position on the British West Indian Federation? What are the strategic means Maraj is willing to use to realise his vision of Indian hegemony? Moreover, what does the colonial office intend to do to thwart Maraj's agenda for Indian hegemony?

In the monthly political report for April 1954 the governor reports on the activities of B.S. Maraj as follows:

"On the religious side, the Hindu Sanatan Dharam Maha Sabha of which Mr. Maraj remains President-General, continues to propagate a political religion of Indian racial superiority."

(CO 1031/1804)

On Maraj's campaign for the single representation of sugar workers and cane farmers under the umbrella organisation named the Federation of Sugar Workers and Cane Farmers Trade Union the report states:

> "The Honourable Mitra Sinanan is at present supporting the Federation not because of any desire to associate with Mr. Maraj but because of political expediency."

(CO 1031/1804)

Both Seukaran and Mitra Sinanan have now been named as Indo-Trinidadian politicians that are not under the thumb of Maraj's vision. But are they assets to be utilized in the covert/overt war on Maraj?

By way of secret letter to Ormerod of the Commonwealth Relations Office dated the 26th April 1954 the assault on the Commissioner of India to the West Indies was pushed one step further. The letter states:

> "This seems to be a more serious and flagrant breach of the Commissioner's instructions than Sahay's indiscretion at the end of 1952 which was dealt with in correspondence with Morris and Hampshire (your reference SA 10/91/2), or the similar indiscretion by his colleague in Mauritius at about the same time."

> "If Nanda makes any difficulty or such material appears again, we should be obliged to ask you to take the matter up officially with the Government of India."

(CO 1031/1804)

The Commissioner of India to the West Indies Nanda is now under the microscope and the mechanism that would end in his recall to India was activated. What is noteworthy is that all Commissioners of India to the Indian Diaspora in the British Empire were in fact under the gun, Sahay was recalled in 1952 as a result of Colonial Office machinations and it was so in Mauritius. There is then a fear of Indian nationalism infecting the Indian Diaspora in the colonial empire in the early 1950's.

In response to the monthly political report for March 1954 the relevant folio note by Robertson to Rogers states:

> "Mr. Bhadase Maraj seems to be making considerable progress in his designs."

(CO 1031/1804)

The monthly political report for June 1954 by the acting Governor Dorman reports on East Indian matters as follows:

> "It has never been easy to distinguish between the political arm of the East Indian movement, the PDP, the trade union arm, the Federation of Cane Farmers and Sugar Workers and the religious and educational arm, the Sanatan Dharma Maha Sabha. Mainly through the medium of the Sanatan Dharam Maha Sabha, and with the encouragement of the Indian Commissioner, the East Indian population continue to show a general tendency to build up their racial organisation in practically every sphere."

> "There can be little doubt that the aims of the East Indian population, organised as they are affords this colony its most serious problem."

> (CO 1031/1804)

Dorman, the then acting governor has now indicated to the colonial office in June 1954 that the most serious problem in the colony is the coolie problem. In the same monthly political report the surveillance of Bhadase Maraj continues apace as indicated by this report when it states as follows:

> "There is some evidence of discontent amongst his followers in his own constituency of Tunapuna and even amongst his immediate henchmen over his high-handed methods of dealing with the funds of the Sanatan Dharam Maha Sabha, but fear of the consequences of open opposition has so far stifled any desire to lodge a complaint which might make a police investigation possible."

> (CO 1031/1804)

Bhadase Maraj is then a thug, a common criminal that has galvanised a semi-educated one third of the colony's population bent on racist Indian hegemony posing the most concerted threat to the colonial order in June 1954.

In the monthly report for July 1954 acting governor Dorman reports on the coolie problem as follows:

> "Over the end of July and the beginning of August two significant rumours gained ground, first that an Indian group was prepared to offer $200,000 for the Port-of Spain Gazette and had deposited this sum in a bank, and second that Bhadase Maraj was going to come out in the open and oppose Federation. Both of these rumours must be regarded as well founded and likely to be confirmed."

> (CO 1031/1804)

Ward in folio note 10 to Wallace, Rogers and Jefferies states:

> "The latest development in the East Indian problem is the rumoured preparation for buying out the Port of Spain Gazette."

(CO 1031/1804)

Wallace responds at the margin by writing:

> "I don't like this."

(CO 1031/1804)

The monthly political report for August 1954 by acting governor Dorman on Bhadase Maraj states as follows:

> "He has been much bolder and forthright in his political utterances of late and he does not try to conceal his associations with the Honourable Roy Joseph and Adjodhasingh. His blatant display of his authority is known to have caused the latter considerable embarrassment on more than one occasion."

> "One thing emerged more clearly during the month and this is Maraj's attitude to Federation. He appears to consider this the right time to come out strongly against Federation and is using all his power and influence amongst the East Indian community to resist Federation at all costs."

> "It appears that Maraj cannot expect the unqualified support of the East Indian community as there have been indications at public meetings and elsewhere that his attacks on the Sinanans and his overbearing manner have earned him some unpopularity."

(CO 1031/1804)

The comment in the left margin of the last segment of the report quoted above was:

> "There is some small encouragement here."

(CO 1031/1804)

The report highlights the continuing surveillance on the Commissioner of India Shri Badri Nath Nanda as follows:

> "It is however reported that Sinanan was invited to meet Maraj in the presence of the Indian Commissioner, the understanding being that the Commissioner, Shri Badri Nath Nanda would act as conciliator. It is not known if the meeting has yet taken place, but the participation of the Commissioner in this move indicates

that he is taking a close and not wholly objective interest in local East Indian politics."

(CO 1031/1804)

The note in the left margin of the report dealing with Commissioner Nanda states:

"I hope the Governor will not hesitate to pull him up."

(CO 1031/1804)

In folio note 11 Wallace of the Colonial Office states:

"The activities of the Indian Commissioner need very careful watching."

(CO 1031/1804)

The said monthly political report for August 1954 under the heading "East Indian Matters" states as follows:

"As indicated earlier attention is beginning to focus on the attitude of the East Indian population towards Federation of the British West Indies. To those who visualise a closer relationship with 'Mother India' Federation is a threat which must be resisted to the full. It is perhaps understandable, therefore, that considerable pressure is being exerted throughout the East Indian communities to bring about a united front in opposition to the Federation proposal on which a decision is likely to be made by the Legislature early in the 1954-55 session."

"It appears from information received that Shri Badri Nath Nanda is anxious to bring together the prominent East Indian politicians at least to ensure a common East Indian front on the Federation issue."

(CO 1031/1804)

The monthly political report for August 1954 indicates that for the colonial overlord in Trinidad and Tobago and in Britain, Bhadase Maraj and the East Indian political movement crossed the line by opposing the Federation of the British West Indies. Would the colonial overlord stand idly by and allow the East Indian political movement to win a majority of seats in the general elections for the Legislative Council due in 1955? Would they postpone the said general elections to September 1956 to allow them the time and space to enable a viable counter political movement to arise to ensure defeat of the East Indian political movement? To give themselves the time and space to execute a covert operation to ensure that there is no amalgamation of political forces that would propel the East Indian political movement into a position of dominance in the Legislative Council in the post general elections 1955 scenario?

The monthly political report for October 1954 by the Governor reports:

> "A meeting was held at Chaguanas on 17th October when Simboonath Capildeo, Mitra Sinanan and Bhadase Maraj addressed a gathering of 350 persons. The main purpose of the meeting was the propagation of the anti-Federation attitude being pursued by the two Honourable Members, and the predominantly East Indian audience was left in no doubt that their interests will be most adversely affected by Federation. The main line of objection put forward was to 'freedom of movement' and great care was taken to avoid mention of racial interests; in fact, Sinanan went so far as to deplore what he described as 'rumours of the development of racialism' by the East Indians."

(CO 1031/1804)

Mitra Sinanan as reported is now moving to counter the discourse of the racist East Indian political movement but the battle lines already drawn are becoming fixed in time as the colonial overlord is only repelled by Indo-Trinbagonian intransigence seen in their rejection of the colonial vision articulated via British West Indian Federation. The discourse of the hostile recalcitrant minority was then formulated and unleashed from Government House, St. Anns, Port of Spain and Solomon Hochoy amongst others was part of the colonial team at Government House.

The monthly report for December 1954 states:

> "It is reported that consultations were held between the Indian Commissioner, the Honourable Bhadase Maraj, A.C. Rienzi and Capildeo on one or two occasions with the object of formulating plans for the launching of the Party and the Party's policies for this year's General Elections."

(CO 1031/1804)

The political reports for February and March 1955 in its section on East Indian Affairs would report:

> "The Commissioner for India, Shri Badri Nath Nanda, paid a visit to British Guiana from 6th February to 24th February. It was, however, significant that the Honourable Bhadase Maraj accompanied by Simboonath Capildeo and Bholai Maraj also paid a three-day visit to British Guiana during Nanda's stay there."

(CO 1031/1804)

The said report for April 1955 continued reporting on the surveillance mounted on Nanda by stating:

> "He was in surreptitious contact with Capildeo and Rienzi. He now believes that his activities have come to the Government and, in conversation with the Acting Colonial Secretary, he intimated that New Delhi had taken up with him the question of his association with Bhadase Maraj and its effect on this Government's attitude to him. On the following day he held a conference at his home with Maraj and Rienzi."

(CO 1031/1804)

On Bhadase Maraj the report states:

> "Bhadase Maraj, having resigned in protest against deferment of the elections, is confident that he has gone a long way to consolidate his position in his East Indian community, and this may well be so."

(CO 1031/1804)

The Trinidad Guardian of the 4th June 1955 would report that Commissioner Nanda would be recalled to India.

The monthly political report for June by the new Governor Beetham would report on the attempt via B.I. Lalsingh and A.C. Rienzi to create an African-Indian political coalition. The report would state:

> "This is the first serious approach by the East Indian faction to the African faction; although Bhadase Maraj was not present it is understood that he was invited, as were several Members of the Legislative Council who accepted but did not attend."

(CO 1031/1804)

Given the depth of reporting as to who were present and what was said at the meeting held under the auspices of afternoon tea at the residence of B.I. Lalsingh, it is apparent the concern the colonial overlord held with attempts at political unity across the racial divide with Bhadase Maraj. What is obvious is that persons who were present at the tea party were assets of the colonial covert security structure.

What is clear from the file under review is that A.C. Rienzi became a target of surveillance as a result of his political praxis in the 1950's. Folio notes number 15 of CO 1031/1804 by Wallace of the Colonial Office states:

"The way Mr. Rienzi, a serving Crown Counsel is allowed to go on in Trinidad strikes me as rather surprising. I should have thought that the conduct described in paragraph 6 was at least getting near to an infringement of Colonial Regulations."

(CO 1031/1804)

What is the historical reality is that the political union of Afro-Trinbagonian political leaders with the Bhadase Maraj led Indo-Trinbagonian political party did not materialise for the September 1956 general elections, which would favour the PNM. Rienzi was not a candidate in the 1956 general elections and simply faded from the politics of the twin island colony thereafter.

The monthly political report of July 1955 by the Governor reports on East Indian activities as follows:

"Bhadase Maraj and Capildeo found their grip on the political machine slackening and started to create confusion among union leaders. But I am afraid that there is good reason to think that the management of Caroni Limited (one of the Tate and Lyle group) believe that the company's interest lies in supporting Bhadase Maraj; they close their eyes to his reputation; they believe that he will be a controlling influence in the next Government and they calculate that they cannot go wrong by supporting him."

(CO 1031/1804)

Governor Beetham is clearly disturbed by Tate and Lyle breaking the common front of the sugar manufacturers against dealing with Bhadase Maraj as the dominant union leader in the sugar industry in Trinidad. What the report is in fact highlighting is the special relationship that existed between Tate and Lyle and Bhadase Maraj.

The monthly political report for November 1955 reports on a meeting held by Bhadase Maraj and political organisations in the colony as follows:

"On the 23rd of the month representatives of the West Indian Independence Party, Trinidad Labour Party, National Democratic Party and the People's Democratic Party met at the Honourable B.S. Maraj's warehouse at Laventille, most notable personalities at this meeting were John La Rose (W.I.I.P.) and B.S. Maraj (P.D.P.). The meeting was convened primarily for the purpose of discussing a common role amongst political parties having common aims."

"It is not yet clear if this group has formed any definite plans for the future but the fact that the W.I.I.P. leaders were included in any such scheme indicates a distinct change of attitude on the part of the other factions."

(CO 1031/1804)

For B.S. Maraj to meet with the W.I.I.P. sounded further alarm bells for the W.I.I.P. was the resident evil of the politics of Trinidad in the 1950's before the advent of the East Indian Problem. The W.I.I.P. was the evil incarnate of communism and the communist threat to Trinidad and Tobago and the rest of the British West Indies. The report again exposes the level of surveillance and the assets in the room that reported on the nature and purpose of the said meeting. Any hint of a Maraj/ WIIP alliance for the 1956 general elections must trigger colonial pre-emptive and reactive actions. Colonial Office official W.W. Wallace in reference to the above states:

> "if the Butler Party joins this group and if a united front is presented at the general elections, the group would be large enough to provide the next government of Trinidad."

(CO 1031/1804)

A clear and present danger is constituted and the question remains what are the measures adopted both overtly and covertly to pre-empt this danger?

The declassified file CO 1031/1804 contains the monthly political reports for Trinidad for 1956. The high point of the file is the lead up to and the final results of the general elections of September 1956. From June 1956 the officials at Government House Trinidad now included the monthly report of the Local Intelligence Committee. From July 1956 Solomon Hochoy would figure publicly in the administration of surveillance of the Colonial Agencies in Trinidad. Hochoy in his capacity of Colonial Secretary would sign the local Intelligence Committee's monthly intelligence report. Beetham as Governor was effectively supplanted as the single voice the Colonial Office officials listened to on intelligence realities in Trinidad such was the singular strategic importance of the general elections of 1956.

Hochoy's central importance to the colonial overlord in Britain would culminate in his appointment as Governor after Beetham and the first Governor General of the independent Trinidad and Tobago. Hochoy's elevation to Colonial Secretary, the apex of the colonial surveillance structure saw no change in the virulence of the discourse of the coolie problem in Trinidad. In fact its intensity, virulence and paranoia constituted a crusade for the preservation of the colonial agenda and the colonial vision for Trinidad and Tobago.

The monthly report for February 1956 reports on East Indian Affairs as follows:

> "The efforts of Bhadase Maraj to take a leading role in forming a coalition front and also his victories in two of the counties following the County Council Elections have been mentioned above. During the County Council Elections, Maraj bitterly opposed Chanka Maharaj, Member of the Legislative Council and one time member of the Maha Sabha, who was supporting a rural candidate for St. George. This flux between coalition and schism keeps us all guessing."

(CO 1031/1805)

B.S. Maraj would carry this flux between schism and coalition into the general elections of 1956 thereby making a stellar contribution to the PNM securing 13 seats in the Legislative Council. Was this flux, this bi-polar praxis influenced by colonial covert pressures? What of Maraj's alliance with Tate and Lyle, did this leverage his electoral strategy?

The monthly report for March 1956 on B.B Maraj states:

> "Maraj, courted from more than one direction, can thus afford to play his cards slowly."

(CO 1031/1805)

Jenkins in Folio note 29 of the said file would state on B.S. Maraj as follows:

> "Mr. Maraj on the other hand is courted by many and can afford to delay his public campaign."

(CO 1031/1805)

W.W. Wallace of the Colonial Office in the same folio would write:

> "Party groupings are still obscure but these will no doubt be a changed picture after the Legislative Council is dissolved on 26th May. Meantime the Tang, Joseph, Bhadase Maraj line-up, or its possibility is disquieting."

(CO 1031/1805)

The monthly report for March 1956 would condemn local politics in 1956 as follows:

> "From the above it is apparent that party politics in Trinidad is still very much in a rudimentary stage. At the present time

personal politics still carry more weight than party politics and individualistic values penetrate deep into the whole society."

(CO 1031/1805)

Any hint of success at the 1956 general elections by the Maraj movement triggers racist angst from the colonial officials in Trinidad and Britain. What then did they do to ensure that their horror never materialised in September 1956?

As of May 1956 the monthly political report became the monthly intelligence report. The said report on East Indian Affairs states as follows:

> "Maraj continues to hold his hand. Various reports in the Press that he had been approached to intervene in the sugar strike were parried with the comment that 'he was giving the matter his consideration' and it is that he may still come forward at the instance of Caroni Ltd."

(CO 1031/1805)

Again the working relationship between Tate and Lyle and B.S. Maraj. In folio note 30 of CO 1031/1805 W.W. Wallace Colonial Office official writes:

> "The main event of the month was the strike in the sugar industry (which ended a day or two after the report was written) and it is clear that strenuous but unsuccessful efforts were made by both internal and external influences to bring about a more general stoppage of work.'

(CO 1031/1805)

Did Bhadase Maraj pre-empt the moves to shut down the sugar industry as a result of the intervention of Tate and Lyle? Clearly the relationship between Bhadase Maraj and Tate and Lyle did not resonate with the strategy to ensure Maraj's political demise.

The monthly intelligence report for May 1956 reports on the activities of the People's Democratic Party (PDP) as follows:

> "As far as can be seen at this stage, the two main objectives being pursued by Joseph, Maraj and Capildeo in concert are:-
>
> (a) the playing down of the racial stigma attaching to PDP, by formation of an alliance with a Socialist Party with influence amongst the Afro-West Indian population towards consolidation of the National Front alliance and,

(b) ensuring as far as possible that the PNM gains no support from other parties of socialist tendencies to strengthen it."

(CO 1031/1805)

Again the report states:

"Maraj is also reported to be planning another approach; he is awaiting the return to the colony of Butler (Home Rule Party) with a view to seeking an alliance with this party."

(CO 1031/1805)

Again:

"The People's Democratic Party has been manoeuvring within the political pattern to such a degree that its position in the final picture is still difficult to foresee."

(CO 1031/1805)

The objectives of Bhadase Maraj as stated in the report for May 1956 would be bolstered by a warning written by Dorman on the imminent threat posed by the PDP in the report for June 1956. The report states as follows:

"Of the other parties the Maha Sabha People's Democratic Party of Bhadase Maraj needs careful watching. Maraj and his followers are quite ruthless in using racialism to serve their own ends and the possibility of his numerous East Indian votes (about 40% of the total) returning a large East Indian bloc in the Legislature must always be reckoned with."

(CO 1031/1805)

Dorman in his last monthly intelligence report from Trinidad as acting Governor repeats the discourse of the coolie problem. But he also hazards a prediction as to the outcome of the 1956 general elections as follows:

"As they stand none of these six parties alone would appear to be able to return a majority in the next Legislature but there is still time for major developments."

"As this will be my last report from Trinidad, I will hazard a guess at the make-up of the new legislature as the field appears at present-30% Williams, 30% Maraj Indian, 30% independents and a mixture of labour groups (TLP, CNLP and Butlerites not in coalition but willing to coalesce on terms with others) and 10% POPPG; in this a maximum of three of the present ministers."

(CO 1031/1805)

The final results of the 1956 general elections falsified Dorman's prediction. What role did the covert interventions and the manner in which the electoral boundaries were de-limited for the 1956 general elections play in consigning the PDP to sterile opposition?

The report of the intelligence committee for June 1956 affords an insight into the discourse produced at the primary organisational committee governing colonial surveillance in Trinidad and Tobago. The report states on the PDP as follows:

> "The party has not yet made public the names of its candidates who will contest the General Elections, but Special Branch reports that the Maraj faction (Joseph, Capildeo/Maraj) is actively engaged in plotting to ensure that in the final outcome at the polls, East Indians will control the Legislature."

(CO 1031/1805)

The intelligence committee is then the focal point of the constituting of the discourse of the coolie problem. The report of the Trinidad and Tobago Intelligence Committee for July 1956 reports on the activities of the PDP as follows:

> "Unfortunately, the factor of race has begun to receive greater prominence in many of the campaign speeches and activities. Smarting under attacks from the PNM that denominational schools had been used by the Hindus for selfish purposes, the PDP has seized the opportunity to use this statement as an attack on East Indians generally and accused the PNM of being anti-East Indian."

(CO 1031/1805)

The PDP then unleashed the factor of race into the general elections campaign of 1956 and the PNM stands innocent of this travesty in official colonial discourse. The report continues as follows:

> "The record and reliability of the sources plus the fact that such tactics are in keeping with the behaviour of Bhadase Maraj and his associates tend to confirm that the leader of the PDP may employ criminal methods to achieve his personal ends and those of his party."

(CO 1031/1805)

The report of the intelligence committee for August 1956 was forwarded with Beetham's summary, which states on the PDP as follows:

> "The East Indian People's Democratic Party with Bhadase Maraj, Ashford and Mitra Sinanan, Ajodhasingh and Pat Mathura, the young mayor of Port-of-Spain, has had little to say that is constructive and is mainly concerned with consolidating the East Indian vote and splitting the 'West Indian' vote of its opponents. There are, however, many East Indians, Hindus as well as Muslims, who would prefer not to be associated with Maraj and his party so that the PDP will not have it all its own way with the East Indian electorate."

(CO 1031/1805)

Beetham has merely recorded or summarised the discourse of the intelligence committee's monthly report on the PDP and Bhadase Maraj. It is noteworthy that the August 1956 Intelligence Committee's report was signed by Solomon Hochoy in his capacity of Colonial Secretary and member of the said committee.

The culmination of the discourse of the coolie problem from 1953 to 1956 is the Appendix "C" titled "Brief Histories of Candidates for the Legislative Council Elections 1956" produced by the Trinidad and Tobago Intelligence Committee of which Solomon Hochoy was part of and attached to the monthly intelligence report for August 1956. The assessment of Bhadase Sagan Maraj is as follows:

> "Trinidadian-age 37 years-East Indian (Hindu) Proprietor-President of Sanatan Dharma Maha Sabha Association and leader of People's Democratic Party political arm of Maha Sabha. An associate of former Indian Commissioner, Shri Badri Nath Nanda. Former President General OF FEDERATION of CANE FARMERS AND SUGAR WORKERS UNION. Successfully contested 1950 General Elections. Strong racial tendencies. Ambitious to ensure East Indian control of Legislature. Has visited India. Employs known criminals and 'strong-arm' men to intimidate anyone who stands in his way of gaining control of the Legislature. Not adverse to using violence and even resorting to murder to achieve his ends. Has a record tainted with illegal activities. A megalomaniac, outwardly plausible, completely unscrupulous and ruthless. Against Federation of the West Indies."

(CO 1031/1805)

Assessment of Simbhoonath Capildeo in the report states as follows:

"Trinidadian-age 51 years-East Indian (Hindu) Solicitor and Conveyancer-a close associate of the former Indian Commissioner in Trinidad, Shri Badri Nath Nanda. Executive Member of the Sanatan Dharma Maha Sabha Association and PEOPLE'S DEMOCRATIC PARTY- a founder of the UNITED FRONT of 1946 and CARIBBEAN SOCIALIST PARTY (now defunct). Co- organiser with Bhadase Sagan Maraj of the PEOPLE'S DEMOCRATIC PARTY in 1953. Has visited India. Has strong

racial tendencies and another of the Maha Sabha's most active members with known ambition for an East Indian controlled Legislature. A crafty, unscrupulous and treacherous individual-has worked against Federation."

(CO 1031/1805)

And the assessment of Roy Joseph in the report is as follows:

"Trinidadian-age 48 years-Syrian-Proprietor. 1939 elected to San Fernando Borough Council. Served as Mayor of San Fernando from 1943-45 and again in 1948. Has been a member of Legislative Council from 1941 to present time. Elected Minister of Education and Social Services from 1950-56.

Honours: O.B.E. in 1950

C.B.E. in 1955

Joseph is known to have alliance with the PEOPLE'S DEMOCRATIC PARTY but is campaigning as an Independent. A self-seeker, prepared to sacrifice anything or anybody to his own advantage-a vicious, vindictive person."

(CO 1031/1805)

Maraj, Capildeo and Joseph were in the words of Appendix "C" prepared by the Trinidad and Tobago Intelligence Committee, the trinity of evil incarnate in the politics of the colony of Trinidad and Tobago. What would have been the reaction of the colonial overlord in September 1956 faced with a victory at the polls by the trinity of evil incarnate? The praxis of British Guiana when the constitution was suspended in 1953 thereby evicting the duly elected Peoples Progressive Party government from office was definitely on the agenda of the colonial overlord.

The final result of the general elections of September 1956 in fact questions the thuggish potency of Bhadase S. Maraj and his faction comprising

Capildeo and Joseph. The PNM won 13 of the 24 seats and the PDP 5 of 24 seats. Non-PNM members of the Legislative Council commanded 11 of the 24 seats. Of the 13 seats the PNM won, Tunapuna was won by 179 votes over the PDP, and St. Joseph was won by the PNM by 109 votes from Chanka Maharaj who ran as an Independent. In the case of Tunapuna, Rattan Kumar Harracksingh the Butler Party candidate clearly split the PDP vote when he polled 703 votes thus ensuring a PNM victory. Rattan Kumar Harracksingh according to Appendix "C" of the August 1956 report of the local intelligence committee was a Bhadase Maraj foot soldier who joined the Butler Party after falling out with Bhadase Maraj.

With all his thuggish resources why then doesn't Bhadase Maraj simply persuade Harracksingh by any means necessary not to contest the Tunapuna seat in September 1956 on a Butler Party ticket? At minimum the failure to forge a common electoral strategy with the Butler Party cost the PDP the Tunapuna seat in 1956. In the case of the St. Joseph seat the Independent candidacy of Vivian Raphael Kangalee cost Chanka Maharaj the seat with the PNM being the beneficiary. Appendix "C" reports that Kangalee was a former member of the PNM and chose to contest the election as an independent after being passed over by the PNM as the candidate for St. Joseph. Kangalee's candidacy could have only hurt Chanka Maharaj and given the fact that Kangalee was close to Bhadase Maraj why didn't Maraj utilise his personal influence and/ or his thuggish resources to ensure the victory of Chanka Maraj in St. Joseph?

In St. Patrick (Central) the Independent Alexander C. Alexis won the seat by one vote from the candidate for the Butler Party. The PDP fielded no candidate but an Independent Seusankar Seunarine, according to Appendix "C" a member of the Maha Sabha contested the election polling 2,448 votes. Seunarine was a foot soldier of Bhadase Maraj raising the question of why didn't B.S. Maraj allow Seunarine to draw PDP votes away from the Butler Party thereby ensuring Alexis' victory who then promptly defected to the PNM in the Legislative Council?

B.S. Maraj therefore held the means, the power to deny the PNM three of the thirteen seats in the 1956 general elections and failed to do so to the detriment of his alleged grand vision of East Indian domination of the 1956 Legislative Council. Why? A man with the required resources to affect the outcome of the 1956 general elections according to the discourse of the coolie problem failed miserably to execute, to intervene, to ensure the grand vision of Indo racist hegemony in Trinidad and Tobago. Why? To intervene strategically the alternate result in 1956 would have been: PNM 10 seats, PDP 6 seats, Butler Party 3 seats, Trinidad Labour Party 2 seats, Independents

3 seats for a grand total of 24 seats. In this alternate scenario the PNM in need of 3 seats and 2 pro PNM nominated members to constitute a majority would have been forced to either invite the Butler Party or the Independents into government. What a minefield for the PNM and the colonial overlords to traverse constituting a political history of Trinidad and Tobago vastly different from the history that exists today.

The October 1956 monthly intelligence report of the Trinidad and Tobago Intelligence Committee by Solomon Hochoy states:

> "There is no apparent security danger in the political situation of Trinidad at the present time; the main potential risk lies in the racial division between East Indians and the Afro-West Indians which for the present is more clearly defined than before, as a result of the consciousness of race brought to the fore during the pre-Election period, and it remains to be shown whether the government can allay the prevalent fears and emotions of the East Indian population sufficiently to neutralise and discredit the racial propaganda of the Sanatan Dharma Maha Sabha and its political front, the People's Democratic Party. The possibility of the emergence of 'racial politics' instead of 'party politics' remains the most immediate security danger."

(CO 1031/1805)

The single most potent threat to the security of the colony was now defused with the results of the 1956 general elections and the swearing in of a PNM government headed by Dr. Eric Williams. From October 1956 the main potential risk was now racial division between Indo and Afro Trinbagonians. The security threat posed by the 'coolie problem' was now defused without the stated interventions of the colonial overlord covertly and or overtly. The denial of Hochoy and the committee is palpable for in order to address the threat of the coolie problem a racist discourse that demonised the Indo-Trinbagonian was unleashed which engendered Afro-Trinbagonian racist hegemony and Williams would adeptly flail away at the Indo- Trinbagonian to ensure PNM hegemony with the full support of the colonial overlords by any means necessary. The colonial discourse of the coolie problem demanded Afro-Trinbagonian racist hegemony to avert the ever present danger of coolie hegemony.

CO 1031/1972 reveals that Dorman the then Colonial Secretary of the colony of Trinidad and Tobago held a meeting on the 21st December 1954 at the Colonial Office, Britain with colonial office officials Rogers, Robertson, Wallace and others on the role of the Indian Commissioner in Trinidad. The Draft Note of the discussion states:

"there was no doubt in Mr. Dorman's mind that the Indian Commissioner was having a unifying influence on the Indian political leaders. There was no doubt that an Indian influenced government in Trinidad would never agree to federation or would wash their hands of it if they gained control before federation was in being."

(CO 1031/1972)

"Nanda's involvement in opposition to federation sounded the most effective basis for demanding the Commissioner's recall from Trinidad. It would no doubt help if Executive Council expressed an opinion but care would have to be taken as East Indians on Executive Council would presumably support the Indian Commissioner."

(CO 1031/1972)

It is then a strategy to ensure that the coolie faction that was problematic did not win the next general elections due in Trinidad and Tobago for they posed the most potent threat to Federation of the British West Indies. It is then a covert strategy for every Indo-Trinbagonian was a potential ally of the coolie agenda and by extension an enemy of the colonial agenda. The salient importance of Dr. Eric Williams and the PNM in 1956 and thereafter was framed and defined by the coolie problem.

CO1031/1548 reports the existence of an undated, unsigned memorandum on Bhadase Maraj handed to P. Rogers of the Colonial Office by Hugill the then new general manager of the West Indian Sugar Company, owner of Caroni Limited in Trinidad in 1954. Rogers by way of Folio Note 1 states that he suspects that Gilbert, General Manager of Caroni Ltd. Trinidad wrote the memorandum. The alleged Gilbert Memorandum is included in the file and clearly Caroni Ltd. is batting for its ally Bhadase Maraj. The memorandum states:

> " There is no doubt that he is a gangster and completely ruthless, as well as being unappetizing. (His wife, mother-in-law and sister-in- law are said all to have produced babies for him in the same month). But he has no interest in disrupting the status quo or going in for ill informed Socialism or Communism. He is, after all, a big businessman on the make, and as such does not have much liking for Communism. It would seem that the Indian Party he has started is infinitely to be preferred to the thing which has emerged in B.G. although Bhadase Maraj himself may not be as 'respectable' as Cheddi Jagan and his madam."

(CO1031/1548)

P. Rogers in Folio Note 1 dated 21ˢᵗ April, 1954 would comment on the memorandum as follows:

> " The general feeling in Trinidad, and from what I saw I certainly share it, is that a political party in power, dominated by Bhadase Maraj would be very unpleasant indeed. Just because he might not happen to be a Communist does not mean that this kind of boss rule might not be just as much a danger to public life and ultimately to public order as Communism, to which indeed it might well open the way."

(CO1031/1548)

Caroni Ltd. so prized the relationship they enjoyed with Bhadase Maraj that they attempted to convince the Colonial Office of Maraj's strategic importance to the British multinational corporation that then owned Caroni Ltd. in the colony of Trinidad. Rogers is adamant that the colonial engagement with the Coolie problem trumps Tate and Lyle's interests in the sugar industry of Trinidad.

CO 1031/2491 contains a secret inward telegram from the Colonial Attaché in Washington, DC to the Secretary of State for the Colonies dated 11ᵗʰ March 1959 which states as follows:

> "Bhadase Maraj.
>
> State Department have informed us that persons named, who is leader of the opposition in Trinidad arrives New York 12ᵗʰ March to enter hospital. Consul General has told the State Department confidentially that his purpose is in fact to undergo treatment for long addiction.
>
> 2. You will appreciate that if on arrival person named should be found to be in possession of drugs, an embarrassing situation would ensue and immigration officials will have no alternative but to prohibit his entry. State Department have decided to extend 'the normal courtesies' which should mean that his baggage will not be examined, though this cannot be guaranteed."

(CO 1031/2491)

The surveillance of Bhadase Maraj by the colonial state both locally and internationally is of the requisite intensity to request of the US Federal agencies that Maraj's entry into New York in March 1959 does not result in Maraj being debarred from entering the US as a result of possession of a prohibited/

controlled substance. Faced with an unrelenting covert/overt strategy to deal with the coolie problem in Trinidad by the colonial overlord how does a drug addict wage a strategically sustainable war against the colonial strategy?

An extract from a Trinidad Despatch of the 21st March 1959 states:

> "Bhadase Maraj is now in the United States for medical attention. It is said that he is suffering from cancer; I have been informed by a delicate source that drug addiction of long standing and not cancer is his trouble."

(CO 1031/2491)

The report is then confirmation of the depth of the surveillance in 1959 on Bhadase Maraj. Such sensitive information intensifies the impact of the overt/covert strategy to marginalize politically Bhadase Maraj.

The monthly intelligence report for March 1959 reports on the Democratic Labour Party (DLP) as follows:

> "22. The preponderance of East Indians in the membership of the Maraj faction of the DLP and the fact that the top posts are held by them will, it is felt, lead to a revival of racial feelings in the community. The racial composition of the faction approximates to that of the defunct People's Democratic Party."

(CO 1031/2491)

The Democratic Labour Party (DLP) has replaced the PDP in 1959 but the hatchet job on the political organ of the coolie problem continues. The struggle for power within the DLP is then a struggle by a racist PDP Indo-Trinbagonian faction to dominate the DLP. The Trinidad Despatch of the 22nd April 1959 in reporting on the internecine warfare within the DLP states as follows:

> "The negro element in the Bryan faction think that even though the PNM is far from being the ideal party to govern the country, it has nevertheless done a lot to ease the racial tension and cites the appointment of two East Indian Ministers, two East Indian Mayors and an East Indian as head of the Polytechnic School; in comparison the DLP, which has cried out most against alleged racialism in the PNM, has revealed itself, openly and defiantly, as being more prone to racialism than the PNM."

(CO 1031/2491)

The colonial discourse of the coolie problem is in 1959 insisting that the DLP is a racist Indian hegemonist political party. A reality that exonerates the PNM from all charges of racist hegemony made by the PDP then the

DLP against the PNM government. The reality that Bryan with no electoral base of the quantum to assault the PNM towards electoral victory in the next general elections due was demanding to be made political leader of the DLP is simply dismissed. Three Indo-Trinbagonian cabinet ministers and two Indo- Trinbagonian mayors is enough window dressing to dissuade the belief that the PNM is a racist hegemonist political party. Moreover when the Indo head of the Polytechnic School is Rudranath Capildeo brother of the denizen of evil in the DLP: Simbhoonath Capildeo.

The infamous speech Williams made in Woodford Square, Port-of-Spain in the aftermath of the PNM's defeat by the DLP in March 1958 Federal Elections was the subject of reports to the Colonial Office in 1958. On the 8th April 1958 Marnham instructs Baxter, all of the colonial office, to analyse the speech sent to the colonial office by Governor Beetham of Trinidad and Tobago. Baxter reports to Marnham that Williams had in fact proven that (a) the PNM share of the popular vote in 1958 had risen from that of 1956, and (b) that the DLP voters were mainly Indian. Baxter finds no racist hegemonic agenda in the discourse of the speech but dismisses Williams' demonisation of the supporters of the DLP as the words of a demagogue. Marnham comments on Baxter's allegation of Williams' failure to prove his allegations against the supporters of the DLP and the DLP in the left margin of Folio 3 as follows:

> "All the same, I wonder if there's not something in them"

(CO 1031/2490)

The letter by Beetham on the said speech states:

> "The racial aspect is to say the least worrying and we are keeping a
> very careful watch on the position."

(CO 1031/2490)

Marnham in Folio Note 6 of CO 1031/2490 reports to Sir J. Macpherson on various issues including the infamous speech of Williams. Marnham states on the said speech as follows:

> "I also attach WIS 105/12/06 containing Dr. Williams' 'racial'
> speech to which the Governor refers (3 thereon). There is a useful
> analysis of it in Mr. Baxter's minute on the file. It has nasty bits but
> I shouldn't myself have thought it was too awful."

(CO 1031/2490)

Marnham and Baxter do not then agree with Governor Beetham that Williams' 1958 speech was in fact racist and Williams is in fact exonerated by Marnham of the Colonial Office.

Mr. Profumo would visit Trinidad and Tobago in April 1958 and Marnham of the Colonial Office would depend on reports arising out of the Profumo visit to detail the realities on the ground in April 1958. As a result of this visit a confidential report undated and unsigned titled: "Racial Tension in Trinidad" would be generated. The report details conversations held between Profumo, Albert Gomes, Sinanan (whether Mitra or Ashford) and Bhadase Maraj on the 22nd April 1958 and the 28th April 1958. The report indicated that the said Sinanan spoke to Profumo on the issue of Federation allowing the speculation that it was in fact Ashford Sinanan. The report states as follows:

> "He declared that he was as strong a Federation man as anyone, and said he personally would not mind 10 or 15 years on the Opposition benches because the DLP would be a constructive opposition party. (Mr. Sinanan was no doubt being sincere in his way but he would have made a better impression if he had put his point a little less emphatically). He and Mr. Gomes were confident that the most effective speakers in the House were on the D.L.P. side."

(CO 1031/2490)

The lesson of the conversations reported above is not the boot licking and complete surrender of Sinanan and Gomes to the colonial overlord. The lesson is not that by their surrender, their complicity with the colonial overlord they exposed the DLP to machinations to ensure the political demise of the DLP. The lesson of the report is the complete, palpable contempt the colonial overlord held for, and acted upon, the politicians identified as being part of the coolie problem in Trinidad in 1958. The report continues:

> "2. They then raised a whole series of charges against the P.N.M. and their supporters, who they said were inflaming racial tension with the connivance of the police, and Government authorities. Mr. Gomes and Mr. Sinanan spoke in turn, adding fresh details to the picture and Mrs. Gomes added her share of allegations."

(CO 1031/2490)

Mr. Gomes, Sinanan and Mrs. Gomes have then used the opportunity of a luncheon hosted by Solomon Hochoy to lay the case to Profumo of a race war being waged by the PNM against the opposition. The presenters of the case also implicated the complicity colonial overlord in the race war being waged by the PNM against the Opposition. The report continues:

> "On Monday 28th April Mr. Bhadase Maraj called on Mr. Profumo and spoke along similar lines though he did not go into detail

to the same extent. Mr. Profumo asked what the Opposition had done to tax Dr. Williams personally about these allegations; Bhadase Maraj gave the impression that their personal relations with the Chief Minister were not good and that Dr. Williams had refused to take any real interest."

(CO 1031/2490)

Bhadase Maraj meets with Profumo and delivers the discourse of PNM racist oppression and Profumo questions Maraj on the opposition's response to this alleged racist war. The colonial overlords' utter disdain and contempt for the denizens of the coolie problem in 1958 is summed up in the report as follows:

"Two general comments: first, racial tension and threats of personal violence are nothing new in the political life of Trinidad, and second, it is more a question of tacit connivance by the Chief Minister in the actions of his supporters than explicit direction by him of a full-scale campaign."

(CO 1031/2490)

Williams is then exonerated and above censure for in the face of the coolie problem Williams is all the colonial overlords have and they must make the best of it. In fact the report would state that Williams' indiscretion was his infamous Woodford Square speech following his defeat in the Federal Elections in 1958. The report states:

"Nevertheless Sir Edward Beetham agreed with Mr. Profumo that the situation was potentially extremely ugly, and that wherever the blame may have lain in the past, the Chief Minister was very seriously at fault having made a most injudicious speech on racial lines earlier in April which brought a strong reaction from the Opposition."

(CO 1031/2490)

Williams' sin was then to make an injudicious speech that gave energy to the Opposition, to the coolie problem for they were one and the same. The substantive issue was not then a racist war being prosecuted to attain racist hegemony in favour of the PNM. It was the damage done to the agenda of the colonial overlord by Williams' injudicious post Federal Elections speech. For this reckless act the files would show that Williams paid his pound of flesh to the colonial overlord.

In the note of the conversation between Profumo and Williams there is no report of Profumo raising the claims of Gomes, Sinanan and Maraj of racist oppression by the PNM and government to Williams. The denizens of the coolie problem in 1958 clearly failed to understand that appeals to the colonial overlord about the PNM and the Government's racist oppression meant nothing, simply not registering on the radar screen of the colonial office. For the denizens of the coolie problem did not generate a viable, acceptable alternative to Williams and as such Sinanan, Gomes, Bryan and Maraj were in deep denial and they paid dearly for it in the politics of Trinidad and Tobago leading to constitutional decolonization in 1962.

Likewise Basdeo Panday and the UNC would be doomed to repeat the denial in December 2001 at 6pm when the then President of the Republic of Trinidad and Tobago invited the opposition PNM to form the government in the face of a hung general elections of 18 seats for both the PNM and UNC out of a total of 36 seats. The coolie problem had returned to haunt the politics of Trinidad and Tobago as in 1956 and was put down by Presidential coup d'état on the 24th December 2001.

The watershed that the September 1956 general elections constituted on the path to constitutional decolonization in Trinidad and Tobago necessitated the preparation of a document titled "Appreciation of the security situation in Trinidad and Tobago-1956" by the Police Security Officer, I.S. Paton. The report states:

> "11. Since the Elections the consciousness of racial origin has not been quite so apparent-although on January 2nd, 1957, the publication of the Report of the Commissioners on the Federal Capital site did some harm-and the new government has done a number of things to gain the confidence of the East Indian community. There remain many factors of influence against racial unity, however, not the least of these being the SANATAN DHARMA MAHA SABHA ASSOCIATION and the presence of the Indian Commissioner and staff."

(CO 1031/2594)

The Bhadase Maraj faction of the coolie problem is then the stumbling block to racial unity. Williams, the PNM even the racist Federal Capital site report are not hindrances to racial unity. The report continues as follows:

> "12. From the strictly security point of view the volatile atmosphere, created by the activities of political factions prior to the Elections was the main security danger, while continuous study of the MAHA SABHA and kindred racial organisations as well as the persistent, if fruitless, labours of the few remaining Communists was ever necessary."

(CO 1031/2594)

The coolie problem exists and demands continuous surveillance and action to ensure the security of the colony. The report dealing with the East Indian Problem states:

> "18. There were no apparent changes in the ideals of the East Indian leaders during the year. The true strength of the MAHA SABHA was shown clearly during the pre-General Election campaigning when, under the name of the PEOPLE'S DEMOCRATIC PARTY (P.D.P.), the Hindus and those Christians of Hindu origin organised into a racial party and returned five (5) members to Legislative Council-and nearly returned three (3) more."

(CO 1031/2594)

The intensity of the coolie threat is seen not in the fact that they won 5 seats in the 1956 Legislative Council but in the reality that they should have in fact won 8 seats in the 1956 Legislative Council. Continued potency of the coolie threat demands continued surveillance and covert action. In speaking on the "Report of the Federal Capital Site Commission" the report states:

> "This Report contained several references to the disquieting influence of the East Indian minority in TRINIDAD which, though containing a great element of truth, could not be calculated to improve the situation."

(CO 1031/2594)

The racist invective of the report is in fact truth for Paton the author of the document being reviewed. The discourse of the coolie problem is then premised upon a near pathological fear of the threat to a specific order, a power relation that the coolies of Trinidad constituted in the 1950's. The report continues:

> "By the time that the new Legislative Council was opened at the end of October it was apparent that there was no unity within the P.D.P. and the gap widened towards the end of the year. This was due mainly to the fact that the two SINANANS showed no inclination to accept the views of Maraj as leader of the Party. The year closed with MARAJ bearing his grudges hard against them and against CAPILDEO who, having gained his own seat in Council, no longer needed a 'mouth-piece'."

(CO 1031/2594)

The Sinanans are then one means by which to destabilise and shatter the PDP. They danced with the colonial overlord walking away from Butler and in the post 1956 scenario are locked in battle with Maraj. The report sums up the political threat of the coolie problem as follows:

> "24. As an all-over assessment, therefore, it is fair to state that power of the East Indian in politics has been weakened to a great extent. No leadership of quality has been seen and influence of the MAHA SABHA appears to be receding. Still there is distrust and even fear of Federation and their place in such a scheme, and it seems likely that they will need proof that their interests will be protected before 'bowing to the inevitable'.
>
> 26. Nonetheless, there are well over a quarter of a million East Indians of Hindu origin in Trinidad with the common bond of race who are within or sympathetic to the MAHA SABHA-or the P.D.P.-and the problem still exists."

(CO 1031/2594)

The PDP presents no viable challenge to the hegemony of the PNM but the coolie problem persists. History would show from 1958 to 1962 Williams and the colonial overlord saw no need in the soft touch, the strategy executed was to co-opt weak, ineffectual leadership that ensured acquiescence of the "East Indian". The question of the willingness of the Indo-Trinbagonian population to confront is then of central importance for they failed to confront the colonial overlord, Williams and the PNM in 1956, and Robinson and the NAR, and in 2001 Robinson as President of the Republic when faced with blatant public political marginalisation which is evidence in support of Simbhoonath Capildeo's discourse of the Indo- Trinbagonian as a servile race.

The Report of the British Caribbean Federal Capital Commission 1956 states:

> "A disturbing element in the political life of Trinidad, to which importance is attached in the other islands, is the presence of a large population, 35 percent of the whole, of East Indian descent. East Indians it is alleged, have ideals and loyalties differing from those to be found elsewhere in the Federation and they exercise a disruptive influence on social and political life in Trinidad which would vitiate the social and political life of the capital if it were placed on that island. We pass no judgement on these allegations, except to say that the existence of such a large minority, differing in so many ways from the rest of the people of the island, is bound

to introduce complications which will make the growth of healthy political conditions in Trinidad even more difficult than it would otherwise have been."

(Federal Capital Commission 1956 Pg. 20)

The East Indian minority in 1956 is then dead weight retarding the growth and development of healthy political conditions in Trinidad. The coolie problem is then arresting the development of Trinidad in the manner expected by the colonial overlord. An intractable problem that demands solution.

The monthly intelligence reports contained in files CO 1031/ 3718 Part A and CO 1031/3719 Part B reveal the reality that for the period 1960-62 the discourse of the coolie problem was no longer part of the official discourse of the Governor of the colony of Trinidad and Tobago. The concept of the East Indian problem was notably absent from the political discourse leading to the 1961 general elections and formal independence in August 1962. What are present in these reports of the then colonial Governors are reports on the schisms that ripped apart the DLP.

The monthly intelligence report for January and February 1960 dated the 17th March 1960 states:

"5. The D.L.P. opposition have not set up a Committee to reconsider the matters in issue on Constitution reform. Ashford Sinanan has made no secret of the fact that Albert Gomes in his discussions with you in London, went right outside his brief in opposing the Senate. Gomes is now in very bad odour with the Opposition and is not a member of the Committee."

(CO 1031/3718)

What then is the importance of Gomes' refusal to toe the DLP line on the creation of a Senate in the Parliament of Trinidad and Tobago? The report states as follows:

"As I understand it, Gomes' brief was to oppose not the Senate itself but its composition and the method of appointment to it. The Opposition may not find it too difficult to accept as a compromise the composition, term of office and method of appointment to the Senate, as has already tentatively been agreed with the Government delegation."

(CO 1031/3718)

The Governor is then part of a move by the colonial overlord to ensure an acquiescent and obedient DLP Opposition in the formulation of the constitution for at minimum full internal self- government for Trinidad and Tobago in the post 1961 general elections period.

In the monthly intelligence report dated the 27th April 1960, reports on developments within the DLP are as follows:

> "6. The stock of the D.L.P. Opposition Party has hit a 'new low'. The ailing Bhadase Maraj has at last handed over the leadership of the D L P to Dr. Rudranath Capildeo, Director of the Trinidad Polytechnic, who has a distinguished academic record matching that of Eric Williams. Capildeo is alleged to have paid a substantial sum of money for the leadership! Dr. Capildeo's first move was to suspend and subsequently expel from the D.L.P. his brother, Simbhoonath Capildeo, at the time acting leader of the Opposition in the Legislative Council, and Mitra Sinanan."

(CO 1031/3718)

Then Governor Beetham cannot mask his satisfaction with developments within the DLP. Bhadase Maraj is no longer the political leader of the DLP, Simbhoonath Capildeo has been expelled by Rudranath Capildeo and the internecine warfare that was fully revealed publicly can only work to the benefit of the colonial agenda. Beetham in the said report would write reporting on "some shameful exposes including an allegation against Stephen Maharaj" made by Simbhoonath Capildeo in the Legislative Council. One such shameful expose on the issue of Pethidine addiction was in fact known by the colonial overlord and acted upon has already been revealed in this text. Simbhoonath Capildeo's revelation therefore made public secrets which served the agenda of the colonial overlord to use such secrets to their benefit.

The monthly intelligence report for October 1960 by then Governor Solomon Hochoy reports on the DLP as follows:

> "7. The Democratic Labour Party is making another effort to re-establish itself. On his return from the United Kingdom recently, Ashford Sinanan, Leader of the Opposition in the Federal House of Representatives, announced that he had accepted the invitation to serve as acting Leader of the Democratic Labour Party of Trinidad and Tobago. This was the result of the consultations in London with the Leader, Dr. Rudranath Capildeo, who expects to be absent from the Territory for longer than was at first anticipated."

(CO1031/3718)

Hochoy is reporting that Ashford Sinanan and Rudranath Capildeo have by October, 1960 announced publicly their working political alliance and no opinion is offered on this alliance concerning a political threat to the

Colonial State. Unlike the alliance between Bhadase Maraj and Simbhoonath Capildeo, the alliance of Ashford Sinanan and Rudranath Capildeo constitutes no threat to the Colonial Order. It leaves one then to infer that no threat was constituted as any threat was possible from Sinanan and Capildeo in 1960.

In the report for November 1960 then Governor Hochoy reports on the rejection of the Boundaries Commission by Bhadase Maraj. Hochoy states:

> "6. In the midst of the re-organisation of the D.L.P. Bhadase Maraj, shortly after the composition of the Boundaries Commission was made public, announced that he had quit the 'DEMS' as the D.L.P. is referred to locally."

(CO1031/3718)

> "Maraj accused the Secretary of State of failing to set up an impartial Commission which he had promised to do during his visit to the Territory last June."

(CO1031/3718)

Bhadase Maraj is mounting opposition to the Electoral Boundaries Commission. Hochoy reports no such protest by the "new" DLP and in fact he reports glowingly on the developments within the DLP for November 1960. Hochoy states:

> "5. The re-organisation of the DLP under Ashford Sinanan is proceeding along well planned lines. The Party has recently set up its Executive Committee which includes a number of prominent persons. Sir Gerald Wight of Alstons Ltd. is reported to be contributing substantially to the Party funds and is a member of the Executive Committee, which wisely does not include any member of the splinter groups of the old DLP."

(CO 1031/3718)

Hochoy has revealed that the new DLP was in 1960 consorting with the white oligarchs. Having purged themselves of the undesirable coolie elements namely Bhadase Maraj and Simbhoonath Capildeo the new DLP was now a fit vehicle for the aspirations of all elements opposed to the PNM deemed fit to rule by the colonial overlord ending the need for the discourse of the coolie problem.

DLP assaults on the report of the Boundaries Commission and on the Electoral Registration Ordinance, 1960 Rules would place on the political agenda the issue of free and fair democratic elections when due in the colony of Trinidad and Tobago. Hochoy in his report of March 1961 reports on the debate in the Legislative Council on the Boundaries Commission Report and the manner in which the PNM government rebutted the charges Stephen Maharaj made of gerrymandering in favour of the PNM. Hochoy states:

> "Williams in his speech effectively dismissed Maharaj's gerrymandering accusation by laying the blame for any such accusation at the feet of the former government."

(CO1031/3718)

For Hochoy, Williams effectively dismissed Maharaj's claims by indicating that the 1956 general elections were in fact executed upon gerrymandered electoral boundaries, but it was the colonial overlord that drew the 1956 electoral boundaries. Hochoy has then to be guilty of electoral gerrymandering given his complicity with the colonial overlord. Moreover the Hochoy/Williams argument that general elections from 1946 to 1956 were all gerrymandered by the colonial overlord but that would end in 1960 with Williams. As is the case with Patrick Solomon's and Williams' retort to the charge of gerrymandering made in 1960, Hochoy's retort does not deal with the substantive issues raised.

In the monthly intelligence report for April 1961 Hochoy reports on the budget debate as follows:

> "The Opposition attack of the budget produced little if any constructive criticism."

(CO 1031/3718)

> "S. Capildeo (Independent) received the applause of both sides of the House for what Williams termed the only speech by a Member of the Opposition worth listening to. His criticisms were obviously well thought out and equally well presented."

(CO 1031/3718)

The new DLP had then in the words of Hochoy failed to live up to its duty as the alternate government in waiting. It was the sole voice of the old DLP that of Simbhoonath Capildeo that would indicate in his brilliance the paucity of thought and moral rectitude that sat on Opposition benches in April 1961, a sole, single voice that does not constitute an alternate government in waiting. Hochoy reports in April 1961 that Rudranath Capildeo would now become a topic, a reality reported on in Hochoy's monthly intelligence reports leading up to the general elections of 1961 and independence in August 1962.

The monthly intelligence report for June 1961 by then Governor Hochoy reports on the activities of the DLP and the Opposition in the Legislative Council. On the activities of the Opposition, Hochoy reports:

"7. The DLP opposition in the Legislative Council have been at it again. On this occasion during the debate on the Central Tenders Board, Simbhoonath Capildeo (Independent Opposition Member for Caroni South) among other things, accused the Government of knowingly appointing as the head of the Industrial Development Corporation, Mr. David Weintrauls, who has been investigated by the United States Government for Communist activities. He referred also to C.L.R. James as having been harboured in the P.N.M. Central Organisation and charged the government for being sympathetic to communists in spite of its 'pious platitudes' against Red infiltration."

(CO 1031/3719)

Hochoy reports to his colonial overlords yet another instance in which the old DLP in the person of Simbhoonath Capildeo raises an issue in the Legislative Council that exposes the hypocrisy of colonial rule in Trinidad and Tobago in June 1961. Declassified files for the Local Intelligence Committee and the Police surveillance reports reveal the priority afforded to the activities of so-called communists in the colony of Trinidad and Tobago. The surveillance of communists in Trinidad would intensify with the rise of Cheddi Jagan and the PPP in British Guiana and the Cuban Revolution in 1959. Simbhoonath Capildeo would then raise the issue of Williams consorting with alleged reputed communists as Weintrauls and known Marxists as C.L.R. James under the protection of the British colonial overlord.

In fact in declassified files read by the author there are no monthly reports made on the activities of C.L.R. James whilst he served Williams and the PNM before August 1962 in the colony of Trinidad and Tobago. One suspects that if such reports were made they were never part of the monthly report made in writing to the Governor of the colony. Clearly the colonial security structure gave Williams space in which to consolidate his grip on political power that was not forthcoming to other political players in Trinidad and Tobago. In the June 1961 report Solomon Hochoy lauds the call the DLP made to its supporters to be registered as electors under the new system of electoral registration introduced by the PNM government.

Clearly there is anxious concern by Hochoy on the timely completion of the exercise of registering all electors who present themselves to be registered to vote in the next general elections. He would report on a campaign event of the DLP as follows:

"8. The re-organised DLP continue to hold electioneering meetings and to open new constituency offices all over the territory. At one meeting in one of the PNM strongholds, they were given a rough time by a booing, jeering and laughing crowd."

(CO 1031/3719)

In the monthly intelligence report for August 1961 Hochoy reports on the reaction of Rudranath Capildeo to the Representation of the People Bill 1961. He states:

"At the same time, Dr. Capildeo, the Party Leader, made public a statement in which he condemned the Bill and threatened to use every constitutional means to see that the election was fought by the ballot box. The statement, strangely enough, continued on the strain 'failing this we are issuing a grave and serious warning, that while we have no wish to break any reasonable law, we will have to consider the possibility if this ordinance is allowed to violate our sense of right and justice as it undoubtedly does'."

(CO 1031/3719)

Hochoy continues his report on the activities of Rudranath Capildeo as follows:

"Dr. Capildeo followed this up by holding a mass meeting in the centre of the sugar-producing area, where the population is almost entirely Indian. Again he voiced another astonishing threat, declaring that he had taken the irrevocable stand, i.e. the ballot box or boycott and after the boycott, civil disobedience."

"This meeting was noteworthy also for the presence of the most prominent leaders of the Opposition Party, all of whom had been at variance with one another up to quite recently including a few like the Honourable Simbhoonath Capildeo, who had at one stage left the Party."

(CO 1031/3719)

Rudranath Capildeo is not according to Hochoy playing the role expected of him as political leader of the new DLP. To assault the PNM agenda for electoral reform in Trinidad and Tobago was one thing but to launch such a vitriolic attack that hinted at the end of schism between the 'old' DLP and the 'new' DLP and the rehabilitation of Simbhoonath Capildeo and Bhadase

Maraj politically in the 'new' DLP sounded the alarm bells for Hochoy with nightmarish visions of the coolie problem of 1956.

The unease that the new electoral registration system and the voting machines constituted in the mind of Hochoy is indicated in the following statement of his:

> "Much capital is being made by the Opposition Leader of the ease with which voting machines can be tampered, and of the difficulty which illiterate voters who are mostly Indians will experience in registering their votes on the machine. But I understand that these fears are very highly exaggerated."

(CO 1031/3719)

Solomon Hochoy never reveals the source of the information that debunks the DLP position on the reliability and efficacy of the voting machine used in the 1961 general elections. What he does indicate is the refusal of the colonial oligarchs in the run up to the 1961 general elections to entertain any criticism of the electoral boundaries, the electoral registration system and the voting machines made by elements opposed to the PNM.

Hochoy in the monthly intelligence report for October 1961 reports on one speech made by Rudranath Capildeo at the Grand Savannah, Port of Spain. He states:

> "At a very large meeting held by the D.L.P. at the Grand Savannah in Port of Spain to present the Party's candidates which was attended by a majority of party supporters, there was considerable heckling by an organised crowd of P.N.M. supporters near the platform. This caused the D.L.P. Party Leader to lose his temper and he called on the crowd to 'go to war against the P.N.M.; break up every P.N.M. meeting wherever they are held; wherever Dr. Williams goes to speak chase him away; run Dr. Solomon out of town; arm yourselves to take over this country'. A vast majority of the community supporters of both political parties have strongly objected to this attitude by the D.L.P. Leader."

(CO 1013/3719)

In a series of public statements reported by Hochoy, Rudranath Capildeo had clearly sown the wind and in November 1961 would reap the whirlwind but the tsunami would come in December 1961. For Hochoy, Rudranath Capildeo had recklessly and irresponsibly played with fire from his return to the colony on the 1st May 1961.

In the monthly intelligence report for November 1961 Hochoy would report on the whirlwind of November 1961 as follows:

"4. I reported separately on the outbursts of violence at electioneering meetings, necessitating proclamations of emergency in localized areas to enable police search for suspected caches of weapons and ammunition. While this measure did not produce the expected result, it served as an effective warning to the lawless, so much so that there were no further major disturbances. The Opposition Party's decision not to hold any further public meetings contributed to this improved situation."

(CO 1031/3719)

By way of a report dated the 25th November 1961 Hochoy details the said events as follows:

"3. The labour unions and the dock workers had staged demonstrations in the city about 10 days ago in support of the Government Party for the General Elections. A second demonstration held by them in Port of Spain on Monday the 20th instant, decided to march out to the eastern suburbs. On arriving at an area about four miles east of Port of Spain which is a D.L.P. stronghold, the demonstrators were attacked by gunfire, bottles and stones. In the ensuing fracas, one man was shot dead and two others were severely wounded. Further acts of violence followed in the form of shooting up the houses of residents, beating up people and damaging motor cars."

(CO 1031/3775)

"With the outbreak of violence firm action was imperative and, on the advice of Cabinet, I proclaimed a State of Emergency in the affected areas with effect from the 22nd November. This enabled the police to search for arms, explosives and ammunition reported to be cached in the district. The police received reports of further caches in two adjoining electoral districts, both D.L.P. strongholds. On the advice of Cabinet, I issued a further proclamation declaring a state of emergency in these areas as well."

"5. The results of the general searches by police have produced little of real value. Ammunition and odd firearms were found but nothing on an organised scale. Either the hideouts are exceedingly well concealed or the information concerning their existence was inaccurate."

(CO 1031/3775)

The reply from the Colonial Office to Hochoy's report of the 25th November 1961 states:

> "The D.L.P. seem to have been up to their old game of causing trouble and then seeking to blame their political opponents. No doubt we shall hear more of this from Capildeo and his colleagues in due course if as it seems likely the P.N.M. win the elections. It is encouraging that Williams seems to have taken firm steps to prevent further trouble and I only hope that he will be able to restrain his own people."

(CO 1031/3775)

The colonial overlord and his local minion Hochoy, insist that: (a) the DLP was involved with the acquisition of the military materiel necessary to a planned strategy of societal violence which was revealed in November 1961. (b) The DLP military arm deliberately attacked a peaceful demonstration in support of the PNM in Barataria in November 1961. (c) Prompt and effective action by the PNM and the Police of Trinidad pre-empted the DLP attempt at a coup d'état.

In the absence of corroborating evidence in support of a military adventurist DLP one can contend that the said union that entered Barataria being a pliable arm of the PNM willingly entered Barataria for the express purpose of waging war on DLP supporters. In the battle that ensued firearms were used by persons unknown, but the abiding reality of the engagement is that DLP supporters perceived or otherwise were the losers of the engagement. The social violence justified the limited State of Emergency in the Barataria electoral district and the pressing need to uncover DLP arsenals resulted in the extension of the State of Emergency to the St. Augustine and Chaguanas electoral districts.

The violence of Barataria and the Police actions under the State of Emergency had the desired effect as the DLP formally withdrew from the 1961 general elections campaign. Rudranath Capildeo led the DLP along the path of engagement with the PNM utilizing empty vitriolic discourse, which empowered the colonial overlord and Williams to brand the DLP as an armed, violent, insurgent grouping necessitating the actions of November 1961. In fact the DLP was never an insurgent grouping and Rudranath Capildeo spoke a role whilst being servile in his worldview.

Evidence of this is seen in a telegram sent by Rudranath Capildeo to the Secretary of State for the Colonies. Capildeo states:

> "We of the Democratic Labour Party, one of the main contending parties, are worried that the intimidation and violence will be used

to prevent our supporters from getting to the polls on election day. We are equally determined that our supporters shall vote. We are not afraid of a fair election. We would kindly request that you send down as many observers as possible so that their presence may help to ensure freedom to vote."

(CO 1031/3775)

The denial of Rudranath Capildeo in 1961 is in fact highly reminiscent of the denial of Basdeo Panday and the UNC in December 2001. How can international observers solve the problems listed in the said telegram? Can a colonial order allow international observers to a colonial general election in 1961?

The deep abiding fallacy of the telegram is the appeal to the colonial overlord for democracy and fair play. Rudranath Capildeo appeals to the colonial overlord but the colonial overlord only has contempt for him and the DLP. Between 21st-24th November 1961 the political back of Rudranath Capildeo was broken and the results of the general election of the 4th December 1961 would reveal a 20 seats to 10 seats victory for the PNM over the DLP. The PNM victory was in fact a rout of the DLP giving Williams the means to move to Independence by 31st August 1962.

The Colonial Office prepared a brief for the British Prime Minister on the new electoral registration procedure adopted by the PNM in 1961 for the visit of the British Prime Minister to the West Indies during Easter of 1961. The brief states:

"7. As far as possible, however, it is suggested that the Prime Minister in replying to any questions on this subject, should say that as Trinidad is now virtually self-governing, he would prefer not to comment on a procedure which he understands, has been adopted by the Trinidad Government with the approval of their Legislative Council. He has himself no experience of voting machines; but the experience of them in the United States, where their use is widespread and where Trinidad acquired both the idea and the machinery, shows that voting machines are perfectly compatible with normal democratic practices. If there are still complaints about the registration practices, these should be directed at the Trinidad Government and not at the Prime Minister."

(CO 1031/3774)

Reginald Maulding, Colonial Secretary in his reply to the letter of Derek Walke-Smith states:

"Finally, a general point. Trinidad has, as you know, enjoyed de facto full internal self-government for sometime past and will continue to do so de jure when the new constitution is brought fully into its operation after the forthcoming elections. You will appreciate, therefore, that the matter of election procedures is within the competence of the local ministers. This is not to say that I should not act if I felt that the new election procedures were being abused. I am, however, satisfied that the Trinidad Government are fully alive to their responsibilities in this respect and that they have made determined efforts to ensure fair elections."

(CO 1031/3774)

The Colonial Secretary has then given the PNM government a clean bill of health on the issue of electoral reform in Trinidad and Tobago in 1961. The discourse of the briefing for the British Prime Minister and Maulding's letter both of 1961 amount to a tour de force that emasculates the DLP for in the face of PNM majority in the Legislative Council 1956-61 and a hostile recalcitrant colonial overlord, the political appeal of the DLP to cross voting lines premised on race faltered and collapsed with the active help of Rudranath Capildeo and his politics of vocal bravado backed up with cowering servility. The refusal of the Colonial overlord to intervene and take action on the charges of electoral fraud against the PNM in 1961 heightened the case for the PNM as the party destined to rule Trinidad and Tobago and the obverse being the reality that applied to the DLP.

In a secret and personal report by then Governor Hochoy dated 19th September 1961 Hochoy states:

"10. There can be no doubt that Dr. Capildeo's utterances concerning the smashing of voting machines could find favour only in certain areas and among the most boisterous followers of his party. Generally speaking, the statements evoked mixed feelings of surprise, concern and resentment. It has been reported that Dr. Capildeo has more recently stated that he has been accused wrongfully of advocating violence, but the only violence threatened was violence against the machines. 'We do not threaten violence against anybody else'. There is, however, an inescapable latent threat of something more sinister."

(CO 1031/3555)

On the 18th January 1962 the Secretary of State met with Rudranath Capildeo in Trinidad. By way of a confidential report on the said meeting of 18th January 1962 D. Williams of the Colonial Office would state:

"It seems to us therefore that Capildeo's charge concerning the Ordinance and incidentally, the validity of the 1961 Registration Rules, are without merit. If you agree with us in this, perhaps you would arrange for Capildeo to be told that the Secretary of State has looked into this matter and is satisfied that no irregularities occurred in connection with the enactment or bringing into operation of the Ordinance.

3. Turning to the rest of Capildeo's complaint, since those are, we believe, all or nearly all, at the moment before the courts, it would be improper for us to comment. Nevertheless, I shall be grateful for your views as to the substance of these complaints, and in due course, when they have been disposed of by the Courts, for your advice as to the terms of the reply which the Secretary of State should send to Capildeo."

(CO 1031/3555)

The following are obvious from the extract of text quoted above: (1) the effective manner in which the Colonial Office played Dr. R. Capildeo and the 'new' DLP. Clearly the colonial overlord effectively strung along R. Capildeo until Independence in August 1962 ended the need for engagement with him. It was then obvious that by the Independence Conference in London all was lost for R. Capildeo and his 'new' DLP. Hence his return from London a broken and spineless politician and his subsequent retreat to the University of London.

(2) The servile worldview of R. Capildeo and his 'new' DLP enabled the colonial overlord to defeat them at the level of the idea.

(3) The colonial overlord in turn played Hochoy as they effectively took a back seat in the management of the colony in the flow to Independence in 1962. They utilised their discourse of de jure and de facto internal self government to ensure that the two major races became the villains of the piece exonerating the white colonial overlord and the effective covert and overt roles played in ensuring the transition to Independence was in keeping with their geo-political agendas.

(4) The colonial vassals at the Governor's House in Trinidad exploited their relatively new positions of power to play both the colonial overlord and Williams to their personal benefit especially in light of an independent Trinidad and Tobago being on the cards. The DLP and their supporters were then the common playthings of abusive suitors namely the colonial overlord, the local colonial officials and Williams and the PNM.

Ellis Clarke by way of a report dated 25th April 1962 to A. Thomas of the Colonial Office would reveal two realities: (a) the discourse of R. Capildeo as a threat to the order in keeping with the discourse so ably articulated by Hochoy. Clarke states:

> "We are not unduly perturbed by Capildeo's threats but at the same time the situation is a grave one and requires careful watching."

(CO 1031/3555)

(b) The covert roles played by the Colonial Officials executing the strategy to ensure the rule of Williams and the PNM at the point in time when independence comes into force. Clarke states:

> "You will, I am sure, realise that my telegram No.69 of the 23rd April, which you will have seen by this, was not wholly uninspired. Let us hope that an early public announcement will not be without effect."

(CO 1031/3555)

The telegram No.69 of the 23rd April 1962 Clarke speaks of was sent from Williams to the Secretary of State for the Colonies by Ellis Clarke. In this telegram Williams calls for the date of the Independence Conference to be announced by the Secretary of State for the Colonies. Williams also requested that the Secretary of State announce the composition of the Trinidad and Tobago delegation:

> "… would be comprised of members of the two main political parties as well as representatives from the Senate and of major economic and political interests in the territory."

(CO 1031/3555)

Clarke clearly boasts of his initiative to convince Williams to give assent to the said telegram that enables the Colonial Office to set in motion the means to effectively kill the court actions launched by the DLP following their decimation in the 1961 general elections.

Governor Solomon Hochoy by way of secret and personal report dated 19th May 1962 to Douglas Williams of the Colonial Office reports on the progress of the pending election cases filed by the DLP. Hochoy states:

> "In the note of the Secretary of State's meeting with the members of the opposition appended to the second letter above-mentioned, the Secretary of State reserved his opinion until the judgment of the courts was delivered pending election cases."

"No news has yet been received with regard to the appeal in the Bleasdell-Thomasos Case and the other election petitions are due to come up for hearing on May 28th. In view, however, of the opening of the Independence Conference on that date..."

(C0 1031/3555)

The depth of strategic incompetence of the 'new' DLP and the manner in which the local colonial officials and the colonial overlord in tandem played the DLP is apparent from the extract of the text quoted above. The DLP was told that the Colonial Office had no position on the general elections of 1961 until the electoral petitions filed by the DLP are settled in the courts of Trinidad and Tobago. Until such time that the petitions were settled the DLP was simply in limbo, but during this state of nothingness the move to Independence accelerated on the 28th May with the start of the Independence Conference in London.

In his monthly intelligence report for May 1962 dated the 8th June 1962 Hochoy would report on the election petitions of the DLP as follows:

"4. As a result of the refusal by the Privy Council to grant leave to the petitioner against the decision of the Supreme Court in his election petition against Dr. Solomon, all the remaining petitions have been withdrawn by the respective petitioners who were ordered to pay costs."

(CO 1031/3719)

R. Capildeo and his 'new' DLP capitulated and came away from the Independence Conference cowed and defeated. Clearly the colonial overlords and their vassals in Trinidad and Tobago delivered a broken, cowed and malleable 'new' DLP to the PNM at the Independence Conference in London 1962.

The Trinidad and Tobago Special Branch Monthly Intelligence Summary for February 1962 reporting on racial, religious and political matters states:

"15. There was evidence of a resurgence of racialism during the month. It was a direct sequel to the recent political development in the territory and might in fact be described as an inflation of the racial tension that had subsided to some extent after the legislative elections in December. The moving figure in this was H.P. Singh, a merchant tailor in Port-of-Spain, whose machinations have been mostly covert."

(CO 1031/3720)

The Special Branch Monthly Intelligence summary for May 1962 reports on the racial, religious and related matters as follows:

> "The Indian Association of Trinidad and Tobago (I.A.T.T.) held several meetings during the month for the purpose of raising funds for financing a four man delegation headed by Jang Bahadoorsingh, President of the Association, to go to the United Kingdom to protest the Draft Constitution for Independence."

(CO 1031/3720)

> "25. At one of these meetings Kenneth Lalla, a member of the managing committee of the organisation, advocated civil disobedience and urged members to 'be ready at a moment's notice to march'. Other speakers, including H.P. Singh, Secretary and Public Relations Officer, suggested that they should resort to violence if the wishes of the association were not granted."

(CO 1031/3720)

> "26. Meanwhile, there have been reports of internal dissension in the association. Controversy arose over the selection of delegates for the London Conference with special regard to the choice between Ramdeo Sampath, a Hindu, and Lennox Dialsingh, a Presbyterian."

(CO 1031/3720)

> "28. The I.A.T.T. has formed an 'action committee' allegedly for the purpose of planning acts of violence and sabotage, as well as training men for this purpose. It is reported that Conrad Gonzales, a Trinidadian whose occupation is given as engineer, was appointed the field organiser of the committee."

(CO 1031/3720)

> "31. A report indicated that on 24/5/62 a decision had been taken to attack Police Stations and bridges, and Negroes residing in areas where there was a predominance of East Indian origin. This was not implemented, however, because it was subsequently felt that such action would have been precipitate, especially as Dr. Rudranath Capildeo had said that he was confident of success in his talks in the UK."

(CO 1031/3720)

"33. As the time for the Independence Conference in London approached, leading members of the D.L.P. of East Indian origin continued to play a major role in the organisation and activities of the I.A.T.T. and, in so doing, exhibited some lack of confidence in and loyalty to their political party. Although the I.A.T.T. had been founded as a racial organisation and not as a political party, it would appear that the possibility of it emerging as a political force must be taken into account."

(CO 1031/3720)

By February 1962 the coolie threat to security was summed up in the person of H.P. Singh and the organisational base of this coolie threat was the Indian Association of Trinidad and Tobago. The Special Branch Intelligence Summary signed by one L.J. Rodriguez insists that the I.A.T.T. possessed the military capability to engage in military adventurism in 1962 in the run up to Independence. If the I.A.T.T. possessed such a capacity why was it never unleashed and moreover where were the pre-emptive strikes to prevent this action by the I.A.T.T.?

This is then a question on the accuracy of the intelligence supplied especially given the political potency of the said intelligence. There were no arms caches discovered during the state of emergencies of the 21st-24th November 1961 as there was no evidence of a military arm of the DLP trained and mobilised to engage in military adventurism with the colonial state.

Likewise in 1962 no evidence was presented of a military arm of the I.A.T.T. trained and equipped to engage in military actions against the state. Secondly the names called in the report with the exception of H.P. Singh as being leading activists of the IATT became noted ones in the realm of business, the law and governance in the post independence era of Trinidad and Tobago noted for the hegemony of Williams and the PNM. Why would the military arm of the IATT hold off on its military adventurism on the expectation of the impact on the Independence Conference and the promise that Rudranath Capildeo would deliver the goods?

The IATT sent a delegation to London seeking an audience with the Secretary of State for the Colonies on the grounds of their rejection of the proposed constitution. Was the reason for the IATT holding off on military adventurism because of their presence in London seeking to influence the outcome of the Independence Conference? The likely reality is that the IATT possessed no credible military resources and posed no threat to the security of the colonial state.

What is apparent then is the deliberate and conscious manufacturing of a coolie threat to security by local colonial officials to ensure that the agenda of

Williams and the PNM became hegemonic in the face of a near precipitous withdrawal from the daily governance of the colony by the colonial overlord in the post 1956 general elections scenario. The colonial overlord in the Colonial Office bought into the process as it served their agenda to pass the colony of Trinidad and Tobago into the hands of Williams and the PNM as all other political forces in the colony from September 1956 to the 31st August 1962 were deemed unfit to rule.

What realities are then afforded by de-classified files for the post-independence era of the National Archives of the United Kingdom? The British High Commissioner based in Port-of- Spain, Trinidad to the newly independent Trinidad and Tobago was required to send fortnightly summaries to the British Foreign Office. These fortnightly summaries would in fact commence before independence on the 31st August 1962 commencing on the 4th July 1962 reporting on the period June 19th to 2nd July 1962.

The fortnightly summary dated the 18th July 1962 would state on the Democratic Labour Party as follows:

> "3. Speaking to a meeting of the Opposition Party (Democratic Labour Party) shortly after his return from London, Mr. Ashford Sinanan, Deputy Leader of the Opposition reported on the Independence Conference and stated that a concerted effort was going to be made by Government and Opposition 'to wipe out race and racial intolerance and all forms of racialism once and for all'."

(DO 200/84)

The fortnightly summary dated the 1st August 1962 states:

> "2. The London talks have certainly resulted in a better atmosphere in Trinidad which has been particularly reflected in the much better tone in Government/Opposition relations in the Legislature. Dr. Williams has commented separately that he has already brought the Deputy Leader of the Opposition into discussions in the absence of the Opposition Leader who has remained in London for medical treatment."

(DO 200/84)

The fortnightly summary dated the 28th August 1962 states:

> "Both Government and Opposition are still showing every intention of honouring their pledge of bipartisan consultation on major issues given at the London Conference."

(DO 200/84)

The fact that political summaries from the 12th September 1962 ceased reporting on race relations at the political level in Trinidad and Tobago indicates that the colonial overlord insisted on a specific type of political behaviour from the end of the constitutional conference in London to formal independence on the 31st August 1962. Thereafter, it was no longer an issue with the colonial overlord.

The fortnightly summary dated the 3rd July 1963 would state:

> "Dr. Capildeo, the East Indian Opposition Leader, returned to Trinidad on the 21st June from his temporary post at London University.
>
> He attended a session of the House of Representatives on the 28th June, but said nothing of substance. He is, however, due to make a major public speech on the 7th July."

(DO 200/84)

The fortnightly summary dated the 17th July 1963 reporting on Dr. Capildeo and the Democratic Labour Party (DLP) states:

> "On 7th July, Dr. Capildeo, the Opposition Leader, made his first political speech since his return to Trinidad after 7 months as lecturer in mathematics at London University.
>
> 2. His speech was bluntly racial, his main theme, and that of certain of his supporting speakers, was that the Peoples National Movement (P.N.M.)Government were ignoring the rights of the Indian community, and one of the D.L.P. MP's said: 'What has happened in British Guiana would be a joke to what could happen in Trinidad'. Dr. Capildeo subsequently spoke in Parliament on the themes that people were afraid to oppose the government because of the threat of discrimination, and that there was actual discrimination against the Indian community.
>
> 4. Dr. Capildeo's descent into racialism was strongly criticised in the main daily 'The Trinidad Guardian', and responsible members of his Party are known to be increasingly dissatisfied with his erratic leadership."

(DO 200/84)

Clearly the personnel had changed but the discourse of the racist East Indian opposition to the PNM in Trinidad and Tobago crossed the independence divide. That there existed an organic bond between the strategic imperatives of Britain and those of Eric Williams is clearly illustrated by Williams' role in the execution of British policy on British Guiana in the early 1960's.

The fortnightly summary dated 8th May 1963 states as follows:

> "Dr. Williams has used this High Commission as the channel for receiving information about the developments in British Guiana and for expressing his own views to the British, British Guianian, Jamaica and Barbados Governments."

(DO 200/84)

The fortnightly summary dated the 17th July 1963 states:

> "Secretary of State's visits to Trinidad.

> 3. These discussions, which were mainly on the subject of British Guiana, confirmed Dr. Williams' concern about the dangers of the spread of racialism and Communism in the region from British Guiana; his loss of patience with Dr. Jagan; and his objections to a solution based on proportional representation because of possible repercussions in Trinidad. One immediate practical outcome has been that Dr. Williams has been persuaded to discourage a visit to Trinidad by the British Guiana Sub-Committee of the United Nations Committee of 24."

(DO 200/84)

The fortnightly summary dated the 4th December 1963 states on the topic of British Guiana as follows:

> "Dr. Williams who had previously said in private that 'Jagan had brought it all on himself', made an outspoken speech on the subject of British Guiana in the House of Representatives at the end of November.

> His speech amounted to an impressive and formidable indictment of Dr. Jagan and though Dr. Williams was careful not to comment on the particular decision you had taken (to have done so would have been politically difficult in Trinidad) his speech was understanding and helpful towards our policies the tone of the debate in the Trinidad Parliament makes it more unlikely than ever that any mediation involving Dr. Williams will be acceptable to Dr. Jagan."

(DO 200/84)

The fortnightly summary dated the 18th December 1963, states on the topic of Trinidad and British Guiana as follows:

"The Trinidad delegate alone among new Commonwealth delegates abstained, along with Britain and the old Commonwealth, on the Ghana motion in the General Assembly demanding the fixing of a date for independence for British Guiana. The Trinidad delegate, who had been instructed by Dr. Williams also spoke against the resolution."

(DO 200/84)

British Guiana ruled by Dr. Cheddi Jagan and the Peoples Progressive Party (PPP) constituted a perceived danger to Williams' hegemony in Trinidad and Tobago. Williams saw the danger in terms of Indo hegemony and Communism and executed his role of marginalizing Cheddi Jagan within the British Caribbean enabling the removal of the PPP via an electoral system that Williams himself feared. Cheddi Jagan and the PPP therefore constituted an Indo, Marxist-Leninist threat that had to be banished from the politics of British Guiana given its threat to the stability of the politics of Afro hegemony under the rule of the PNM in Trinidad and Tobago in 1963.

CHAPTER 2

FLASHPOINTS 1956-1962

The de-classified files accessed dated from 1956 indicate specific flashpoints between the colonial and ex-colonial British overlords and Dr. Eric Williams in his capacities of Chief Minister, Premier and Prime Minister of Trinidad and Tobago.

The general elections of the 24th September 1956 resulted in the PNM winning thirteen of twenty-four seats. In a unicameral chamber termed the Legislative Council consisting of twenty-four elected members, five nominated members and two ex-officio members, Williams did not command an absolute majority.

In the Monthly Intelligence Report of the Trinidad and Tobago Intelligence Committee for September 1956 the then Governor Edward Beetham would report on the said results as follows:

> "2. By securing seats in thirteen of the twenty-four constituencies the People's National Movement obtained a majority among the elected members but not an absolute majority in the Legislative Council as the Constitution also provides for two ex-officio and five nominated members.
>
> Accordingly on the day following polling day when the preliminary results had been made known I called in Dr. Eric Williams, Political Leader of the People's National Movement, and expressed the hope that he would form a Government under the New Constitution, at the same time offering him my fullest co- operation in his task. This action on my part set off a great deal of surmise in the press and elsewhere-including a public hint by Dr. Williams himself-that I had implied, in effect, that the People's National Movement would be entitled to 'nominate' at least two of the five nominated members from among other members of the Party to enable it to

run the Government. At an interview sought by the Press, I made it clear that the interpretation placed upon my 'offer of co-operation' was incorrect: that the two ex-officio members would naturally vote with the PNM. Government (or any Government in power) and that I would appoint nominated members who would not be unsympathetic to the People's National Movement but that Her Majesty's Government's standing instructions precluded me from appointing any person who is a member of the Party or subject to Party discipline. After further discussions with Dr. Williams we reached an understanding in the matter and he confirmed on the 3rd of October that the People's National Movement would form the Government. Throughout this period Dr. Williams and his Party treated the matter in a most dignified manner and preserved a strict silence with the press."

(CO 1031/1805)

Governor Beetham is then initially adamant that he cannot fit two nominated members out of five that are PNM Party members or are willing to toe the PNM party line in the Legislative Council of 1956. Beetham by his position placed the decision to be made whether to assure Williams a majority in the Legislative Council squarely in the lap of his superiors in the Colonial Office.

Appendix A to the Monthly Intelligence Report for September 1956 as signed by Solomon Hochoy states:

> "Whether P.N.M. will form the government is not clear and constitutional crisis is possible, but it will be difficult to explain to the country at this stage exactly why P.N.M. cannot at least try to run the Government. From the security point of view this may constitute a serious threat as P.N.M. with its popular appeal can, if desired, convince the electorate that the fault lies with the Administration and thus create dissatisfaction amongst its supporters.
>
> This in turn could lead to unrest of a serious nature but such is likely to depend on the interpretation of events put out by Williams and the other P.N.M. legislators-elect."

(CO 1031/1805)

Solomon Hochoy, the Colonial Secretary and the other members of the Intelligence Committee had then warned the colonial overlord that there was a price to pay by refusing to avert the upcoming constitutional crisis.

Foreign Office Intel No. 198 to certain of Her Majesty's Representatives dated November 8th, 1956 reports on the 1956 general elections in Trinidad and Tobago as follows:

> "Dr. Williams then asked that his nominees should be appointed to fill the nominated seats and this request at first threatened to give rise to some constitutional difficulty. The basis on which Nominated Members are appointed remains as it was set out in 1949 in a despatch from the Secretary of State to the Governor, namely that such members should 'strengthen the experience and knowledge of the Council in dealing with the complex issues of Government' and should be appointed not to represent any particular interest but 'to serve the broad and best interests of the Colony as a whole'.
>
> In one or two other colonial territories with advanced constitutions, it has, however, been recognised recently that nominated members could not be appointed to a Legislature to oppose the policy of the majority of the elected members, and in those territories the Governors have consulted with the Leaders of the majority parties as to how the nominated seats should be filled.
>
> In Trinidad, therefore, the emergence of a majority party was recognised as calling for some modification of the principles of the 1949 despatch. The Secretary of State therefore authorised the Governor to 'take such steps by way of nominating suitable persons to the Legislative Council, after consultation with the leader of the majority party. As will provide a reasonable working majority for that party'.
>
> Discussions between the Governor and Dr. Williams have now taken place and two Nominated Members who may be expected to support the P.N.M. have been appointed."

(CO 1031/1301)

The decision to grant Williams two pliant nominated members was then a strategic imperative given the rejection of the colonial office of the PDP and the Butler Party. But it was the report of the Intelligence Committee in the hand of Solomon Hochoy the then Colonial Secretary that would indicate the need to not invoke the 1949 mechanism of the constitutional coup d'état that was so effectively used against the Butler Party in 1950. It was Hochoy's report that would confirm that it was now necessary to review the policy on the appointment of nominated members to the Legislative Council in the Colony of Trinidad and Tobago in 1956.

By way of a handwritten letter dated the 9th April 1958 by the then Governor Edward Beetham to J.S Macpherson of the Colonial Office, a case was being made for the destabilisation of the PNM Government. Beetham states:

> "1. P.N.M. got a hard smack in the elections. One of two results of this were possible (a) that it would have a sobering effect on the Government generally, or
>
> (b) that it would have exactly the opposite effect and that it would harden their hearts and that there would be no holding them.
>
> The effect to date has been (b) with Eric Williams and his Deputy, Solomon, and perhaps the majority of his party, and (a) with a minority of the party and with three of the Ministers-Montano and Mahabir (the best two of the bunch) and Mohammed.
>
> We are therefore very near a split-Mahabir will probably go first, followed by Montano and later, possibly Mohammed. The actual reason for the split (though Montano and Mahabir have been out on a limb for sometime) is: -
>
> 2. Both parties, P.N.M. and D.L.P., are exploiting 'race' (Negro versus East Indian) and Williams last Tuesday night made a speech in Woodford Square which made the position far worse (I sent Rogers a copy of this). The position is becoming extremely serious with Negroes boycotting Indian shops and professional men. A few sparks (which may well happen during the forthcoming bye- elections for Leg. Co) and the whole country could become involved, resulting in a state of emergency, troops, etc., etc.
>
> All I can say is that we are watching things very carefully and that the necessary 'orders' are being drafted. You will realise that the personal position of Mahabir and Mohammed (both Indians) is becoming intolerable."

(CO 1031/2490)

Beetham's worse case scenario for Trinidad in April 1958 is then social instability even civil war premised on race war involving the two majority races of Trinidad who happen to be non-white. The elections Beetham speaks of is the Federal Elections of 1958 which the PNM lost to the DLP.

Beetham's hand written letter to J.S. Macpherson continues as follows:

> "3. The position in the oil industry is serious. After much talking between the Oil Companies, there was a meeting with the C.M.

While the Oil Companies were prepared to play to a certain extent, their offer had not a hope of success with Williams and, in my view never had a hope. I understand that BP, Shell and the others were prepared to make a far better offer which might at least have been a basis for negotiation, but that Texas alone held out. The result was a declaration by the C.M. something on these lines 'I have done my best to keep the oil industry out of politics, now you will see what happens when you force me to involve you in them.' This bodes ill for the future of the Trinidad oil industry (with the world drop in production), of the revenue of Trinidad, and of peace and tranquillity in this Island. However all is not yet lost, since another meeting is to be held: I had feared the total breaking off of all talks."

(CO 1031/2490)

Beetham is then insisting that Williams' intransigence in negotiations with the oil companies operating in the colony of Trinidad for the revision of the oil taxation regime was now posing a dire threat to the interests of the colonial overlord.

Beetham continues:

"4. The hot-heads in the Government are forcing a head-on collision with:

(a) The Americans on Chaguaramas, and

(b) The Governor General over the appointment of Senators in which they are unfortunately backed if one can believe newspaper reports, by Manley.

The whole situation is very tense and unfortunate.

(CO 1031/2490)

Beetham's case against Williams is then premised upon:
(a) The present state of negotiations concerning the oil taxation regime of Trinidad.
(b) The assault on US interests on Chaguaramas.
(c) The assault on the Governor General of the Federation of the British West Indies, and
(d) The threat to the stability of the colony of a race war between Afros and Indos.

In April 1958, John Profumo of the British Government visited Trinidad and Tobago. A series of notes of the various meetings held by Profumo in

Trinidad provides insight into the issues raised. The note on racial tension in Trinidad states:

> "Mr. Hochoy, while not admitting that there was substance in all of these allegations, agreed that there was cause for concern, and added that some of Dr. Williams' Ministers (i.e. Mahabir and Montano in particular) were seriously concerned."

(CO 1031/2490)

The note on the meeting between Beetham and Profumo on the 22nd April 1958 states as follows:

> "The Governor asked if the Secretary of State would be prepared to authorise him to fly to the United States to see Mr. Long, the President of Texaco whom he knew, if circumstances were such that this seemed to him to be the only way of bringing Texaco into line with the other companies and averting a first-class row between the Government and the oil industry. The Governor said if the oil industry broke off negotiations with the Chief Minister it might well mean the end of Dr. Williams present Government and new elections."

(CO 1031/2490)

Beetham is now seeking permission to intervene directly into the negotiations between Texaco and the PNM Government over the oil taxation regime. He is then talking the talk of the collapse of the PNM Government and new elections if the negotiations with the oil companies are not amicably resolved.

The note on the meeting between John Profumo and Dr. Eric Williams on the 24th April 1958 states as follows:

> "Constitutional Demands
>
> The talk took place with Dr. Solomon and Mr. Hochoy present. The Chief Minister began by referring to the P.N.M.'s demand for a Ministry of Home Affairs with an elected minister at its head on the Jamaican model.
>
> 2. The discussion even turned to the P.N.M's demand that the nominated members should be appointed by the Governor on the advice of the Chief Minister. (It is worth noting that in a talk beforehand the Governor had told Mr. Profumo that the P.N.M. had themselves been brooding over their constitutional programme for a matter of months: Mahabir, the Governor added, had not

been in the picture at all-an instance of the inner party group of negro ministers not consulting their non-negro colleagues)."

(CO 1031/2490)

Beetham is then in April 1958 unrelenting in his assault on the PNM Government led by Williams. Beetham in a hand written letter dated the 2nd May 1958 to J.S. Macpherson states:

> "Unfortunately for me, it looks as if any political blow up amongst Ministers that may come, will come at the end of this month."

(CO 1031/2490)

A telex from REUTER dated the 11th May 1958 reported on the report of the Sunday Guardian Newspaper of the same day as follows:

> "Three Trinidad Government Ministers have informed the Governor that they wish to resign from the Executive Council following dissension in the top ranks of their People's National Movement (P.N.M.) the Sunday Guardian reported today. Their resignations which have been temporarily deferred, will probably cause the Government's downfall and a general election, the newspaper said.
>
> The Sunday Guardian said the resigning Ministers are Mr. Gerard Montano, Minister of Housing and Local Government, Dr. Winston Mahabir, the Health Minister and Mr. Kamaluddin Mohammed, Minister of Agriculture. The resignations were deferred because of Princess Margaret's recent visit the newspaper adds, but are likely to take effect after the Governor goes to Britain for a holiday next month."

(CO 1031/2490)

A folio note to the hand written letter of Beetham to J.S. Macpherson dated the 2nd May 1958 by Jenkins states as follows:

> "This can be put by. But I should record that in a postscript to a letter dated 20.5.58 on another subject Sir E. Beetham predicts that the three Ministers referred to in (11) will hold back now in order to have a greater chance of defeating Williams if he plays the fool over oil taxation."

(CO 1031/2490)

The minute numbered 11 is the telex from Reuters quoted previously. What is revealed is the destabilization of the PNM Government in 1958 to force Williams to accept an oil taxation regime as dictated by the oil companies operating in Trinidad. The three named ministers would be used in a covert operation, which forced Williams' capitulation. Mahabir would leave the PNM at the end of its first term in 1961 and Montano would be removed from the Cabinet following the army mutiny in 1970. Mohammed would remain in successive PNM Cabinets until the defeat of the PNM by the NAR in 1986.

In the Sunday Express of December 11, 2005 Selwyn Ryan revealed instances of a taped interview he had with Gerard Montano former PNM Cabinet Minister. Ryan reports Gerard Montano's words as follows:

> "Williams was ruling his Cabinet with a very rough hand. I saw him make Kamal cry, and I mean cry. He licked up Winston Mahabir. He licked up Solomon, and so on,

> One day he lashed out at me. It must have been in early 1957. Some of the fellows began to rally behind me. One was Granado, one was Kamal, and the other was Winston Mahabir.

> I was kept at arm's length. So when the subject of Chaguaramas was being discussed, he would discuss it with his close colleagues, and certainly I wasn't close. Winston wasn't close because he supported me. Kamal wasn't close because he supported me and, Granado wasn't close because he supported me. So we were like a team outside. One morning, in our Executive Council meeting, Williams looked directly at the four of us, said: 'Your Excellency, there are reports emanating from this Executive Council which are being leaked to the Americans.'

Montano confirms the existence of the Gang of Four in the PNM Cabinet in 1958 at the height of tensions between Williams and the oil companies especially Texaco on the issue of revision of the oil taxation regime of the colony. Montano would in fact mention a subservient flash point of the time used to mask the conflict over the proposed changes to the oil taxation regime i.e. the issue of the return of the US military base at Chaguaramas to Trinidad and Tobago.

The declassified file CO 1031/2595 reveals the flashpoint in 1959 involving Julian Amery and Eric Williams and the then PNM Government of Trinidad and Tobago. The single folio note on the file is signed by Jenkins and states as follows:

> "N.B The Governor of Trinidad has destroyed all his personal correspondence on this file addressed to or sent from Trinidad.

Care should therefore be taken to avoid references to these telegrams since no copies will be on record."

(CO 1031/2595)

Jenkins is then sanitising the records of an event in Government in 1959 thereby raising the question of the nature of the events: A message from Troopers to Commander Caribbean area dated 26th June 1959 1800Z classified Top Secret reads as follows:

"Preliminary warning order (.) There is unrest in TRINIDAD which may possibly call for IS reinforcement (.) You need NOT REPEAT NOT take any action to alert troops or contact charter aircraft companies (.) You should avoid all publicity but should hold yourself ready to act on receipt of further orders."

(CO 1031/2595)

A telegram from the Secretary of State for the Colonies dated the 27th June 1959 to the West Indies and Trinidad reads as follows:

"Situation in Trinidad

You should know that the following action has been taken: -

(!) Frigate 'TROUBRIDGE' has been ordered to sail from Bermuda at normal speed for Trinidad. She leaves later today 27th. Steaming time to destination four (repeat four) days at normal speed, just under three if ordered to increase speed.

(11) Commander, Caribbean, has been given preliminary warning by War Office that IS reinforcement may be needed. Troops have not (repeat more) been alerted nor have charter aircraft companies been contacted.

2. If you decide that troops are required grateful if you will give earliest possible warning to Commander, Caribbean, since air transport may take some time to arrange."

(CO 1031/2595)

This telegram was classified Top Secret and Personal. Beetham replies to the telegram of the 27th June 1959 on the 27th June 1959 in the following manner:

"Addressed to S. of S.

Repeated to Governor General, the West Indies No.17.

Your telegram Personal No.45.

I can think of nothing (repeat nothing) more calculated to provoke the highly explosive situation and make possible settlement with Amery out of the question than the arrival of warship or troops at this stage.

I must therefore request you Immediately to cancel the sailing orders of the Frigate TROUBRIDGE.

I have discussed with the Governor-General who is personally in full agreement with the view expressed above.

If naval or military assistance should be required I will let you know immediately."

(CO 1031/2595)

Beetham's reply of the 27th June 1959 is classified "EMERGENCY, TOP SECRET AND PERSONAL". On the 27th June 1959 Beetham sends another telegram to the Secretary of State for the Colonies classified EMERGENCY, TOP SECRET AND PERSONAL. Beetham states:

> "I am most grateful for your assistance and indeed we had considered carefully on afternoon of 24th June advisability of warning military and seeking naval assistance. On 25th June on learning of Amery's visit I did (? group omitted) possible to persuade Premier and through him other Ministers that they should accept visit as constructive effort to find a solution. The result was that, as reported in my telegram Personal No.49 and 200, the situation eased sufficiently to enable me to decide to await further events. Since then there has been no signs of deterioration and I do not (repeat not) believe there will be any significant change for the worse unless and until talks with Amery break down.
>
> The position continues to be potentially dangerous but there is no (repeat no) imminent threat to public order. It is therefore necessary to be alert but it is essential that nothing should be done to spark the latent dangers of the situation.
>
> The Ministers' present calm, if tense, restraint should be matched by corresponding tact and reserve on our part. Moreover nothing should be done to give the slightest evidence of lack of confidence in normal guardians of public order or to suggest reliance on external aid is even contemplated.

2. I have considered advisability of TROUBRIDGE visiting one of the other islands close by but danger of speculation in Trinidad is too great to take this risk. If talks with Amery break down and we have trouble it will take some days undermine police morale to such an extent as to make outside assistance necessary.

3. I shall be very grateful for immediate confirmation that TROUBRIDGE's sailing orders have been cancelled."

(CO 1031/2595)

Beetham has intervened personally convincing Williams to accept Julian Amery's visit to Trinidad and Tobago hence obviating the need at that specific moment for British military intervention in the colony.

The Secretary of State for the colonies by way of a telegram dated the 30th June 1959 to Beetham states:

"Following personal for Julian Amery from Secretary of State.

Begins

My telegram Personal No.49.

Please explain following to the Governor.

I was told in his telegram Personal Nos. 47 and 48, that a situation of utmost gravity would arise if I did not send (forthwith) an affirmative answer. For reasons given in my telegram Personal No.41 I was not prepared to send such an answer.

I therefore thought that a situation of utmost gravity might arise and took the essential precaution of asking Admiralty to alert TROUBRIDGE (and troops) with necessary precaution against leaks. At no time was it intended TROUBRIDGE should go to Trinidad unless situation became very grave."

(CO 1031/2595)

The Personal telegrams from Beetham Nos. 47, 48 and 59 to the Secretary of State for the Colonies are not in this declassified file i.e. CO 1031/2595. Likewise the Personal telegrams 41 and 49 of the Secretary of State for the Colonies to Beetham are not in the said declassified file. The picture that has emerged is the refusal of the Secretary of State to give an affirmative answer to a demand relayed by Beetham. Beetham had indicated to the Secretary of

State that his refusal to give the answer desired would result in instability in Trinidad and Tobago. The Secretary of State given his refusal to give the answer desired by Beetham played the military card to protect colonial interests in Trinidad and Tobago in 1959.

Beetham would literally cringe and beg upon receipt of the telegram confirming that the military card was in fact played indicating that the political situation in Trinidad and Tobago was now much more stable. Beetham in fact indicated that Williams would now meet with Julian Amery and he begged that military intervention be postponed until such time that the talks with Amery have collapsed. Clearly the Secretary of State played the military card to change the power relations between Beetham and Williams and between Beetham, Williams and the British government.

Williams (1969) in his autobiography provides the context to fully appreciate the content of the telegrams presented before. Williams states:

> "We decided to request from the Secretary of State to appoint a ninth Minister, to whom we would transfer control of the police. Everything was set for the inauguration of the new Legislative Council and the celebration of Cabinet Day on June 26th, 1959. We sent the telegram to London one week before. The day before, on June 25th, a telegram came back stating, that there had been 'misunderstandings' on our part and that the Secretary of State was sending his Parliamentary Under Secretary Julian Amery, to discuss things on the spot.
>
> We cancelled all the arrangements for the inauguration of the new Legislative Council on June 26th. Amery was as rude as possible. He saw the Chief Minister only after he had seen the Chief Secretary and the Commissioner of Police.
>
> He went around meeting people including members of the opposition, and eventually capitulated."

(Williams 1969 Page 170)

In April 1958 Williams would discuss with John Profumo the constitutional reform proposals of the then PNM government. As previously noted the keynote proposals were for the ninth minister in control of the Police and for the nominated members of the Legislative Council to be appointed by the Governor on the advice of the Chief Minister. Williams' strategy of negotiation was to commence at the level of the impossible and then move to the possible. He therefore started with the position that the Governor of Trinidad and Tobago must now be demoted to the position of Lieutenant Governor. In excess of one year after discussions with John Profumo the

Secretary of State for the Colonies throws a spanner in the works on the issue of the ninth minister as the other proposals of Williams were now not on the agenda. Beetham attempts to cajole the Secretary of State and wilts under the pressure of the thought of military intervention on his watch in Trinidad and Tobago. Beetham passes the message to Williams, the festivities of July 26th 1959 are cancelled and there is no manifestation of the social unrest that Beetham attempted to bend the will of the Secretary of State with. Amery visits Trinidad, plays himself and the British government gives Williams his ninth minister. The question is: What did Williams give them? Is it an oil taxation regime acceptable to the British and the Americans? Is it Williams' active support in the destabilization of the duly elected PPP government, led by Cheddi Jagan of British Guiana?

In his budget presentation on the 30th December 1957 Eric Williams in speaking of oil taxation states:

> "The Government is of the opinion Mr. Speaker, that the only way to ensure that both these considerations are met, that the oil industry is taken permanently out of politics, is by the introduction of the Venezuelan legislation, and it proposes to do this to take effect by January 1st, 1959. This will not only ensure a maximum of 50 per cent of profits to the Government, but it will also encourage rapid exploitation by a progressive system of taxation for unexploited areas, and provide for a surrender to the government, on a chequer board system, at the end of the period of exploration, of 50 per cent of all areas leased for exploration.
>
> The Government has further decided, Mr. Speaker that as from January 1, 1958, all new exploitation leases, land or marine, will be offered for competitive bidding and sold to the highest bidder, on the basis of a minimum price fixed by the Government."

(Hansard 30 December 1957 Col 710)

Williams has then indicated his intention by the 1st January 1959 to overturn the oil taxation regime presently in operation in Trinidad. Williams' stated aim is 50 cents of every dollar of profit declared by the oil companies accruing to the Government. Williams proposed legislation would significantly add to the costs of production and would impact the maximisation of profits particularly in the marine oilfields which would impact the operation of Texas Oil Co. Williams continues:

> "Mr. Speaker, negotiations have been going on for some time now between the Government and the oil companies. I am happy to report that they have been conducted in an atmosphere of cordiality,

that the companies are very sympathetic to the development needs of Trinidad and Tobago, and that they fully appreciate the desire of the Government to bring Trinidad and Tobago's oil legislation and practices in line with the more progressive oil countries. I do not propose to disclose any details of the negotiations.

Suffice it to say, Mr. Speaker, that the negotiations are simplified by the fact that there can be less doubt today with respect to the profitability of marine drilling than there might have been two years ago."

(Hansard 30th December 1957 Cols. 714-715)

Williams adopts a non-confrontational stand with the oil companies in public and his discourse is one of the moral high ground premised upon the position that marine oil especially can afford the new oil taxation regime he intends to implement. Williams' discourse reflects then the salient reality of the power relations between Williams, the oil companies and the colonial overlord over the new oil taxation regime. What does Williams give to the oil companies and the colonial overlord in order to acquire agreement on the form and shape of the new oil taxation regime? The conclusion is then obvious that the myth of William the conqueror is simply a discourse of Williams that served his quest for political hegemony in the politics of Trinidad and Tobago nothing else.

The colonial overlord viewed the rise of an Indo-Trinbagonian dominated political movement as a threat to the security of the colony of Trinidad and Tobago in the early 1950's. The paranoia over the Maha Sabha and Bhadase Maraj was heightened with the assault of the colonial overlord on the duly elected P.P.P. government headed by Cheddi Jagan in British Guiana. That there was a covert operation to ensure the defeat of the PDP in the 1956 general elections and the DLP in the 1961 general elections is indicated by the content of declassified files of the colonial office on Trinidad and Tobago. Why then in 1958 and 1959 does the Secretary of State for the Colonies choose to precipitate successive flashpoints with Williams and his PNM government over constitutional developments for Trinidad and Tobago on the grounds that the Opposition DLP were not in support of the said constitutional developments? The Secretary of State for the Colonies plays the rejection by an opposition that the colonial overlord does not view as a desirable alternative to the then PNM government to halt Williams' momentum.

The Secretary of State for the Colonies would never therefore hurt the prospects for PNM re-election in the 1961 general elections in fact the British colonial overlord must work assiduously for PNM re- election in 1961 both overtly and covertly. Both Williams (1969) and Solomon (1981) insist that the flashpoint in 1959 over constitutional development was linked to US activities at the Chaguaramas Naval Base especially the alleged presence of radiation levels that posed a threat to Trinidad. What they both do not speak of is very instructive i.e. the issue of a new oil taxation regime and the agenda to remove Cheddi Jagan and the PPP in British Guiana. Williams would state:

> "Thereafter there was silence-until May of 1960, after our famous march for Chaguaramas, the Secretary of State decided that since Mahomet would not come to the mountain, the mountain must perforce come to Mahomet.
>
> He decided to visit Trinidad himself in June 1960. We met, discussed pleasantly, settled all outstanding problems in one or two sittings of a few hours, and Trinidad and Tobago had its full internal self-government with a bicameral legislature which came into effect after the General Elections on December 4, 1961."

(Williams 1969 Page 172)

CHAPTER THREE

MACHINATIONS/CORRUPTION

By way of letter addressed to P. Rogers of the Colonial Office dated the 5th September 1957 Solomon Hochoy then Acting Governor of Trinidad and Tobago presented the case for the transfer of Attorney General Inniss who was replaced as Attorney General by Ellis Clarke. Hochoy's case is as follows:

> "A most disturbing situation has developed as an offshoot of the Car Loan and the more recent disqualification issues, in which the Government and certain of its Party members are directly involved.
>
> A few weeks ago the PNM Party released a statement which was published by the daily press and the 'PNM Weekly', to the effect that members of the legal profession who were members of the Party did not give legal advice to the Government and were not responsible for such constitutional issues as had arisen; that it was the duty of the Government's legal department to advise on all such matters; that any blame for what has occurred should be placed at the doors of the Government and of the Crown Law Officers; and that this statement was necessary since the professional reputation of such Party members was being adversely affected by the prevailing erroneous impression that they served as legal advisers to the Government.
>
> This statement itself caused much embarrassment to our Attorney General who at no time was ever requested in advance to furnish his opinion on their constitutional implications.
>
> Williams' statement in Executive Council has done much to avoid what could have developed into a serious administrative problem and for the moment the matter is closed but I do feel that it would

no longer be of advantage to the administration to have Inniss continue in Trinidad apart from the embarrassment it must cause him as the conventional leader of the Trinidad Bar.

Our Attorney General has given devoted service. It is most unfortunate that through a series of circumstances for which he cannot be held blameworthy, not only his professional reputation but also his official career is seriously jeopardised. I strongly urge that in the circumstances consideration be given for his very early transfer and in doing so I recommend that he be favourably considered for promotion."

(CO 1031/2154)

The influence Hochoy wielded with the colonial overlord is indicated by the reality that the necessary measures to transfer Inniss to British Honduras as its new Chief Justice were being put in place by the 12th September 1957. Inniss was played and Hochoy was the conductor of the symphony as Williams chose not to demand the removal of Inniss. Inniss is attacked by the PNM both in the PNM Weekly and the daily press with the PNM Weekly relentlessly assaulting him. Hochoy insists that Inniss is innocent as charged but defending Inniss would not resolve the conflict it would only escalate it. The only solution is to remove Inniss quickly and the replacement for the post was Ellis Clarke. Was it coincidence, conspiracy or the machinations of Hochoy?

In November 1959 Solomon Hochoy replaced Edward Beetham as Governor of the Colony of Trinidad and Tobago. In his capacity of Colonial Secretary Hochoy wrote a letter in manuscript to J.S Macpherson dated the 4th February 1958 on the topic of Edward Beetham the then Governor of Trinidad and Tobago. Hochoy states in the said letter as follows:

"In so far as Sir Edward is personally concerned there is no position that he has seemingly, albeit not actually, suffered a severe diminution of status. Even the Countess Mountbatten within 24 hours of her arrival here gave me the distinct impression that she sensed this. The admiration in which Sir Edward and Lady Beetham were held for their generous and willing sacrifice is fast turning into sympathy and pity. It may be only a question of time for the Ministers and then the public to develop the feeling that his stay here is purposeless.

I have tried to the best of my ability to put the picture before you as exactly as I see it. I feel, in all sincerity, that a solution must be sought which will relieve Sir Edward of the embarrassment and discomfiture to which he is being subjected and which he has to endure as a result of his status being irreparably impaired. Unpleasant as the thought may be, you may even wish to contemplate the possibility of a replacement, who, being new, will not be in so intolerable a position.

You will appreciate by now my reason for not putting this in the typewriter nor have I shown it to Sir Edward."

(CO 1031/2209)

In February 1958 whilst the pressure builds on negotiations between Williams and the oil companies of Trinidad for the new oil taxation regime Hochoy writes to Macpherson of the Colonial Office making the case for the ineffectiveness of Beetham as Governor of Trinidad and Tobago. It was in December 1957 that Williams in his Budget presentation indicated the decision of the PNM government to implement the new oil taxation regime by the 1st January 1959. The impasse in the negotiations which gave Beetham the room to manoeuvre given his friendship with the Chairman of Texas Oil and Williams' racist invective at Woodford Square following the PNM' s loss to the DLP in the 1958 Federal Elections in Trinidad and Tobago would enable Beetham to launch an attack on Williams which gave him the space and the time to blunt Hochoy's assault.

A handwritten comment by Reese to P. Rogers on the heading of Hochoy's letter states:

"Mr. Rogers

This is a very carefully worded letter. It does not come as a total surprise. I should like to discuss early."

(CO 1031/2209)

"J.S. Macpherson of the Colonial Office replies to the Hochoy letter of the 4th February 1958 by way of letter dated the 12th March 1958. Macpherson's letter states:

"All that I need to say, I think, is that I very greatly appreciated your action in writing; that your letter-which cannot have been an easy one to write-was impeccable in tone and phrasing; and that the contents, and every nuance, are fully understood at this end.

Thank you very much indeed for writing as you did."

(CO 1031/2209)

It is then apparent that Hochoy's letter of the 4th February 1958 did not harm his career, as he became the first Governor appointed in the British West Indies who was then a native of the British West Indies. What is clear is that the move on Inniss, which culminated in Ellis Clarke becoming the Attorney General in 1957, was again executed in 1958 by Hochoy this time on Governor Beetham. By November 1959 the three fathers of the independent nation of Trinidad and Tobago were in the positions of power necessary to the genesis of a post-colonial political elite: Williams, Hochoy and Clarke. This was a political elite holding allegiance to the Trinity of fathers of Trinidad and Tobago premised upon the hegemony of Williams and the PNM.

CORRUPTION

In the run up to the General Elections of the 4th December 1961 Simbhoonath Capildeo would on the 8th September 1961 in the Legislative Council present his case for collusion, machinations and corrupt practices involving the Swiss West Indies Bank in Trinidad and various PNM Government Ministers. Five PNM Cabinet Ministers commencing with Learie Constantine and John O'Halloran followed by Kamaluddin Mohammed, Gerard Montano and Winston Mahabir sued for libel the publishers of "the Statesman" of September 30th 1961. The persons sued were Ramdeo Dowlat Singh, H.P. Singh and Errol Peyson. The Statesman was in September 1961 the organ of the Democratic Labour Party (DLP).

The concern here is the contents of the declassified file CO 1031/4078 which dealt with the issue of the relationship between the Swiss West Indies Bank in Trinidad and the then PNM Government. The file CO 1031/4078 was closed until 1993 but in 1992 some Seven Minutes and their relevant enclosures were closed until 2012. This action indicates that the Seven Minutes and their accompanying enclosures were so sensitive that they were closed for some fifty years. Within fifty years it is expected that persons named in the said seven minutes and their enclosures would be dead. This action of the British government immediately leads to the conclusion that there was indeed evidence to be suppressed by the British government, which proved that the accusations of Simbhoonath Capildeo were in fact accurate. Hochoy the Governor wrote to A.R. Thomas by way of letter dated the 10th October 1961 stating as follows:

> "In my Monthly Intelligence Report I referred to the Opposition charge of corruption during a debate in the Council. I enclose

a copy of a relevant publication sponsored by the Opposition Party.

With General Elections in the air, it is more difficult than ever to sift the wheat from the chaff, but the allegations are causing much speculation."

(CO 1031/4078)

Hochoy by way of letter to A.R. Thomas dated the 24th October 1960 states:

"I understand from the Premier that the Ministers mentioned have all denied the charges of corruption and that they prepare to take legal proceedings. But some doubts remain."

(CO 1031/4078)

A.R Thomas would reply to Hochoy's two letters listed above on the 31st October 1961 as follows:

"Many thanks for your two letters sending me copies of publications by the Opposition Democratic Labour Party on alleged corruption by certain Cabinet Ministers. It remains to be seen how much this affair will be worked out during the elections which I now see are fixed for December 4th.

Incidentally, any assessment-or gossip which you care to send again us in as much detail as you like will be of great interest to us against the background of how much depends for the future of Federation on the likely attitude of the Government Party."

(CO 1031/4078)

Thomas is simply not interested in the accusations of corruption in October 1961. In fact what interests him is the attitude of the PNM Government to the British West Indies Federation.

The list of minutes of the said file also shows that enclosures were removed from the file to other files and enclosures were sealed until 2012 even though the minutes remain listed. The minutes numbered 18 and 19 were removed from the file and the minutes remain listed. The enclosure for Minute 17 was removed whilst the minute is still listed. Minute 17 indicates that the issue of the Knighthood proposed for Learie Constantine was impacted by the matters arising out of the Opposition charges of corruption and the actions taken by the five PNM Cabinet Ministers. A folio note to a sealed minute states:

Mr. A.R Thomas

The conclusion to be drawn from this would appear to be-unhappily-that the recommendation should not proceed while the court case is pending. Should we not write to the Governor at once pointing this out and asking when the case is likely to be heard and the verdict known."

This folio note was dated the 8th November 1961.
The folio note to Minute number 17 states:

"Further action regarding the "K" for N. Constantine has been taken in OSA 71/92/06-

S. Phillips

14/12/1961"

On the 8th September 1961 Simbhoonath Capildeo read into the record of the Legislative Council an affidavit of Archibald Chapman, Managing Director of the Swiss West Indies Bank and a letter of Archibald Chapman. The affidavit states:

"Trinidad- I Archibald Chapman, Managing Director of the Swiss West Indies Bank make oath and say as follows:

1. On the morning of September 7th, 1961, I received a communication that I was to meet the Hon. Kamaluddin Mohammed, the Minister of Lands, Agriculture and Fisheries at 6pm with instructions that I was to wait in my car until such time as his car drove into the Ministry grounds.

4. The Minister told me that the talks in the Legislative Council were very regrettable and that the Government felt sorry for me, but that the Premier was in a political position where he had to defend himself politically.

5. The Minister warned me, however, that I should keep quiet, say nothing about it, in other words, he would very much regret any incident which might affect the name of his country should any untoward accident befall me through violence from the more hot headed members of his party.

6. There is no doubt in my mind that this was a threat of violence against my person put to me by the Minister on behalf of Dr. Eric Williams.

7. This is not the first time that I have received such threats on behalf of the Government through persons connected with Mr. John O'Halloran, Dr. Eric Williams and Mr. Alan Reece.

I attach herewith a letter written by me in connection with the failure of the sanitation bonds loan in reply to threats received on their behalf by Dr. Rodrigues.

Sworn to this eight-day of September, 1961, at No. 25 Chacon Street in the presence of A. Carmichael, Commissioner of Affidavits of 35 Abercromby Street."

(CO 1031/4078)

The letter of Archibald Chapman is as follows:

"Swiss West Indies Bank Limited

Officina de Ingenieria S.A.

15 Tragarete Road

Port of Spain

(Attention Dr. C. Rodrigues)

Dear Sir,

Reference is made to the conversation between Dr. Rodrigues and the Managing Director of this Bank last week. We wish to put on record that at no time have we divulged any information as to the status of the negotiations on the sanitation bonds loan.

The verbal threats of violence and the use of such phrases as 'blasting you out of existence' by Dr. Rodrigues are not appreciated.

It is well known in Port of Spain that the actual leakage of information took place when Mr. Alan Reece discussed the matter with Mr. Joor and Mr. Neal Lau. This was later confirmed to them by one of the Government Ministers.

It is also to be presumed that if leakages of this description are given to one set of persons, they have probably been given to many others as well, and we wish to tell you that we ourselves have heard these rumours coming back to us from various sources of business people in Port of Spain.

We as a bank acting as agents for the Government of Trinidad and Tobago and OFISA in the negotiations with Compagnie Francaise de Transactions Internationales and in no way undertake to discuss matters of such a confidential nature with third parties. This rule evidently does not apply to the Ministry of Finance and it is their prerogative to tell to whom they wish whatsoever they may wish to say.

We, therefore, cannot be responsible for any such leakages of information when we have definite proof that they have come from the Government and we therefore, ask you to give us immediately a written and a retraction of your threats otherwise we shall be forced to send a copy to the Colonial Office and to the Governor General of the West Indies.

Chapman

For and on behalf of

Swiss West Indies Bank, Limited."

(CO 1031/4078)

The letter in the hand of A. Chapman reveals the business relationship that was the base from which the allegations of corruption surfaced in early September 1961. The Swiss Bank was the agent of OFISA and the Government of Trinidad and Tobago in negotiations with Compagnie Francaise de Transactions Internationales.

A secret telegram dated the 11th September 1961 from Trinidad to the Secretary of State for the Colonies states:

> Grateful for any particulars concerning-Henry Davernas, Chairman Transaco SA, 17 Boulevard Henry IV Paris (4), France and Compagnie Francaise de Transactions Internationales (Transaco), 17 Boulevard Henry IV, Paris (4), France."

(CO 1031/4078)

The Secretary of State for the Colonies would reply to the said telegram on the 11th December 1961 giving a clean bill of health to Henri Davernas and Transaco. The telegram of the 11th December 1961 is but another indication of the colonial officials of Trinidad and Tobago seeking the interests of Williams and his government. Interest in Trinbago and Henri Davernas arose as a direct result of Simbhoonath Capildeo's revelation in the Legislative Council on the 8th September 1961. There was simply no interest before in the Swiss Bank and Transaco by Hochoy et al before the 8th September 1961.

In December 1958 in his budget presentation for 1959 Williams announced as a capital project under the 1959 budget the creation of a sewage schema to serve the urban areas of Trinidad such as Port of Spain. The contract for the creation of the sewer system is awarded to a Venezuelan company OFISA on the grounds that it was the lowest bidder. The funding for the project is a government bond placed on the international financial markets. OFISA is charged with the task of placing the bond on the market and selling the said bond. The sale of the bond funds the contract to erect the sewer system and the government of Trinidad and Tobago services the debt created by the bond. The bond would then be a government guaranteed foreign debt payable in foreign currency by the government of Trinidad and Tobago.

From the outset the colonial overlord held responsibility to oversee the process of letting the contract to OFISA and the placing of the government bond in international markets as Williams and his PNM government were not the political directorate of an independent sovereign state charged with the power to contract guaranteed foreign debt payable in a foreign currency. OFISA was clearly inadequate to the task at hand as it had no experience on the international financial markets as it was a small company by multinational construction standards. OFISA therefore failed repeatedly to successfully place the bond to finance the sewer system on the international market.

Enter Transaco and Henri Davernas seeking to finance state projects through government guaranteed foreign debt. Transaco's entry into the sewer scheme project was in itself a contravention of the existing contract between the government and OFISA. Transaco appoints Swiss Bank West Indies Ltd as its agent in Trinidad and Tobago with reference to the sewer scheme, OFISA and the government. By the 8th September 1961 the PNM government had failed to vary the contract with OFISA naming Transaco and its agent the Swiss Bank West Indies as the entity charged with placing the sewer scheme development bond on the international financial market. A war therefore broke out in the political directorate and the state bureaucrats between the allies of OFISA and those of Transaco/ Swiss Bank West Indies Ltd. Transaco/ Swiss Bank complained bitterly of OFISA's continued efforts to place the bond via Merill Lynch of the New York financial system whilst Transaco was also involved in the same financial activity. Both OFISA and Swiss West Indies Bank purchased on an ongoing basis political influence to realise their given ends.

Internecine political infighting literally blew the lid off the project and the supply of documents to Simbhoonath Capildeo and others indicated that the war was now threatening the sustainability of the Williams' government as a credible entity internationally. There is no internecine political infighting within a ruling political party in the absence of gain: monetary and hegemonic. The end result of the internecine political struggle was the mortal wound to the proposed sewage scheme. Although it was executed eventually it never grew to the size and scale envisaged in 1958. The initial and basic flaw of the process of erecting a sewage system for Trinidad was letting a contract to OFISA, which was premised on a scope of works and financing structure that was outside the experience and structure of OFISA.

Herein lies the basic stench of purposeful mistakes to facilitate corruption. Then there was the purposeful invitation to Transaco to contravene the contract with OFISA without any amendment to the said contract. Again a purposeful mistake by which influence would be bought and paid for. But the legal quicksand in which Transaco found itself in scuttled its attempts to finance the project leading to its exit from the quagmire it found itself in. A. Chapman of the Swiss Bank West Indies Ltd. upon recognition that they were played on the project simply decided to blow the whistle failing to understand that this would backfire in the face of the Swiss Bank West Indies Ltd.

Williams would then with plausible denial apply damage control by seizing control of the financing of the project from OFISA and successfully negotiating a million USD credit from the Export- Import Bank of the USA on the 25th October 1961. In order to purchase US made materials, which were conditional to the credit, OFISA was forced to become partners with a sewer pipe factory in Puerto Rico. The US based government consultants to the project Metcalfe and Eddy had estimated a cost of 8.7 million USD for the Port of Spain sewers and 2.1million USD for the Port of Spain treatment plant and pumping station. The credit of 9 million USD was some 1.8 million USD short of the estimate for the Port of Spain sewer system, which was the only one, constructed. Metcalfe and Eddy gave a costing for the original 1958 project design at 16.5 million USD. Why let a contract to a construction firm that had no capacity to float a government guaranteed sewer bond for some 16.2 million USD on the international market? Why conceptualise a project without due regard to the state's capacity to service the debt to only have the project collapse with realized financing being only 9 million USD out of an estimated project cost of 16.2 million USD? After the initial phase the project has never continued to date in Trinidad nor commenced in Tobago. What transpired in 1961 has therefore impacted the environmental sustainability of Trinidad and Tobago to this day. The sewer project bore all the hallmarks of a state development project that was a covert feeding trough for ruling politicians and their allies.

Simbhoonath Capildeo would make his revelations in the Legislative Council and call for a commission of inquiry to determine the veracity of the allegations. The publishers of The Statesman were used by the functionaries of the Swiss Bank to print allegations of corruption against PNM ministers, which neither served the interests of the DLP and the Swiss Bank in 1961. The DLP lost the 1961 general elections 20 seats for the PNM and 10 seats for the DLP. And the colonial officials did not intervene to embarrass Williams, as their geo-political interests demanded a Williams/ PNM landslide in 1961, another potent indicator that power is amoral.

Under the provisions of the FOI Act of the UK the Minutes and enclosures closed until 2012 were opened in response to the request made by the author. By way of letter dated the 18th November 1961 by Solomon Hochoy to A.R Thomas of the Colonial Office it is revealed that Hochoy nominated Learie Constantine for the Knighthood. In the said letter Hochoy indicates the weakness of Constantine's libel case against the publishers of The Statesman and the folly of Constantine's lawsuit especially the impact it was having on the knighthood to be conferred on Constantine. But Hochoy ends the said letter insisting that the recommendation must go forward in spite of the libel suit.

CHAPTER 4

WILLIAMS AND THE BRITISH: 1962 TO 1971

The British High Commissioner to Trinidad and Tobago N.E. Costar, in a letter dated the 5ᵗʰ February 1964 to Chadwick of the Commonwealth Relations Office states as follows:

> "2. I said in the despatch that Dr. Williams had noted that the Labour Members of the House of Commons delegation met 'privately' with elements of the Trinidad Opposition, while they were here as guests of the Trinidad Government.

> 1. The meeting, as I said in the despatch took place against our advice, Mr. Shinwell and Mr. Royle were pressed for a meeting by a slippery lady Senator, and they reluctantly decided that politeness demanded some compliance and agreed to have a chat. They expected a private meeting but were tricked, and next day found themselves on the front page of the local DAILY MIRROR."

(DO 200/248)

The Daily Mirror article of the 28ᵗʰ January 1964 names the three DLP Members of Parliament as Senator Thomas Bleasdell, Senator Margaret Lucky-Samaroo and Balgobin Ramdeen. It must be noted that in January 1964 the Labour Party of Britain formed the Opposition in the House of Commons. Costar continues:

> "4. I hoped at the time that the incident might prove to be a storm in a teacup, and I much regret that Dr. Williams has not taken it up formally. His tiresome letter 'conveys the serious view that the Cabinet takes of the report … that two members of the visiting Parliamentary Opposition in Trinidad'. The letter ends with a request for an assurance from the British Prime Minister

that the British Government is not a party to these unfortunate developments, and requests that he (the British Prime Minister) will convey the Trinidad Cabinet's concern to the proper quarters."

(DO 200/248)

That it was two opposition members of a British Parliamentary delegation that met with a delegation of the DLP means that the British Government bears no responsibility in this flashpoint. Costar therefore seeks to explain Williams' bitching to the Government of the UK as follows:

"5. My first tentative diagnosis is that Dr. Williams' grumbles about the two Labour M.P.'s are connected with the possibility that Learie Constantine might get a peerage and Ministerial Office under a Labour Government. Once again there is a reference to interference in Trinidad's internal affairs. Constantine's advancement would be anathema to Dr. Williams who is a man of intense personal fixations, and who wants to see Constantine 'drove down'. He now sees that Constantine may be elevated instead and this is naturally upsetting him considerably, especially as a substantial element in the original row between Dr. Williams and Constantine was the latter's reaction to Dr. Williams siding with the Secretary of State over Constantine's indiscreet utterances. In this small local episode affecting the Labour M.P.'s he may think he has a lever to keep Constantine down."

(DO 200/248)

Costar is insisting that Williams persistently seeking to pick rows with the British Government is directly linked to a perceived embrace of Constantine by an incoming Labour Government if they are successful in the next general elections in Britain. The Commonwealth Relations Office brief on Williams dated March 1964 states:

"Dr. Williams, the Prime Minister of Trinidad and Tobago, has been upset in recent weeks by various actions which he considers – unreasonably in our view-to be the fault of the British Government.

(a) Various passages in the Trinidad newspapers have displeased him. Since the newspapers belong to the Thompson Group and the Daily Mirror Group respectively, Dr. Williams has 'registered a formal protest with the United Kingdom Government'.

(b) The possibility that the British Labour Party might put forward for a Life Peerage the name of Sir Learie Constantine formerly High Commissioner for Trinidad in London, has incensed Dr. Williams. He has indeed warned our High Commissioner that if the proposal were carried out, he would resign his Privy Counsellorship, despite the fact that he has shown eagerness to be sworn a member of the Privy Council when he visits London just before Easter."

(DO 200/248)

Williams is then willing to pick petty spats with the British Government in an attempt to continue his personal war with Learie Constantine. That the British are willing to dance with Williams indicates that he has strategic value to them in 1964. What then is Williams' value to the British political elite in 1964?

N.E Costar reports to Saville Garner by way of letter dated the 2nd May 1964. Costar reports on Williams' overseas visit as follows:

"Dr. Williams is with us again. I saw him briefly at the airport on his arrival last night when his manner towards me was cordial, but judging by his public statements I think we may be in for a somewhat difficult time once more.

1. Since Dr. Williams has returned from Canada and the U.S. without any specific commitment on aid, whereas Britain did at least offer a commitment, I suspect that Dr. Williams' mood is due to something more than the question of aid. I gather that in Canada and the U.S. (as well as in the African countries he visited), the red carpet was rolled out. I suspect that the red carpet treatment pays great dividends with Dr. Williams and our own more informal methods which to us appear to be more friendly, to him seem somewhat offhand. I will let you know if I get further confirmation of this impression.

2. I am sure that you in London are well aware of the point which would of course have wider application than Trinidad. It is possible that other ultra sensitive leaders of newly emergent Commonwealth countries like the red carpet treatment which they get elsewhere, including iron curtain countries and harbour resentment against us for not providing the same."

(DO 200/248)

Costar's discourse immediately takes one back to the writings of Franz Fanon. Costar is insisting that leaders of these newly emergent states of the British Commonwealth suffer with psychological impediments, which prevent them from appreciating the welcoming nature of the manner in which the Commonwealth Relations Office (CRO) and the Foreign Office (FO) treat with them when they visit the UK. Costar is then suggesting that the CRO and the FO pander to the inferiority complexes of colonized non-white races to ensure the compliance of said black political leaders to the geo-political strategies of the UK. Since these black political leaders lack the mental and cultural faculties to understand the rationale of the UK's methodology in treating with them then the CRO and FO must change their methodology to deal with a lesser race. Costar's position reeks of North Atlantic white racism and the contempt for inferior races.

N.E Costar by way of despatch No.7 dated the 6th May 1964 reports on Dr. Williams' trip to Africa "Williams' African Safari" to Duncan Sandys, M.P. Secretary of State for Commonwealth Relations. Costar states:

> "3. Dr. Williams' journey was by chartered B.O.A.C. Britannia wearing B.W.I.A. livery and its cost (to which I shall refer later may have exceeded $ WI 500,000. Dr. Williams' entourage of fifteen included Mrs. Isabel Teshea, his Minister of Health, no doubt to show a woman in his Government, Mr. Kamaluddin Mohammed, Minister of Public Utilities, presumably to show that Indians and Africans work in harmony in Port of Spain and that Trinidad has its Muslims who support the Government, and Sir Ellis Clarke, Trinidad's Ambassador in Washington and her representative at the United Nations. Sir Ellis Clarke's inclusion in the party may well have been a demonstration of confidence, as his moderation at the United Nations has apparently been criticised by some of the African representatives in New York.

> Dr. Williams' Objectives.

> 5.Shortly before he left for Africa, Dr. Williams broadcast to Trinidad on the aim of his tour. In part, he said, it was to 'embrace the sources of our African heritage'. But Dr. Williams is not a Negro racialist in an extreme sense, and when this phrase was criticised in Trinidad he added a postscript that 'Trinidad was not a negro country'.

> Finally Dr. Williams had the natural wish to put Trinidad on the map and to project his own (anti-Jagan) views on British Guiana.

> East Africa

9. In some ways the East African programme was the mixture as before.

Public speeches, some anti-Jagan lobbying, return invitations and occasionally a quiet chat with the British representative.

10. Dr. Williams also seems fully to have sensed the risk of subversion in East Africa, perhaps especially of subversion from China, and he has spoken in comparable terms of Cuba and Zanzibar (again in March).

North Africa

12. Dr. Williams last landfall in Africa was Algeria. Here of all places he visited he was most impressed, and both in private (with the British Foreign Secretary and with me since his return) and in public he has praised Ben Bella as an outstanding leader in Africa.

13. While in Algiers, Dr. Williams also saw President Sekou Toure of Guinea but managed to avoid contact with Mr. Brindley Benn, one of Dr. Jagan's most militant colleagues, no doubt present in Algeria on militant business.

The Local Reaction

14. The cost of Dr. Williams' African 'Safari' inevitable came under fire from the largely Indian opposition in Parliament. There was also strong business opposition: 'all this out of our taxes!' but Dr. Williams' trip has not been greatly resented by the non-Indian man on the street, who, if he thinks about the trip at all, sees it as more 'bigness' for Trinidad and a feather in the cap for the tough little terrier at the top. The East Indian community are less impressed.

The Results of the Tour.

Even so, in the light of discussions with other members of his Party, and following a conversation which I have had with Dr. Williams himself, some results of the tour can already be forecast. It also seems that Dr. Williams may have converted some of the African leaders to his view that without effective safeguards independence for British Guiana under Dr. Jagan would have disastrous consequences, and he almost certainly absorbed African views on Southern Rhodesia.

British Guiana

18. I have already reported that almost immediately after Dr. Williams returned, he was visited in Port of Spain by Dr. Jagan. Subsequently, Dr. Williams informed me that at Dr. Jagan's request he would shortly be using his good offices to promote a settlement in British Guiana.

Dr. Williams believes that his tour of Africa, and especially his talks on British Guiana with Dr. Nkrumah and President Ben Bella (hitherto Dr. Jagan's friends) have undermined the position of the British Guiana premier in the Afro-Asian group. Because Dr. Jagan no longer feels able to rely on the support of the Afro-Asian group he has turned to Dr. Williams. Dr. Williams has his own ideas on the solution of the British Guiana problem which include an effective and probably external guarantee of the constitutional arrangements made.

It may be, after seeing Dr. Nkrumah and President Ben Bella, that Dr. Williams feels that the time has come for a little 'expansionism' from Port of Spain.

Southern Rhodesia

19. The price for African support for Dr. Williams over British Guiana will almost certainly be some further hardening of the Trinidad attitude over Southern Rhodesia at the United Nations (so far Trinidad has not been altogether unreasonable on the subject).

Relations with Britain

21. Rightly or wrongly (and he is not a modest man) Dr. Williams feels that he has made an impression in Africa upon which he can build. He believes that he has been recognised in Africa as a, indeed the, unifying leader in the Caribbean. But Dr. Williams has also sensed that moderation toward Britain earns no plaudits in Africa. Against this background, and that of his unsuccessful aid talks in London, I fear that Dr. Williams may in future take a more publicly unfriendly view toward Britain's policies, both in Africa and the Caribbean, than he has in the past. This is not to say that he has shifted his views on British Guiana, but over the Little Eight and elsewhere, we may find him less helpful than recently. Aid from Britain might, however, help to preserve the balance."

(DO 200/248)

What is most striking of Costar's Despatch No.7 is the working relationship that exists between Williams and the British. Williams succinctly serves British geo-political interests in the Caribbean and moreover Williams utilizes the strengths and weaknesses of British geo-political strategies within which to execute a Williams' agenda for the hegemony of Williams. He is then a satellite of the British geo- political agenda; he was simply then Britain's bitch in the Caribbean. It is noteworthy that in the report of Costar the access Costar enjoys to Williams is similar to that of a member of the PNM Cabinet and the state bureaucracy. Furthermore Costar indicates Williams' close contact with British representatives in the states he visited in his African tour. What is apparent is that in 1964 Williams' visit to Africa was justified on the grounds that it served British geo-political interests as he assaulted Jagan's position on independence for British Guiana under the rule of Jagan.

Costar is then insisting to the British political establishment that in exchange for Williams' assault on Dr. Jagan the British must tolerate a changed position on Southern Rhodesia by Williams. Costar expects that Britain has a price to pay for Williams' assault on Jagan of British Guiana which includes Williams' indifference to Britain's policy on the British colonies of the Windward/Leeward Islands with the collapse of the British West Indies Federation. In response to the space that Williams demands in exchange for his assault on Jagan, Costar advises that Britain must respect this space and provide the aid that Williams demands.

Despatch No.7 is but another indication of the central strategic importance the removal of Cheddi Jagan and the PPP as the dominant political leader and political party in British Guianese politics in British geo-political strategy in the Caribbean in the 1950's and 1960's. Williams prime directive in his Africa tour of 1964 was to sever the alliance Cheddi Jagan had established with especially Nkrumah of Ghana and Ben Bella of Algeria and in so doing not only isolate Jagan within Africa but moreover to project Williams as the primary leader of the newly independent former colonies of Britain in the Caribbean.

Costar's despatch poignantly revealed that Williams was a capable servant of British geo-political strategy in the Caribbean hence his importance to the British and the interventions that must follow this reality, into the politics of Trinidad and Tobago. The political behaviour of Rudranath Capildeo then reeks of the allegation that he was under the thumbs of the British covert agencies thereby ensuring Williams' political hegemony from 1961-1966. The sudden breakthrough that broke the deadlock at the Independence

Conference in London and the Leader of the Opposition in absentia whilst employed in London reeks of a deal brokered by covert agencies of Britain to ensure Williams' hegemony.

Despatch No.12 dated the 19th October 1964 by Costar is titled "Trinidad after two years of Independence" reports as follows:

> "On the political front, until we have solved our problems in British Guiana and the East Caribbean, we have a particular interest in remaining on the best terms we can with Trinidad who can help or harm us both in relation to these countries themselves and by her policies in the United Nations. There are also the wider political considerations, of even greater concern to the U.S. than to Britain, of preventing Castroist subversion or take over in Trinidad. Of this at the moment there is no danger whatever, though a deteriorating economic situation or political irresponsibility by her leaders could at any time bring about a change.
>
> 19. At the moment Dr. Williams is pleased neither with Britain from whom his financial expectations have always been too high, nor with the Commonwealth. Dr. Williams in fact has little use for any special connection between Trinidad and Britain, or between Trinidad and the Commonwealth, except as a source of economic aid.
>
> 20. As far Dr. Williams personally is concerned, his mind is I fear closed. Short of an impractically large capital grant without strings from Britain to Trinidad, his views are unlikely to change. In any case, there is not a great deal of gratitude in Dr. Williams make up. In particular, and now more and more, we stress the value of the Commonwealth Sugar Agreement and the extent of Britain's financial help to the poorer West Indian islands."

(DO 200/248)

Costar on the 19th October 1964 is calling for action to ensure Williams' compliance with Britain's geo-political strategies. Costar insists that there is need to engage with Williams as he in 1964 is of central strategic importance, but Costar calls for a hard line against Williams rather than appeasement. He is of the view that in spite of Williams' hegemony over the political process, civil society remains under the influence of a desire for interaction with Britain. Costar outlines the discourse being utilised to assail Williams' position perceived as anti-British and anti-Commonwealth.

Costar wrote to Sykes of the Commonwealth Relations Office (CRO) by way of letter dated the 30th October 1964, stating as follows:

"Dr Williams returned to Trinidad late in the evening of October 28th and I had a talk with him at the airport. He was very affable, and considerably more attentive to me than to his own assembled Ministers.

2. He was clearly flattered by the attention he had received in Britain, and said he thought that the new Government were taking a firm grip on the country's problems. But he thought they had under estimated (before and during) the course of the election the strength of feeling in Britain against immigration. He said he was not a party to Jamaica's wish for an open door into Britain.

3. All this was satisfactory. But he went on to say that his line was that Trinidad should train West Indians for work in Britain. He already had two schemes lined up. I foresee Dr. Williams being touchy on three points. First of all, he has had a bright idea, and if it is thwarted he will be cross. Secondly, immigration and racial prejudice are closely related to his mind, and thirdly any policy which would reduce unemployment in Trinidad is extremely important to Dr. Williams.

6. As I have said, Trinidad immigration into Britain has not in the past been a problem. It has certainly not affected Britain's relations with Trinidad. I am afraid this happy state of affairs may no longer continue.

7. For the rest, I should report that Dr. Williams said nothing on the subject of aid, and appeared to be satisfied that Trinidad products would not be seriously affected by the new import surcharges. He also displayed interest in developments in Southern Rhodesia."

(DO 200/248)

Costar is then reporting that the issue of immigration into Britain would be an expected new flashpoint with Williams thereby raising the need for action to ensure Williams' compliance with British geo-political interests. It is apparent that Costar's access to Williams continues but the salient issue remains the terms and cost of endearment between Britain and Williams. The discourse is clear that Britain insists that the terms of endearment must ensure British hegemony and that Williams must shoulder the burden of an oppressive portion of the costs of endearment.

Costar writes to Sykes by way of letter dated the 13th January 1965 reporting as follows:

"Each week Dr. Williams lays down the law in his party newspaper THE NATION.

2. I enclose a copy of this current piece in which you will see, the Trinidad Prime Minister has been particularly critical of Federations which have stemmed from the British Empire.

5 Warming up to his theme, Dr. Williams added that these Federations were inspired by British interest and had collapsed or were collapsing because they were British inspired. As for the Eastern Caribbean, Dr. Williams stated: -

(a) British policy in British Guiana was bankrupt, a total failure: no attention was paid to Trinidad's views at the Commonwealth Prime Ministers' Conference.

(b) Britain did not know what to do about the Little Seven, and so the Grenada situation hung fire, since assistance to Grenada was dependent upon assistance given to the Little Seven.

6. Despite its world-wide look, Dr. Williams' anti-Federation broadside is in fact almost certainly aimed at the Caribbean, and is a reminder that he is not likely to give an enthusiastic welcome to the new neighbour Federation now in the offing. I therefore enclose a copy of this letter in case you may wish to pass it on to the Colonial Office, bearing in mind Mr. Greenwood's forthcoming visit to this part of the world."

(DO200/248)

Williams' timing is impeccable given the pending visit of the Secretary of State for the Colonies to Trinidad and Tobago. Williams has attacked British policy on British Guiana and on the British colonies of the Windward/ Leeward Islands or the Little Seven. He rejects Federation on British terms and by extension the British quest for a Trinidad and Tobago role in this federation. Williams insists that at the Commonwealth Prime Minister's Conference his policy on the solution to British Guiana's political problems was slighted even dismissed in the face of British policy on British Guiana that clearly was bankrupt. The British Government in January 1965 was now faced with the need to cut a deal with Williams to accomplish its geo-political strategic aims in the Caribbean. Furthermore a letter dated the 18th November 1964 by Costar to Sykes shows that Costar and the officers of the

British High Commission in Port of Spain had in fact executed a propaganda campaign to limit Williams' political power. Costar states:

> "3. We have, as you know, been developing publicity to show the extent of British help to the West Indies,..
>
> This has evoked both surprise and favourable private comment from many influential sources including the Governor-General in conversation with me.
>
> We have also now compiled a memorandum..
>
> 4. We are employing the document in various ways."

(DO 200/248)

Williams faced with a move by the British to foster resistance to his worldview and strategies, responds in the manner expected from him.

Costar by way of letter dated the 13th February 1965 reports to Sykes on the visit of Greenwood to Trinidad and Tobago as follows:

> "You will know from my telegram No.53 that this prompted Stephen Maharaj, the Leader of the Parliamentary Opposition in Trinidad, to write to Mr. Greenwood, and to seek an appointment with him. Fortunately, this appointment was headed off. Maharaj then wrote a second and somewhat woolly letter to Mr. Greenwood. But the meaning of both was quite clear: the Trinidad Opposition firmly oppose unitary statehood with Grenada and now seem more prepared than hitherto to come out in the open in saying so.
>
> 3. Meanwhile, Dr. Williams, who had learned of Maharaj's approach, had Dr. Solomon inquire of me on his behalf about the content of the letter which he claimed to have heard was insulting to the Trinidad Government. Dr. Solomon was also prepared to be huffy about the possibility of Mr. Greenwood meeting Maharaj. But the wind went from his sails when he learned that Maharaj had withdrawn his request to see Mr. Greenwood when he was told that the Colonial Secretary's visit was too brief to permit their meeting; and that even if time permitted, it would first be necessary to consult the Prime Minister."

(DO 200/248)

In spite of the so-called problems the British are having with Williams they refuse to meet and treat publicly with the DLP. What is noteworthy is the servility of the DLP Leader of the Opposition Stephen Carpoondeo Maharaj.

Costar notes their rather belated willingness to voice their opposition to any Trinidad-Grenada union. But what is noted is the servility of the DLP leader seen in the failure to engage with and demand of the British that they meet and treat with the political leaders of a race that would be impacted upon in the event of any form of union with Grenada. Clearly Costar and the British have no respect for the DLP and by extension the race they represent politically. Flashpoints with Williams do not include the destabilization of the political hegemony of Williams. The British made their choice since 1953 and they had to abide by this choice until parted by death, as there was no visible alternative suitable to the British. Costar continues:

> "Dr. Williams is now in an extremely sour mood with almost everyone. It is no doubt a cycle in Dr. Williams' schizophrenia, which would have probably developed anyway.
>
> 1. The Governor General, when Mr. Greenwood called on him, attributed Dr. Williams' state of mind to his reaction to recent developments in Britain in connection with immigration."

(DO 200/248)

For Costar, Williams' sour mood is the product of his schizophrenia. Costar is for the first time in the declassified files unleashing the discourse of the mentally ill maximum leader. He is therefore warning the British Government to expect a worsening of the relationship between Williams and Britain. Costar continues:

> "7. Now to the meeting. Mr. Greenwood did not mention the subject of Trinidad-Grenada union. Nor did Williams.
>
> 8. There was some discussion on British Guiana on which Mr. Greenwood made some effort to draw Dr. Williams. Again Dr. Williams was sour and not very forthcoming. The subjects not discussed included aid and any East Caribbean Federation as well as Trinidad-Grenada union.
>
> 11. Mr. Greenwood found Dr. Williams unforthcoming, in contrast to previous meetings in London. But at the moment this is as much to do with Dr. Williams' general all round mood of dislike as to any string feeling against Britain."

(DO 200/248)

Williams according to Costar is not forthcoming because of problems with his schizophrenia. Williams is not then intrinsically anti-British therefore the onus is on Britain to engage with him to protect their interests and advance their geopolitical agenda.

A Brief FOR UK EYES ONLY dated July 1965 on UK and Trinidad relations reveals the British position that good relations with Williams are premised upon an exchange of gifts. Naturally in the Brief what Williams does for Britain is not revealed. The Brief states:

> "2. Relations with the Government of Independent Trinidad started badly with disagreement over the financial settlement offered by the British Government, which were publicly and discourteously rejected by Dr. Williams. Relations improved in 1963 after the British Government had made a two-year loan to Trinidad and had given her four Viscount aircraft for the Trinidad Government airline. (British West Indian Airways).

> 4. Dr. Williams has shown every sign of being favourably disposed towards the new British Government from when he received a loan of f12m in December 1964 to enable him to nationalise the Trinidad Bus Service. Dr. Williams in the United Kingdom from 25 April to 4 May 1965, during which time he received an honorary degree of Doctor of Civil Law from the University of Oxford."

(DO 200/248)

The formula is then simple and even simplistic. Williams behaves as a bad boy attacking Britain publicly and a deal is struck. What then does Williams want in the second half of 1965 that results in his assault on Britain? What is of note in the said brief is that the nationalization of the bus companies that were the property of predominantly Indo-Trinbagonian entrepreneurs was facilitated by a loan from the British Government in 1964. The question arises of the capacity of the Williams Government to effect such a nationalization, which impacted race relations in Trinbago in the absence of the loan from the British Government in 1964.

Costar in his fortnightly summary dated the 8th September 1965 reports as follows:

> "Dr. Williams continued his attacks on Britain. Dr. Williams has again used his column in his party newspaper The Nation for public criticism of Britain. His fire is concentrated on:

> (a) The conduct of the recent Commonwealth Prime Ministers' Meeting:

> (b) Britain's new immigration measures.

4. In a later article on 3 September Dr. Williams condemned the absence of General Commonwealth discussion on immigration as 'typical of the British technique of divide and rule'. He also made unfriendly comment on his private talks with the Prime Minister on 15 July. Dr. Williams complained that there was no serious discussion of the immigration problem,

In an apparent reference to Sir Learie Constantine, Dr. Williams said 'all that Britain can think of in this explosive situation is the creation of a black peer."

(DO 200/248)

Williams' tirade against the Labour Government of Britain continues in September 1965 with no hint of abating. Costar fails to appreciate that Williams' onslaught is being pushed by much more than a peerage for Constantine, at best a simplistic causal explanation to render a complex character as Williams into a base character.

By the 9th November 1965 the groundswell of the international movement for Black Power washes over the British High Commission in Port of Spain and they are unable to grasp that the groundswell would culminate in the events of 1969-1970 including the army mutiny and the state of emergency in 1970. On the 9th November 1965, J.A. Davidson writes to A. Scott of the CRO stating as follows:

"I write to enclose a copy of a letter dated 27 October written jointly to the High Commissioner by the Presidents of two local bodies, the Afro International Association and the Afro Caribbean Association. The letter, submits a protest on the situation in Rhodesia, has been formally acknowledged but nothing more, and we propose no further action."

(DO 200/248)

The process has commenced that would flower in 1969. J.A. Davidson writing to A. Scott of the CRO dated 18th November 1965 would state:

"I do not want to burden you with too much of the local rudeness to Britain about Rhodesia, ..."

"But I am afraid the present political flavour of the Trinidad Branch of the U.W.I. seems to be such that no great stimulus is needed where anti-British sentiment is concerned!"

(DO 200/248)

Costar writes to Pickard of the CRO on the 24th November 1965 stating for the first time the recognition that initial demonstrations on Rhodesia can spiral and multiply posing a threat to British interests. Costar states:

> "If the Rhodesian situation drags on with the issue of the use of force continuing to be agitated, there is a likelihood that, in the absence of such discouragement by authority have, there will be more and perhaps more serious demonstrations and incidents."

(DO 200/248)

Costar's fortnightly summary-17th November-1st December 1965 reports:

> "Rhodesia-demonstrations against the British Government.
>
> On the 19 November the main editorial in Dr. Williams' party newspaper, which bore the hallmark of the master's hand, dealt with Rhodesia in violent and racialist fashion under the heading 'Commonwealth for Whites'.
>
> 2. The next day (20 November) there was a demonstration at the High Commission over Rhodesia, by students of the University of the West Indies (Pro-Chancellor Dr. Williams).
>
> 4. I wrote to the Trinidad Government to record the facts of the incident in the hope that a repeat performance might be prevented; and it is possible that with The Queen's visit pending Dr. Williams may for his own reasons seek to prevent recurrence during the next month or so. But the demonstration may regrettably have set a new local fashion.
>
> Moreover, the next issue of Dr. Williams' party newspaper following the incident sang praise of the demonstration and referred it as a 'first venture'."

(DO 200/248)

Costar is then insinuating that Williams has orchestrated the UWI student demonstration at the British High Commission in Port of Spain. For Costar Williams has ratcheted up his tirade against Britain with potential future impact on British interests. The Queen's visit is then the overt thin edge of the wedge to counter Williams' assault on British interests in Trinidad. On the 4th December 1965, J.A. Davidson of the British High Commission wrote Cleary of the CRO on the issue of Williams' reply to the letter of Costar on the UWI demonstration. Davidson states:

"2. I now write to enclose a copy of Dr. Williams' reply to the High Commissioner. As you will see it is written in emotional terms-no doubt with the Queen's visit in mind."

(DO 200/248)

Davidson sings the praises for the overt strategy of the British High Commission to deal with Williams' strategy of engagement with the British. Davidson desires a disciplined Williams but this desire fails to see the changed reality of politics in Trinidad and Tobago and the consequent impact upon British strategy for a compliant Williams. The lesser mortals of the British High Commission fail to see that Williams' intransigence stems from partially the impact of a radical resurgent black nationalism spawned in the crucible of African de- colonisation and the civil rights movement in the USA. Williams was then in late 1965 at risk of losing his place in the pantheon of black nationalist intellectuals involved in the process of decolonisation and post colonial development. Williams' dance with the British before and after 1962 left him in late 1965 open to the charge that his supplication to British hegemony failed to deliver a social order that reflected the ideals of black nationalism.

The failure of successive British Governments to be discerning of the impact their geo-political strategies were having on the sustainability of the political enterprise of supplicant black nationalists was apparent. By 1965 it was apparent to Williams that there was no partnership, no mutual respect between Britain and himself and British regimes were increasingly adopting a hard line which was making black nationalist hegemony in a recently decolonised social order tenuous at best. Williams would learn this lesson the hard way from 1965 to 1970. The army mutiny and subsequent state of emergency in 1970 would rock Williams' world and deliver the message to the British that their geo-political strategy was not cognisant of the new political realities of Trinidad and Tobago.

J.H.Walsh of the British High Commission at Port of Spain wrote a confidential file note titled: "Double Taxation Agreement" dated the 18th December 1965 and reports as follows:

"Correspondence on the double taxation agreement between the UK and Trinidad and Tobago had begun before independence.

2. On 1st September 1962 a draft of a new tax agreement with explanatory notes was sent to Trinidad and Tobago authorities for comment. No reply was ever received.

4. On 30 June 1965, the Trinidad Government gave notice terminating the existing agreement-without prior consultation-and invited the U.K. Government to begin the negotiations for a new arrangement.

6. The effect of the notice terminating the agreement of 1947 is that it will cease to have effect after 31 December 1965 in Trinidad and Tobago and after 5 April 1966 in the U.K.

7. The Trinidad team led by Mrs. Patricia Robinson, had discussions in London from 20-24 September and reached agreement on a number of articles."

(DO 200/248)

Walsh writes to T.W. Keeble of the CRO dated the 18th December 1965 on the Budget Speech delivered on the 17th December 1965 by A.N.R. Robinson, Minister of Finance. Walsh states:

"2. In his Budget speech yesterday, the Hon. A.N.R. Robinson, the Minister of Finance of Trinidad and Tobago, attacked Britain on its attitude towards double taxation.

3. We all know that these are in fact the words of Mr. Patricia Robinson speaking through her husband, and if challenged on the point of delay by the U.K. in producing a draft treaty, we shall not hesitate to make known the long delay of the Trinidad Government in coming to grips with the problem and their unreasonable attitude in expecting officials to negotiate on a draft agreement prepared by Trinidad and Tobago which was only produced on the day negotiations were to begin."

(DO 200/248)

Brinksmanship over a new double taxation treaty would reveal the opinion the British held of the capacity of A.N.R. Robinson to execute his tasks as Minister of Finance. Costar by way of a fortnightly summary for the 1st-14th January 1963 titled: "The Budget Muddle" states:

"The Government's reputation has suffered as a result of its extremely inept handling of the 1963 Budget. Mr. A.N.R. Robinson, the Finance Minister announced in his Budget speech that recurrent expenditure for 1963 would be $(WI) 181 million ($(WI) 17 million more than in 1962) and that his main fiscal measure would be the introduction of Purchase Tax. However, when the Government Order purporting to implement these proposals was published the next day it revealed substantial increases in Personal Income Tax which had not been mentioned in the Minister's.

Even worse, the Order applied these new personal tax rates (and reduced allowances) retrospectively to 1ˢᵗ January1962.

4. There is no doubt that the Government's standing, the reputation of the Finance Minister, and particularly the image of Dr. Williams as an efficient leader have all suffered as a result of this mishandling of the Budget. Business confidence, especially the confidence of expatriate firms and individuals, has been shaken by the evidence of the Government's willingness to make ad hoc and ill-considered efforts to increase revenue (even by retrospective measures) instead of considering radical steps to reduce growing expenditure;"

(DO 200/248)

The Budget Speech in 1965 by A.N.R. Robinson triggers flashbacks to his budget muddle in 1963. In both instances for the British, Robinson's incompetence present a threat to British interests in Trinidad and Tobago but on the issue of the double-taxation treaty with Britain the said correspondence would insist that Robinson was simply the mouthpiece of his wife Patricia.

The declassified files now offer the views of the British and the Canadian High Commission in Trinidad on the events of 1970 namely the Black Power Movement and the mutiny of the Trinidad and Tobago Regiment. The valedictory despatch dated the 26ᵗʰ March 1970 of Sir Peter Hampshire the British High Commissioner to Trinidad and Tobago to the Secretary of State for Foreign and Commonwealth Affairs would contain Hampshire's analysis of the reasons for the events of 1970 that preceded the Army mutiny of April 1970. The summary of the said despatch states:

"During the High Commissioner's last month in the post, Trinidad's unemployed (15 percent of the population) made an overdue protest against their plight, over which neither of the two main political parties had hitherto shown urgent concern. They followed the leadership of Black Power groups demonstrating against alleged Canadian persecution of West Indian students involved last year in the George Williams University affair in Montreal."

(FCO 63/589)

Hampshire is insisting that the Black Power demonstrations were the result of the failure of Williams to address the burning issue of unemployment. Hampshire states in the despatch as follows:

> "it is surprising that the unemployed-some 50,000 of them in a population of 1 million-should for so long have accepted their lot with apparent resignation and lack of public protest.
>
> 2. In the final month of my time here the overdue protest has at last been made in what is, as we have reported, an unusually dramatic fashion for Trinidad."

(FCO 63/589)

Hampshire continues:

> "They have now found the missing leadership as a result of the arrival on the Trinidad scene of money, guidance and support from the American Black Power Movement, into which have been recruited university students from the George Williams University in Montreal. Round these have clustered the local leaders of the various small fringe groups here (Communists, Marxists, Maoists, Black Panthers) always ready to jump in when there is a chance to make trouble. The young unemployed, up to a total of about 4,000, have eagerly responded to this new-found leadership, which has organised quite effectively the demonstrations and protests over the past month."
>
> "In terms of Government response achieved, the demonstrators must be judged successful."

(FCO 63/589)

Hampshire's analysis at minimum is a very potently accurate analysis of the nature of the leadership of the Black Power Movement before the State of Emergency in April 1970. What is noteworthy is Hampshire's statement of the links that existed between the US Black Power Movement and the Movement of Trinidad and Tobago.

Hampshire in his despatch proves to be prophetic in his analysis when he states:

> "2. The demonstrations offer no prospect to an ambitious political leader in Trinidad's democratic society. They pose a serious threat to the Government only if the revolutionary trade union leaders, who actively support the Black Power demonstrators, can swing their union members away from the ruling People's National Movement into a full alliance with Black Power."

(FCO 63/589)

Hampshire continues:

> "5. Party politics in Trinidad is organised on a strictly racial basis, the Negro People's National Movement Government party confronting the Indian Democratic Labour Party opposition. Any new party of the radical Left could only be formed if there was a major breakaway from the PNM-the Indians will in no circumstances associate themselves with such a party since they share none of its objectives and are indeed alarmed, not without reason, by the implications of Black Power for their own community."

(FCO 63/589)

There was no major breakaway from the PNM, the radical unions failed to persuade their members to desert the PNM, A.N.R. Robinson was the lone deserter from the leadership of the PNM and the Indo Trinbagonian community were spectators to the events of 1970 as they were in July 1990. Hampshire has been exonerated by history. Hampshire states:

> "6. Accordingly I do not anticipate any major change on the political scene as a consequence of Black Power's arrival."

(FCO 63/589)

Hampshire in the summary of his valedictory despatch states:

> "5. The High Commissioner regrets that it has been left to Black Power to bring to the surface long-submerged grievances. The Prime Minister, Dr. Eric Williams, believes he understands what lies behind the movement and can control it. Trinidad's economic prospects are promising, and the country enjoys a real measure of racial harmony."

(FCO 63/589)

What concerns Hampshire is the impact of Black Power on business and he reports on it as follows:

> "8. The arrival of Black Power is bound to have its impact on business here. The Government has in effect been compelled to take a step to the left in order both to damp down the demonstrators now on the streets and to make sure that Labour does not join them. Business is going to be called on to contribute both financially and in other ways to the speeded-up plans for absorbing as many as possible of the unemployed; to reduce their employment of expatriates; and to free itself of any charge of colour

discrimination, which in practice may involve more employment of unqualified Negroes in jobs normally filled by qualified white or Indian candidates.

This sort of thing is not going to be good for business confidence or for the prospects of much-needed new foreign investment. Nevertheless, it is hard to see that in present circumstances Government has any alternative if developments even more damaging to business are to be effectively prevented."

(FCO 63/589)

For Hampshire business had then to rally around Williams to ensure that Williams retain political power. The key to the strategy was to soften the face of apartheid in 1970 in the private sector of Trinbago.

Hampshire in closing his final despatch would speak of the political leadership of Williams in glowing terms as follows:

"its political leadership as long as Dr. Williams is there is expert, acute and confident;"

"What they have so far bumped into is a Government led by a shrewd pragmatist who has shown himself alertly responsive to those of their demands which are legitimate sensibly firm in insisting only that the manner in which they advance them should remain within the law."

(FCO 63/589)

Hampshire's despatch cannot cover the events of 21st April 1970 specifically the mutiny of elements belonging to the Trinidad and Tobago Regiment. Reports on this reality would be left to the incoming British High Commissioner to Trinidad and Tobago: R.C.C. Hunt. What is apparent from the despatches of R.C.C. Hunt is the position that the army mutiny of 21st April 1970 constituted the most potent threat to the development of Trinbago in 1970 not the Black Power Movement.

R.C.C. Hunt in his despatch of the 21st July 1970 states:

"A few days before I came a State of Emergency had been (belatedly) declared and though the immediate threat of a coup d'état, possibly of a bloody character, by Black Power extremists in conjunction with mutinous soldiers had been narrowly averted, the situation both in Trinidad and Tobago was still very edgy, the police and the Coast Guard were stretched to the limit, and-with the exception of the Prime Minister himself, who kept admirably calm-the Government were a group of frightened men, some of the Ministers were sheltering under armed guard at the Hilton Hotel in Port of Spain. The public at large were confused and apprehensive and, in the almost total absence of guidance from their Government, relied on the BBC bulletins from London, re-broadcast locally, to tell them what was happening just a few miles away from their homes."

(FCO 63/589)

Hunt speaks of panic and paralysis of the state agencies when faced with the army mutiny that commenced on the 21st April 1970. D.K. Middleton on the 27th July 1970 wrote a minute to Mr. Allen on the said despatch. Allen would reply on the 30th July 1970 as follows:

"Mr. Hunt's despatch is very readable and I think, a good analysis. I am not sure he is right in giving Dr. Williams quite so much credit for calm (para 1), given that a number of his immediate reactions to the crisis (e.g. firing off reports for help, inclined to the hysterical but in relative terms I suppose he did remain cool and collected."

(FCO 63/589)

The scenario depicted by Hunt and Allen would be repeated in July 1990.

Hunt speaks of the majority races in Trinbago in 1970 as follows:

"the compromise essential to the future stability and progress of the country is that between the people of predominantly African descent and the East Indians. Behind the compromise is to some extent a division of function-the African predominant in the top echelon of Government in the Civil Service and the police, contributing in a substantial lower middle-class and still larger working class in the towns as well as the bulk of the army of unemployed youths.

The East Indian, active and successful in business and the professions, but with a substantial agricultural proletariat, notably in the sugar industry. As in other Indian expatriate communities, the East Indian is clannish, prefers to remain politically non- aligned if he can, clings to his cultural links with India whilst despising its poverty and backwardness and likes best to be left alone to make a profit. So far many Indians have been willing to go along with the People's National Movement Government, particularly since it contains a proportion of Indian Ministers. But after the Black Power explosion here, from which the East Indians stood aside,

I have the strong impression that their leaders are now giving some thought about their future. With numbers totally about half a million, they are a powerful force in the country, and if the Government were to appear to lean too heavily on their interests in policies designed to placate the more vociferous demands of the African elements at the bottom end of the economic scale, we might see the beginnings of an unhealthy polarisation of the two main communities. This would be a daunting prospect, but I believe that there is enough statesmanship and good sense in the country to prevent it. One would, however, like in particular to see a more genuinely multi-racial political Opposition to the present ruling party instead of what appear largely to be disunited factions of East Indians."

(FCO 63/589)

Hunt articulates the discourse of the servile coolie and is concerned that the political subservience of the coolie can be disturbed by the PNM in response to the demands of the Black Power Movement. Hunt sees this disturbance of the order of race stratification, which the British worked earnestly to complete before Independence in 1962 as the most potent threat to the social order of Trinbago post 1970.

Hunt in the said despatch speaks of Williams and his Government as follows:

"and it is possible that during the recent troubles, Dr. Williams has given some hostages to fortune. He has had to rely heavily on the police and the Coastguard to remain in power. Perhaps more awkwardly he has had to rely on a single man, Brigadier Serrette, to end the army mutiny: and the aftermath of these singular events is still very much with us. The security forces, and their leaders, are now very prominent in the body politic, and new pressures and ambitions may be at work. In the continuing absence of any effective Parliamentary Opposition the threat, if there is one to Dr. Williams' position would most likely come from somewhere inside his own governing establishment. But on the surface at least no such prospects are visible, and I would rate Dr. Williams' instincts for political survival as well developed although they may have to pass further, more searching tests."

(FCO 63/589)

Williams survived until his death in 1981, A.N.R. Robinson and Karl Hudson Phillips paid the price by losing their careers as PNM and Cabinet functionaries supposedly close to Williams.

C.S. Roberts replies to Hunt's despatch on the 31ˢᵗ July 1970 setting out in clear and unequivocal terms the strategic importance of Williams as Prime Minister to the UK. Such a statement clearly indicates the basis for covert and overt interventions in support of Williams' continued political hegemony. Roberts states:

> "3. It seems clear that Dr. Williams is still the keystone in the Trinidad edifice and that much depends on his will to remain in power and the appeal of his peculiar kind of anti-charisma. I presume you see his continuation as head of government as the best possible thing for Trinidad in the immediate and medium term, and that it is in our interest to give him all possible support."

(FCO 63/589)

It was then in the interest of the UK to ensure that the back of the mutiny of the Trinidad and Tobago Regiment was broken and the danger to Williams' government disarmed. It was also in their interest to ensure that there were no further threats to Williams' hegemony in the post mutiny political power relations.

R.C.C Hunt on the 4ᵗʰ September 1970 reported on a meeting he had with Williams. Hunt states:

> "From the stray remark he dropped about political intrigues in the PNM and the latest challenge by A.N.R. Robinson, I assume that he still fears some attempt to unseat him should he leave the country and that he has no intention of going the way of Nkrumah."

(FCO 63/589)

Hunt reports to C.S Roberts of the Foreign and Commonwealth Office that Williams has assumed a threat to Williams' political hegemony. What then was the UK's response to this threat if any?

R.C.C. Hunt reports to H.A.A. Hankey by letter dated the 12ᵗʰ October 1970 on a visit to the Governor-General and the Prime Minister. On his visit with the Prime Minister Hunt states:

> "On the Public Order Bill he said, somewhat disingenuously, that the publication of the Bill was a mistake. It came out at the wrong time and contained provisions which were altogether too drastic. He implied that his Cabinet had not been consulted about it and if they had they would not have agreed to it being published in the form that it was. The Government now proposed to rush through, in separate legal packages, legislation dealing with such matters as

illegal possession of arms, and para-military forces, and this process will be complete before the State of Emergency is repealed."

(FCO 63/589)

Hunt is then reporting to Hankey that Williams had now targeted in the second half of 1970 Karl Hudson Phillips as the person to take the blame for the withdrawal of the Public Order Act. Hunt also reported in the same letter on his visit to Donald Granado in a Port of Spain nursing home. Hunt indicates that although Granado did not tell him he knew that he had undergone surgery for a prostate problem. Hunt reports as follows:

"I found him to be distinctly unhappy about Trinidad and sad that he had such little contact with his Government whilst on leave, he told me he was a close friend of A.N.R. Robinson and thought that Robinson would have done better to groom himself for Prime Ministerial Office, for which he was not yet ready, by continuing to work inside the PNM rather than by breaking away from it as he has."

(FCO 63/589)

Hunt is clearly engaging with Donald Granado for the express purpose of gathering intelligence and cultivating a useful contact. Hunt's report on the meeting with Granado indicates that A.N.R. Robinson at this time was under UK surveillance.

F.D. Milne would write to the British High Commission on the 24th November 1970 concerning A.N.R. Robinson's new political party. John Clarke would reply to Milne via letter dated the 4th December 1970 stating as follows:

"If, for election purposes, a deal could be made with the Jamadar faction of the D.L.P. together with James Millette's party, there is the possibilitythat some of the marginal seats at present held by the P.N.M. might go to the opposition. If Robinson's party went in alone then there is little likelihood of their gaining any seats from P.N.M or from D.L.P. for that matter-although Robinson himself is likely to hold on to his present constituency of Tobago East. However, in going alone, Robinson could win some votes from P.N.M. and in so doing let in the opposition in some marginal seats."

(FCO 63/589)

Milne is informed by Clarke that Robinson's political challenge to Williams and the PNM can at minimum benefit the opposition to Williams and the

PNM that contests the 1971 general elections. At maximum a coalition of opposition forces involving Robinson can result in a diminished majority for Williams and the PNM in the 1971 general elections. Milne would reply to Clarke on the 11th December 1970 stating as follows:

> "Much, it seems is going to depend when the time comes for the election on the degree of cohesion which is reached between the various opposition parties, even if only for electoral purposes."

(FCO 63/589)

For Milne the crux of the issue is the unity of the political parties opposed to the PNM contesting the 1971 general elections. Is it then simply strategic bungling and political immaturity that influenced Robinson's call for a boycott of the 1971 general elections by the electorate and his refusal to enter the ACDC/DLP into the 1971 general elections? The refusal of the ACDC/DLP to challenge the PNM in the 1971 general elections certainly worked to the benefit of the UK's geo-political interests in Trinbago in 1971.

R.C.C. Hunt's record of a call on Sir Solomon Hochoy on the 11th June 1970 summarises Hochoy's position as follows:

> "In his view the marches and demonstrations could have been kept under reasonable control if the trouble had not been compounded by the mutiny of the Regiment which he described as 'unexpected'. The mutiny of the Regiment was not merely the result of dissatisfaction with service conditions and prospects; it was part of an organised plot to achieve a coup d'état. If Captain Bloom and the Coastguard had not prevented the move of the mutineers from Teteron the Government might well have been forcibly deposed."

(FCO 63/589)

The mutiny of the Regiment on April 21st 1970 was then one of the salient threats to the Trinbagonian state and by extension the geo- political interests of the UK. Hunt continues:

> "There was a real danger of a political vacuum developing in Trinidad. This was because the Prime Minister was no longer giving proper leadership to the nation. He had been personally mortified and humiliated by the course of events, which had seemed to negate all the achievements of his long years of service to the nation. His Cabinet consisted largely of non-entities. There was the danger that in his present situation he might either drift indecisively or do something really damaging to the interests of the country."

(FCO 63/589)

For Hochoy the second salient threat was the leadership of Dr. Eric Williams. Hunt continues:

> "There was a danger that his present approaches to business for participation and contributions to the reconstruction fund would boomerang. Sir Solomon indicated that he had warned the Prime Minister of some of the difficulties in getting foreign firms to contribute in the sort of way that had been suggested."

(FCO 63/589)

The third salient threat was to business interests, as Williams demanded from these interests what they could not give. Hunt continues:

> "What the Prime Minister was doing at the moment was largely to react to the demands of Black Power. What he should do would be to put forward a constructive policy of his own based on the second Five-Year Plan, but altering priorities and targets to conform more closely with the political needs of the moment."

(FCO 63/589)

Hochoy on the 11th June 1970 called for a new direction for the PNM and PNM governance in the wake of the events of April 1970. Hunt reports on Hochoy's political analysis as follows:

> "As things stood at the moment the official opposition parties could not provide the basis for an alternative government. The people who could obtain mass support, and were to some extent doing so, were the extremist 'pseudo- intellectuals'. Their well-phrased, though empty, propaganda was exactly what the younger elements of the country wanted to read. The threat to the present Government therefore came largely from what he described as the Radicals and the pseudo-intellectuals. If they gained power it would probably be goodbye to democracy as it is now understood in Trinidad. These people would not be sobered up by the responsibility of power; they had too much of a racial chip on their shoulders. Their aim would be to get rid of the whites from Trinidad. When I asked about the possible reactions of the large East Indian community, Sir Solomon thought that their policy would be to keep their heads down until and unless their own position was threatened. Then they would fight.

(FCO 63/589)

Hochoy pushes every available button to set in train an operation to ensure Williams and the PNM retain power in the 1971 general elections. Williams has to be awakened from his stupor and the radical pseudo-intellectuals halted in their tracks. Failure to do so means race war and the end of Trinidad as Britain wants it. This is in effect Hochoy's message to the then ruling British political elite to ensure that a revitalized Williams retains political power at the 1971 general elections.

Bernard Pennock met with Solomon Hochoy on the 7th October 1970 in Trinidad. Pennock's notes on the said meeting reports Hochoy's position as follows:

> "His Excellency himself had advocated a Public Order Act several years ago. The recent Bill, including as it did some emergency power provisions was too wide in its scope and this was an error of judgement on the part of the Government."

(FCO 63/589)

Hochoy is then by extension blaming the then Attorney General, Karl Hudson Phillips for the withdrawal of the Public Order Act. Pennock continues:

> "The Governor-General found himself in complete agreement with 'Perspectives for a New Society' which he thought brilliant. He confirmed that this had been produced by Williams himself and he had shown it to him before publication ......"

(FCO 63/589)

'Perspectives for a New Society' was then the direction Hochoy sought from Williams and Williams delivered. Pennock continues:

> "The statement in 'Perspectives' on racial amity was more whole-hearted than any statement previously expressed by Williams."

(FCO 63/589)

Williams' statement on race relations in Trinidad and Tobago in Perspectives for a New Society is proof of the new Williams bringing the new dispensation fully supported by Hochoy. And finally the most potent message Hochoy delivered to Bernard Pennock.

> "The Governor-General agreed that there was no one of the comparable stature or competence in the political field to take the place of Williams."

(FCO 63/589)

Given Hochoy's position that Williams is the only viable game in the political arena then it is incumbent upon Hochoy and the British to ensure the re-election of Williams and the PNM in the 1971 general elections. Was the no vote campaign the product of the strategic need for Williams' re-election?

R.C.C. Hunt on the 18th December 1970 gives his last report on the internal political situation for 1970 and it is upbeat and full of praises for the leadership of Williams. Hunt reports:

> "All this seems to have been good for Williams and the PNM; and most people say that Williams' stock has risen sharply in recent weeks. He himself is said to be at the top of his form. The country at large seems also to be in a euphoric and free-spending mood, with the shop-keepers expecting their best Christmas ever."

(FCO 63/589)

What then for Hunt has sent Williams' political stock soaring seen in the bumper Christmas expected by business people in 1970? For Hunt these are: (a) the removal of the State of Emergency without a return to violent political action; (b) the failure of the released NJAC leaders to replicate the demonstrations and marches as in February 1970, and (c) after prolonged delays the hearing of evidence in the Court Martial of the mutineers had commenced. R.C.C. Hunt is then on the 18th December 1970 stating that the decision to support Williams and the PNM by the British was the right decision and it was already paying dividends.

The date for the 1971 general elections was Monday 20th May 1971. The Action Committee of Dedicated Citizens (ACDC) entered into a coalition with the DLP faction led by Vernon Jamadar forming the ACDC-DLP with Robinson as Chairman of the coalition and Jamadar as Vice-Chairman. On Sunday the 9th May 1971 Robinson declared that the ACDC-DLP would not contest the 1971 general elections on the grounds that the general elections of 1971 would not be safe and fair. Robinson's strategy that fateful Sunday in early May 1971 was to call for a no-vote campaign amongst the electorate. The end result was that the PNM won all thirty-six seats of the House of Representatives in 1971. The Democratic Liberation Party of Bhadase Maraj failed to capture the Indo-Trinbagonian vote that would have gone to the DLP and this was Maraj's final political intervention in the interests of his British overlords and Williams.

Vernon Jamadar would pay the ultimate political price for consorting with Robinson in 1971 as the 1976 general elections would signal the arrival of the new Indo-Trinbagonian maximum leader: Basdeo Panday. Some 33.17%

of the electorate voted in the 1971 general elections and the PNM garnered approximately 28% of this total. Clearly Robinson's action channelled the anti-PNM vote to marginalised irrelevance because Hochoy and the British called for victory at the polls and with that victory Hochoy and Williams rode out any constitutional crisis that ensued. The debate about a minority government elected by only 28% of the electorate and the constitutional crises generated by the absence of an Opposition in the House of Representatives meant nothing in the face of the Hochoy/ Williams alliance intent on ruling until general elections were called in 1976. An opportunity Williams embraced with open arms as he won again in the 1976 general elections and then he died in 1981.

In closing it is noteworthy that the "radical and pseudo- intellectual" political forces opposed to Williams and the PNM such as NJAC, TAPIA and UNIP refused to take part in the 1971 general elections. TAPIA would contest the 1976 general elections and was rejected at the polls. Robinson's DAC in 1976 would be rejected in Trinidad but won the two Tobago seats. The various forms of Marxist- Leninist, Maoist dogma would be represented in the ULF only to be cast adrift by Basdeo Panday with the fracturing of the ULF, and NJAC stayed out of "conventional politics" opting instead for "non- conventional politics". By the 1976 general elections the anti- Williams forces that emerged in the politics of February to April 1970 were consigned to the marginalized futility of opposition politics waiting for the death of Williams to move to fill the space created with his passing.

R.C.C. Hunt reports to C.S. Roberts by letter dated 13th July 1970 stating as follows:

> "Captain David Bloom of the Coastguard has been unburdening himself to SLO as well as myself about the Regiment and in particular the personality and motivation of Brigadier Serrette. It has never been very clear exactly how Serrette succeeded in persuading the mutineers to surrender but it is widely believed that in the course of very difficult and indeed dangerous parleys he had with them he may have extended a quid pro quo, which might have taken the form of an assurance that he would in some way protect their interests.

> Bloom has now persuaded himself that Serrette, who had always deeply resented the way in which he was dismissed from command of the Regiment and who has always regarded it as his own personal creation, actually engineered the mutiny in order to discredit his successor and to regain command of it. It is not at all easy to assess his information. It is somewhat disquieting, if only

in its implication that the leaders of the defence forces in Trinidad are clearly at loggerheads. I have observed with my own eyes that Serrette and Bernard, the new Police Commissioner, are not at all happy in each other's company."

(FCO 63/603)

C.S. Roberts by way of letter dated the 31ˢᵗ July 1970 responds to Hunt's letter of 13ᵗʰ July 1970. Roberts states:

> "Our first impression, like yours, was that the story was far-fetched and hard to swallow. True or false, that it is being spread, albeit within a discreet and fairly small circle, seems bound to add to the already dangerous situation of mistrust between the leaders of the various branches of the security forces, and between them and the Cabinet.
>
> 4. But what has caused Bloom to make these allegations now?
>
> We should welcome your opinion on Bloom's motives, and on whether you think that in the very closely-linked army/police community there is any real chance that Bloom's suspicions of Serrette can remain secret for long and I must say that we agree with your assessment that the emerging jealousies between the securities chiefs seem to add seriously to Dr. Williams' problems, and to make his position much more vulnerable."

(FCO 63/603)

Roberts is insisting that Bloom's accusations are in fact heightening the threat against Williams and creating a threat to Bloom's position as Commander of the Coastguard, which is important to UK interests in the aftermath of the events of April 21ˢᵗ 1970. Roberts is then ordered to uncover Bloom's motivation to make such accusations moreover to monitor the activities of Serrette. Hunt replies to Roberts by letter dated the 17ᵗʰ August 1970. Hunt states:

> "The Regiment's present disposition on both sides of the Coastguard base does nothing to relieve Bloom's feeling that if Serrette is planning to use the Army for a political purpose, it will not be stymied next time by the Coastguard.
>
> I think, that Bloom reached his conclusions in early July after assessing the reports which had reached him, via his own officers, from Regiment officers whom he regarded as reasonably trustworthy.

4. My own feeling is that we should be wiser to suspend judgement rather than dismiss Bloom's ideas as wholly far-fetched, while at the same time remembering that Bloom himself is somewhat overstrained."

(FCO 63/603)

Hunt is then refusing to support Roberts' position on Bloom's accusation by pointing out the strategic realities if Bloom's accusations turn out to be true. There is then a quest by the British to penetrate the cover of Serrette to determine if the intention to launch a coup d'état exists, if then a salient threat to Williams' political hegemony exists.

Fawcett by way of letter dated the 24th August 1970 writes to C.S. Roberts stating as follows:

"3. Macintyre nevertheless formed the impression that Serrette does not intend to use the Army politically and is well content with his new appointment and its perquisites and with having levelled the score with ex-Minister Montano. He did not detect any signs of strain or anxiety. He agrees however that if there were to be a threat of disclosures at Courts Martial or at treason trials that would damage Serrette's reputation or endanger his position, Serrette might look around for a political protector other than Dr. Williams. The verdict thus remains an open one."

(FCO 63/603)

Fawcett is reporting to Roberts on the visit of the ASO (Caribbean), Lt. Col. Macintyre to the T&T Regiment on the 20th August 1970. Macintyre provided an assessment that necessitated keeping Serrette on the British watch list of potential threats to Williams and the PNM Government.

In 1968 the Minister of Home Affairs retired Lt. Col. Joffre Serrette at the age of 52 years. Serrette would return in 1970 and stayed until 1978 when he retired at the age of 62. The Minister of Home Affairs in 1968, Mr. Gerard Montano would lose his place in the Cabinet following the army mutiny in April 1970. The Court of Appeal would quash the convictions of Rex La Salle and Raffique Shah by the Courts Martial. In his judgement Justice Fraser of the Court of Appeal would state as follows:

"It is perhaps the acme of irony that the two men who boldly and brazenly proclaimed themselves to be leaders of the mutiny in the Regiment and whose plans and purposes were aimed at disruptive and dangerous courses should escape punishment for their actions. But the law must take its proper course. I can find nothing to commend either of them.

Their behaviour on April 21, 1970 was reprehensible in the extreme; but in military affairs the law, as it now stands, gives a commanding officer power to condone military offences, including mutiny, and such condonation is a bar to trial by a court-martial. The hearing of the plea of condonation was not a fair hearing. The principles of natural justice were cast aside for no apparent reason; and the Act does not provide the alternative of a re-trial. Where there is a substantial miscarriage of justice the Act demands that the conviction be quashed."

(Hylton Edwards 1982 Pg 148)

In 1972 the Privy Council would support the ruling of the Court of Appeal. Justice Fraser insists that the Defence Act No.7 of 1962 demands that the sentences on Shah and La Salle be quashed because of the judicial incompetence of the Courts Martial that found them guilty. Shah and La Salle's defence was condonation of their mutinous actions by their Commanding Officer, Joffre Serrette. But the Court of Appeal comprising Justice Clement Phillips, Justice Fraser, and Justice Georges all ruled in favour of Shah and La Salle on the grounds of procedural fairness and the Defence Act No.7 of 1962 and insisted that on such grounds the sentence of the Courts Martial was to be quashed and there was to be no re-trial. Shah and La Salle walked away as free men not as a result of being exonerated by the Court of Appeal and the Privy Council but by dint of the provisions of the Defence Act of 1962. This reality would be repeated in the aftermath of the Jihad of July 27th 1990. As the Children of Sisyphus we routinely invent squared wheels. It is fitting to recall Simbhoonath Capildeo's assault on the Defence Bill 1962 when it was laid in the Legislative Council by Patrick Solomon. The mutiny of April 21st, 1970 and the freeing of the leaders of the mutiny in 1972 by dint of the provisions of the Defence Act 1962 simply indicate the vision of Simbhoonath Capildeo.

FCO 63/858 deals with the internal situation in Trinidad in 1971. R.C.C. Hunt of the British High Commission, Trinidad wrote to C.S. Roberts of the Caribbean Department, Foreign and Commonwealth Office (FCO) on the 29th January 1971. Hunt would report on a conversation he had with the then Governor General Solomon Hochoy. Hunt would report on two issues: the sale of arms by Britain to South Africa and the Declaration of a State of Emergency in Trinidad and Tobago in April 1970. On the issue of an arms sale to South Africa, Hunt would report that Williams absented himself from the Conference of Commonwealth Prime Ministers to evade having to toe the line at the Conference set by the African members of the Commonwealth. On the issue of the declaration of the State of Emergency in April 1970 Hunt reports that Hochoy indicated that Williams sought Hochoy's advice on declaring a state of emergency in March 1970. Hochoy persuaded Williams to delay the declaration of the state of emergency and when it was declared in April 1970 Hochoy was away on leave. According to Hunt, Hochoy indicated to Williams that a declaration of a state of emergency in a post-colonial state was perilous at best. Hunt states:

> "Since independence however all that lay behind the police force was the Regiment, and who indeed could be sure that they would be ready to open fire on their own cousins, brothers, etc.? Hochoy for one was quite certain that they would not and that in fact they would only support the civil power if they themselves were convinced that things had got completely out of hand."

(FCO 63/858)

On the 3rd February 1971 D.G. Allen of the FCO would report on a meeting Allen had with Eustace Seignoret then Deputy High Commissioner of Trinidad to Britain. Allen states:

> "4. Mr. Seignoret confirmed that it was his impression (like ours) that nothing very solid had yet emerged from the recent forming of a joint party between A.N.R. Robinson's Action Group of Dedicated Citizens and Mr. Jamadar's DLP.
>
> 9. I told Mr. Seignoret that we had been struck recently by several indications, e.g. in Mr. Prevatt's budget speech that Trinidad was taking a leaf out of Guyana's book, e.g. in giving much greater emphasis to the development of cooperatives. Mr. Seignoret said that it was time that Mr. Burnham had made a considerable impact on Trinidad and that the Trinidad Government were to some extent 'keeping up with the Joneses'. Trinidad had been very impressed with the progress Guyana had made under Mr. Burnham's government and were anxious to learn any lessons that they could from the Guyanese example."

(FCO 63/858)

Instances afforded from the contents of a declassified British file indicate: (a) the failure of Williams to articulate an independent stance on apartheid South Africa that resonated with his public stance of a black nationalist, (b) the power Hochoy wielded in 1970 and his foresight in not trusting the newly created Regiment as an instrument to protect the government of the day from the Black Power movement, (c) that the British had dismissed the ACDC/DLP as a potent threat to the hegemony of the PNM in early 1971.

John Clarke of the British High Commission at Trinidad would write F.D. Milne of the FCO on the 18th March 1971 stating as follows on the political parties present:

> "5. The ACDC/DLP led by ANR Robinson and Vernon Jamadar appears to have a very shaky election platform indeed. The party seems to have taken over the leadership of the Black Power Movement from NJAC and this is noticeably demonstrated at their public meetings. But what is disturbing about ACDC/ DLP is the manner in which they are making political capital out of the Court Martial sentences. The public in general remains unconvinced by this catchpenny opportunism. The party has not yet issued a manifesto (although in October they presented a Declaration of Principles) nor at public meetings has it made any positive comment apart from those on the Court Martial issue."

(FCO 63/858)

It is clear that Clarke views the ACDC/ DLP as a threat to the existing order and British interests in Trinidad and Tobago. It is apparent that for Clarke in 1971 the ACDC/ DLP is not fit to rule Trinidad and Tobago.

In a letter to C.S. Roberts of the FCO by RCC Hunt of the British High Commission in Trinidad dated the 24th April 1971 Hunt states:

> "After 14 years in power there is widespread disillusionment with Dr. Williams and the PNM, and it seems likely that this feeling rather than the credibility of the opposition will pose the only real threat to his successful return to office. But as yet Robinson's ACDC/DLP can hardly be regarded as a serious contender, and its prospects were damaged by its courting of extremist elements, such as for instance those who were trying to urge the release of soldiers sentenced by the court-martial. However, these are early days and we shall have to watch developments."

(FCO 63/858)

Those were not early days as elections were held on the 24th May 1971. It is noted that for Hunt on the 24th April 1971 the ACDC/ DLP was Robinson's and the ACDC/DLP was unacceptable to Hunt for its courting of extremist elements in the society. Was it then another coincidence in the political history of Trinbago that on the 24th May 1971 the ACDC/DLP imploded and did not contest the general elections of the 24th May 1971?

Diplomatic Report No. 432/71 from the British High Commissioner at Port of Spain to the Secretary of State for Foreign and Commonwealth Affairs dated the 23rd August 1971 states:

> "3. The blame for this unhealthy state of affairs must rest in the first instance with the Opposition. But the long years of PNM supremacy under Dr. Williams and the consolidation under his expert and unremitting attention of a well organised political movement, largely negro, have demoralised the disunited, mainly East Indian Opposition, reducing it to an almost contemptible irrelevance.

> 21. So far as our interests are concerned we have no real grounds for complaint in finding Dr. Williams still in power after nine years of independence ...on the whole both he and his government have a realistic appreciation of the many links which continue to bind Trinidad and Tobago with Britain. It has been our experience that in the last analysis pragmatism rather than doctrine wins the day."

(FCO 63/858)

In August 1971 the threat of the ACDC/DLP is long gone and Williams as Prime Minister of Trinidad and Tobago is the only game in town that is worthy of British support. What is noteworthy is that the shattering of the anti-PNM political opposition is the fault of the East Indian leadership. But the opposition to Williams is faced with a catch 22 for resistance to the genius of Williams is futile. The hostile recalcitrant minority of 1958 is by 1971 languishing in irrelevance. From 1953 to 1971 the agenda of the British overlord is then made manifest in the "almost contemptible irrelevance" of the Indo- Trinbagonian opposition to Williams and the PNM. Was this simply wishful thinking made reality by coincidence?

On the 28th October 1971, J.P.B. Simeon of the British High Commission in Trinidad would report on the death of Bhadase Sagan Maraj on the 21st October 1971 to F.D. Milne of the FCO. Simeon would report on the impact the death of Maraj would have on the All Trinidad Sugar Estates and Factory Workers Trade Union, the Maha Sabha and the Democratic Liberation Party. Simeon reported on the honour afforded Maraj by the ruling PNM and inevitably repeated the claims, supposedly made by sources to Simeon of Maraj's criminal activities. Simeon reported that on the 25th October 1971 Dickson Emery was appointed by the executive of the Union to act as President General until May 1978 by the Union. Simeon reported that at the time of writing no successor to Maraj was announced by his Democratic Liberation Party. Simeon would report on the war that erupted in the Maha Sabha over the person chosen to act as president general until elections due in 1972. On the 26th October 1971 the daily press reported that Simbhoonath Capildeo was appointed acting President General until 1972 but two days later on the 28th October 1971 the daily press reported that the duly elected acting President General was now Rampersad Bhoolai. Harry Persad Beharry the then secretary of the Maha Sabha denied that the trustees of the Maha Sabha had ever appointed Simbhoonath Capildeo as acting President General. Pundit Jankey Persad Sharma would also indicate that the appointment of Simbhoonath Capildeo as acting President General of the Maha Sabha was null and void.

F.D. Milne would write to JPB Simeon on the 10th November 1971 on the death of Maraj stating as follows:

> "2. It should be useful to have your assessment of any likely shift in the political stance of the sugar union from one of being, under Maraj, broadly pro-government and anti-OWTU. In addition one is tempted to wonder whether the Democratic Liberation Party is likely to be of any continuing significance in the political life of the country."

(FCO 63/859)

It is noteworthy that Milne of the FCO attaches no significance to the Maha Sabha with reference to British interests. In addition Maraj was important, as the union's stance was pro-government and anti-OWTU. One expects that the Democratic Liberation Party was also pro-government even though Milne does not say so. Simeon would reply to Milne's query by reporting that he expects the union to maintain its pro-government, anti-OWTU stance. On the question of the Democratic Liberation Party Simeon states:

> "it is after all difficult to take seriously a newly formed 'party', obviously formed as an expedient to enable Maraj and some of his lieutenants to contest the general election and it is now even more difficult to believe that they have much future since they failed to win even a single seat."

(FCO 63/859)

This textual journey commenced with the British reaction to the political mobilization of Bhadase Sagan Maraj in the early 1950's and ends with his death in 1971. It closes with the collapse of the political vehicle created to contest the 1956 general elections, a vehicle that first collapsed and then shattered into factional pieces in 1971. The colonial alarm over the East Indian Problem in 1953 would then drive specific actions by the colonial overlord that would mould the history of Trinbago in this period. A course of history that our political leaders were in fact spectators as the events unfolded.

ERIC WILLIAMS AND THE CARIBBEAN COMMISSION 1954-1955

CO 1042/404 the file containing the British documents on Williams' dismissal from the Caribbean Commission was only declassified in 2007.

The confidential minute of the meeting of the 20th May, 1954 held by the four co-chairmen of the Caribbean Commission states:

> "The four co-chairmen met on May 20, 1954, at the Fort George Hotel, Belize, to hear a report by the Secretary General on the deterioration in staff relationships within the Secretariat."

> "The Secretary General is of the opinion that the interpretation given by the Head of the Research Branch to his status in the Organisation, and the general attitude adopted by him in the Secretariat as a result of this interpretation has set up highly undesirable stresses in the Central Secretariat. Although thus far these stresses may not have outwardly affected the Secretariat's overall performance, the Secretary General considers them entirely inadmissible and feels that without doubt they will impair the Secretariat's efficiency, and destroy the present commendable level of industrial relations within the organisation."

(CO 1042/404)

The Secretary General of the Caribbean Commission has brought a complaint to the four co-chairmen in 1954 of a Head of the Research Branch of the Caribbean Commission who is openly challenging the power of the said Secretary General in the daily management of the Caribbean Commission. The Head of the Research Branch in 1954 is Dr. Eric Williams.

The four co-chairmen respond to the complaint if the Secretary General as follows:

> "After an exchange of views, the four co-chairmen consider that the contemplated revision of the Agreement for the Establishment

of the Caribbean Commission is likely also to call for a reappraisal of the Commission's research activities.

In view of this consideration, and the internal developments reported above by the Secretary General, the four co-chairmen agreed to instruct the Secretary General to renew the service contract of Dr. Eric Williams with the Caribbean Commission, expiring in June 1954 for a period of one year."

"The four co-chairmen further agreed that a letter should be handed to Dr. Eric Williams as per the copy attached to these confidential minutes."

(CO 1042/404)

The proposed restructuring of the research staffing of the Commission and the charges brought by the Secretary General, are then the grounds to renew Williams' contract for one year.

The four co-chairmen would write to Eric Williams on the 22nd May 1954 stating as follows:

"Dear Dr. Williams:

The Secretary General informed the four co-chairmen of the difficulties which have arisen in the General Secretariat due to the conflict between his interpretation and yours-based on previous commission decisions and directives-of the position of the Research Branch and its Head within the Secretariat organisation.

The four co-chairmen consider the contemplated revision of the Agreement for the Establishment of the Caribbean Commission is likely also to call for a reappraisal of the Commission's Organisation insofar as its research activities are concerned.

In these circumstances, and bearing in mind the above developments reported by the Secretary General the four co-chairmen have instructed the Secretary General that your service contract with the Commission, expiring in June 1954, shall be renewed for the period of one year."

(CO 1042/404)

Williams would reply to the said letter of 22nd May 1954 on the 24th November 1954. Williams states in his reply as follows:

"I have given very careful thought to the communication of the four co-chairmen of May 22, 1954, and discussed it with various people who have been connected with the establishment and organisation of the Commission and its Secretariat, both in the Caribbean and in Europe. I have been confirmed in my opinion that the letter is equivalent to notice of dismissal. It is the type of letter that I would expect to be sent to an employee of an organisation who has been given a chance and who has failed. It implies a factitious opposition on my part to authority. These imputations of failure and faction, combined with the statement that 'the contemplated revision of the Agreement ..... is likely also to call for a reappraisal of the Commission's organisation insofar as its research activities are concerned' give to the final paragraph of the letter a punitive aspect."

(CO 1042/404)

Williams interprets the action of the four co-chairmen of the Caribbean Commission as the first move in a strategy to dismiss Williams from the said Commission. What is instructive is the British colonial position on the action of the Commission and Williams' response to the position of the Commission.

By way of a letter dated 5th August 1955 by M.H. Dorman then acting governor of the colony of Trinidad and Tobago to Sir Stephen Luke, Comptroller for Development and Welfare in the West Indies one of the four co-chairmen of the Caribbean Commission reports on a meeting with Albert Gomes. Dorman states:

"Dear Sir Stephen,

On the morning of the 3rd August Albert Gomes came to speak to me about Dr. Eric Williams and obviously felt very much concerned about difficulties that had arisen between him and the Caribbean Commission.

Gomes was sorry to feel that the matter had been handled in such a brusque fashion.

He then went on to talk about Eric Williams' contacts with politicians throughout the area and said that this might become a West Indian issue if Williams chose to publicise it in a certain way. He also suggested that there might be a demand from R.E.C. to have him appointed as an Economic Adviser. Eric Williams had himself been anxious to join R.E.C. particularly I suppose in the light of the prospects of Federation and had already written to Bradshaw, Manley, Adams, himself and others"

(CO 1042/404)

Albert Gomes then member of the Executive Council of Trinidad and Tobago raises the issue of Williams' treatment by the Caribbean Commission and the political backlash that can result. Gomes cites Williams' influence amongst West Indian politicians but moreover he posits a possible strategy to appoint Williams to the post of Economic Adviser. Gomes' strategy was then to keep Williams out of politics in the capacity of a civil servant attached to the British West Indian Federation. Luke would reply to Dorman's letter on the 16th August 1954 stating as follows:

> "I am most grateful to you for passing on to me the gift of your conversation with Gomes. The whole problem is complicated, and there is definitely another side of the story. I am myself much concerned about Dr. Williams' position on the Caribbean Commission secretariat, and I foresee many difficulties and embarrassments ahead before a solution is found."

(CO 1042/404)

On the 18th October 1954 Phillip Rogers of the Colonial Office wrote to Stephen Luke on the issue of Eric Williams and the Caribbean Commission. Rogers states as follows:

> "My Dear Tommy,

> In the course of a talk on a number of matters last week Albert Gomes told me that Eric Williams was very much upset about recent developments relating to his position with the Caribbean Commission. Gomes was worried about the possibility that Williams might resign and go into politics and that colour bitterness might be enhanced as the result if Williams should ascribe these developments on the Commission to his own colour. Gomes was therefore anxious that I should have a talk with Williams and I duly saw him for a very hurried half hour on Saturday, much interrupted by phone calls.

> I suppose, however, that there are distinct possibilities of bitterness on colour grounds among West Indian intellectuals, if Eric Williams is forced out of the Commission, and in case all these side-winds had not been brought to your notice I felt that I should do so."

(CO 1042/404)

Phillip Rogers has then indicated the potent threat the treatment of Williams by the Caribbean Commission was posing to British colonial interests in the Caribbean. Stephen Luke would reply to Phillip Rogers on the 8th November 1954. The contents of Luke's letter to Rogers would show the impact of Rogers' letter of the 18th October 1954 on Luke. Luke reports as follows:

> "When I was in Trinidad last week, I had a lengthy talk with Williams and did my best to dispel his impression that he was a victim of 'racial persecution'.
>
> I am afraid that I do not think that either the Secretary General or the four co-chairmen have so far been very dexterous in handling a most difficult staff problem, and for this I must bear my share of the responsibility.
>
> I have no doubt that Williams is a source of serious weakness in the Caribbean Commission secretariat, and that it would greatly benefit from the termination of his association with it. But it is most important, not least for the Commission, that he should not leave under a strong sense of grievance. If this should happen, he might well prove a most damaging influence in this area. I very much hope, therefore, we may be able, in French Guiana, to find a solution that will ensure the smooth working of the secretariat without driving Williams into the wilderness. Indeed, I am disposed to think that it may be necessary to sacrifice the interests of the Caribbean Commission generally: and of de Vriendt personally, to the narrower interests of H.G's future relations with the British West Indies. Time may, in any event, solve the problem for us since Williams may take himself voluntarily into Trinidad or federal politics.
>
> My main objective, whatever solution is found, is to try to ensure that we are not left with an embittered and anti-British Williams on our hands."

(CO 1042/404)

What is noteworthy is that Luke is convinced that Williams is disrupting the smooth operation of the secretariat of the Caribbean Commission. Luke wants Williams out of the secretariat but British colonial interests demand an exit strategy for Williams that would not alienate Williams from the British colonial agenda for the British West Indies.

On December 3rd 1954 the Commission acknowledged receipt of Williams' memorandum of November 24th 1954. The Commission by its letter made it clear that Williams future as an employee of the Commission was to be decided by a review of his performance in light of the charges laid against him by the Secretary General of the Commission. The letter states:

> "The Commission has noted with satisfaction your unqualified assurance that you accept the full authority of the Secretary General and his Deputy for the proper functioning of the Secretariat, thus rendering it unnecessary to enter into detailed discussion of the several points raised in your letter, many of which are unacceptable to the Commission.
>
> With reference to the letter of May 22nd addressed to you by the co-chairmen, the Commission hopes that when the question of the renewal of your contract comes up for consideration at its Twentieth Meeting to be held in Puerto Rico the experience of the next six months will justify the conclusion of a further contract with you on a basis satisfactory to all."

(CO 1042/404)

The letter of December 3rd, 1954 by the Commission to Williams makes it clear that (1) the Commission has rejected outright the case made by Williams in his memorandum dated November 24th 1954. The charges made by the Secretary General stood. (2) Williams' job performance and his future employment at the Commission would be assessed on the basis of the charges laid by the Secretary General. It must be noted that Williams' rebuttal of said charges were never called for and formally deliberated on by the four co- chairmen. It is then apparent that Williams' employment was to be terminated in 1955. The question arises of what actions were taken by the British colonial state to ensure that Williams, despite the termination of his employment at the Commission, is not hostile to the British colonial agenda for the British West Indies. The verbatim notes of the secret plenary sessions of the 19th meeting of the Caribbean Commission held on the 2nd and 3rd December 1954 indicate the hard line against Williams' continued employment adopted by the delegations but the fact that in spite of his remonstrations and promises to Phillip Rogers , Stephen Luke was in full support of the move against Williams by especially the French and Netherlands delegations. Luke would write to Phillip Rogers on the 9th December, 1954 carefully crafting a reality for Rogers which omitted the witch hunt against Williams that had consumed the secret plenary session of December 2nd and 3rd 1954. Luke states as follows:

> "As I expected, we spent much more time on this problem than on anything else during our meeting in Trinidad last week. I am happy to say that, after many hours of discussion and consultations, we

managed to find a solution that, for the time being at least, saves the Commission from public embarrassment and offers perhaps some hope of improvement of the state of affairs in the Secretariat.

Unless there is a great improvement in relationships in the Secretariat, we shall be faced in Puerto Rico in May with a choice between dispensing with Williams' services or accepting the resignations of de Vriendt and Beauregard."

(CO 1042/404)

Williams was then marked for death in May 1955 as the Secretary General, de Vriendt and the Deputy Secretary General Beauregard are of the master race, Dutch and French, and one cannot expect white men to choose Williams over their fellow white men.

The crux of the matter is in fact the refusal to investigate the veracity of the charges laid against Williams by Secretary General de Vriendt. In fact during the secret plenary session held on the 2nd and 3rd December 1954, a member of the Dutch delegation demanded that Williams be called upon by the Commission to withdraw the counter charges made in his memorandum dated 24th November 1954. This was not supported by the whole commission.

The staff report of Dr. Eric Williams prepared by the Secretary General dated May 3rd, 1955 states as follows:

"If, therefore, the Commission decides to extend the service contract of Dr. Williams, I strongly recommend that only those tasks be assigned to him for which his capacities and temperament best qualify him, i.e. conducting specific surveys demanding considerable personal participation in the collation and interpretation stages, but with limited responsibility for the supervision of staff members."

(CO 1042/404)

The Secretary General is then giving the Commission an ultimatum: get rid of Williams or retain his services under new terms and conditions of service that render him emasculated . Clearly de Vriendt wanted to exert power over Williams to put him in his place.

On May 19th 1955 the Commission met in Puerto Rico and Stephen Luke presided over his meeting of the Commission. The confidential minutes report as follows:

"After long discussion, the Commission unanimously decided not to renew Dr. Williams' contract."

(CO 1042/404)

The editorial of June 3ʳᵈ, 1945 of the Port of Spain Gazette would raise the most potent issue to arise with Williams' dismissal from the Commission. The editorial states as follows:

> "In more recent times, Dr. Williams' national outlook has veered considerably and now appears to rest on the side of the British. He has argued vehemently for federation-federation of any kind as long as it is a federation, and he would even have it imposed.
>
> On the question of education for West Indians, Dr. Williams also strongly supports the present Colonial Office policy, and, therefore, that of the people who now discard him.
>
> We await with the greatest interest to see the transformation which must take place if he is to 'serve' his country. From a philosopher he may learn if he be not incorrigible; but whatever he does, he cannot, with complete safety, serve two masters. 'Let down your bucket where you are' now."

(CO 1042/404)

But Williams can in fact serve two masters: the colonial master and the master of his desire for power. For they are both joined at the hips in the march to independence in 1962.

On the 4ᵗʰ June 1955 Chief Minister, Norman Manley wrote to Stephen Luke on the dismissal of Eric Williams from his post in the Caribbean Commission. Manley states:

> "I am distressed to see that it has been unanimously decided not to renew his contract. The Commission has got rid of its most useful officer. I know that he is not an easy person to work with but when you are dealing with a man with exceptional qualification much has to be allowed for personal idiosyncrasies. Frankly I begin to regard the Commission as a completely useless organisation.
>
> From the very start of its life it has been bedevilled with international jealousies on a level that is positively childish."

(CO 1042/404)

Norman Manley indicates his position of the utility of the Caribbean Commission to the Caribbean. Stephen Luke would answer Manley's letter of the 4ᵗʰ June 1955 without offering an explanation for the need to dismiss Williams from his post in the Caribbean Commission. Luke chose to defend the integrity and utility of the Caribbean Commission to Norman Manley.

Williams' employment with the Caribbean Commission was terminated on the 21st June 1955. On that date Williams commenced his public political agitation to propel him into electoral politics in Trinidad and Tobago. General Elections were due in 1956 and in June 1955 the Caribbean Commission handed Williams the perfect issue, black educated victim of a white power structure, to launch himself as a politician in Trinidad and Tobago.

The Secretary General of the Caribbean Commission would report on the 20th June 1955 to all Commissioners via typed newspaper reports from the Port of Spain Gazette and the Trinidad Guardian on Williams' meeting in Woodford Square in Port of Spain, Trinidad on the theme: "My Relations with the Caribbean Commission 1943-1955."

On the 27th July 1955 Stephen Luke writes to Hugh Foot, Governor of Jamaica briefing Foot on the person Dr. Eric Williams. Luke states as follows:

> "Unfortunately, he also has some serious weakness of character which should make you very cautious in considering him for Government employment in Jamaica. Those better able to judge than I consider him to be more a publicist than a scholar; even I can see that his work is often superficial and distorted by his preconceived ideas and prejudices.
>
> He is preoccupied with problems of colour and the aftermath of slavery, and his bitterness often clouds his judgement.
>
> From your point of view, however, these characteristics need not, in themselves, be decisive. What is far more important is that, by temperament and bent of mind, he is essentially a politician rather than a civil servant."

(CO 1042/404)

Luke then sinks any hope Williams may have had for a post in Jamaica. Luke insists that Williams' career as a Caribbean bureaucrat ended with his dismissal from the Caribbean Commission. What is of great significance is Luke's bitter assault on the intellectual potency of Dr. Eric Williams.

The Caribbean Commission by dismissing Williams on 21st June 1955 gave the British colonial order in Trinidad and Tobago its greatest gift towards establishing a neo- colonial order in the era of independence since the 31st August 1962. The British colonial overlord needed a creative political leader and a political vehicle that would consign to the opposition benches the threat posed to the colonial state by an Indian Hindu dominated political party seeking to win a majority in the Legislative Council in the 1956 general elections. With the formation of the People's National Movement (PNM) in January 1956 and capturing 13 of 24 seats in the Legislative Council as a result of the 1956 general elections Williams would blunt the Indian political assault for the moment and in so doing merit his agenda to dismantle the white colonial oligarchy in Trinidad and Tobago and the Federation. Revenge is a dish best served cold.

What is most apparent from the material presented in this text is the futility of our existence from 1950 to 2009. As the children of Sisyphus we have relentlessly re-invented square wheels which our denial applauds as circular achievements of glorious creativity. We have moved from constitutional crises from 1950 to 1956 to 1971 to 2001 to constitutional collapse and paralysis in 2009. We have moved from mutiny in 1970 to jihad in 1990, to constitutional coup d'état in 2001 to paralysing criminal insurgency in 2009. We have moved from the March to and for Chaguaramas in the 1950's, to demonstrations and marches in 1970, to frenzied looting in 1990, to blatant looting of the treasury and now governance by corrupt practices.

In 1962 I was seven years old and had ingrained within my psyche the ideals of Independence. I learnt all the patriotic songs and held on to my bronze commemorative Independence medallion. In 1970 I threw away my medallion because Independence was now a cruel lie because as a person of mixed blood every creed and race did not find an equal place in Trinbago of 1970. My generation is the first lost generation of independent Trinidad and Tobago and sadly there are other lost generations since my own. As a nation we have lived many lies and continue to generate bodies of lies that are clearly failing to generate hegemony over those who express their rejection of this brutal, racist, suffocating, elitist social order that was erected from 1956. These generations are expressing their hate with the gun, but their hate pales into insignificance when compared to the hate of the generation that was lied to: my generation. We internalised our hate, which expressed itself in addiction and other expressions of withdrawal from the conventional social order. The difference then is the gun possessed and many of my generation have passed our hate and disillusionment down through the children we have socialised. We all in Trinbago sowed the wind and today we are reaping the whirlwind.

In the history of human civilization there are historical instances where civilizations collapsed, unable to end their decline by addressing the crises created by the civilization. A civilization can therefore reach a point in which it does not have the will and capacity to save itself from collapsing. There is then a point of no return for any civilization and Trinbago is fast approaching this point of no return, this point of collapse. Political leadership from 1956 to 2009 has failed Trinbago for they have used salient threats to the viability of our civilization as the means by which to rule over Trinbago. The two most potent salient threats politicians have embraced are racist hegemony and the illicit drug trade and in 2009 it is now clearly manifest that the politicians lack the will and capacity to arrest the decline of our civilization to the point of collapse. Haiti beckons.

Institutional paralysis, collapse and irrelevance are the direct result of racist hegemony and the illicit drug trade and an alternative civilization rooted in endemic gun violence, lawlessness and impunity with a racist hegemonist agenda is now actively challenging the hegemony of our civilization founded upon the discourse of independence. The civilization of lawlessness, impunity and gun violence is now independent of and sees no profit in subjecting itself to the hegemony of the politicians of all persuasions. The gun has now broken the dependence of this civilization on political largesse liberating itself via an orgy of gun violence, which has the politicians trembling with fear of the gun wielded by persons they do not control. This civilization is apolitical as it has learned that you take what you want when you are armed and you make deals for profit and relative peace when you are armed. They have learnt from the powerlessness of my generation as we talked revolution with empty hands clenched in fists that beat the air but made no difference to our powerless state of existence. This civilization was created by independence 1962 to 2009.

This then is my tribute to Simbhoonath Capildeo who had the vision to see the shit that has now hit the fan and to sound the alarm. Simbhoonath paid the price for thinking, for his praxis that rejected this independence civilization, but he showed the testicular fortitude to sound the alarm, to live his rejection, to live alone, spurned, rejected and persecuted even by his own family. The civilization that he sought to save from itself, the civilization that spurned and rejected him is now faced with collapse. Such is Karma. For it is not only the soul of Simbhoonath Capildeo calling for justice but thousands of others and of special importance to me, the souls of the first lost generation of the independence civilization.

CHAPTER 5

TERRORISM AND RACE WAR: GUYANA 1953-1964

On the 27th April 1953 general elections were held under the new constitution for the first time. Universal adult suffrage for the first time was exercised by the electorate of the British colony of British Guiana. A unicameral legislature consisting of a House of Assembly with 24 elected representatives was elected on the basis of a simple majority in single member constituencies and a State Council consisting of nine non elected members. An Executive Council comprising three ex-officio members, the Governor and six ministers chosen from the elected members of the House of Assembly formed the government.

The Peoples Progressive Party (PPP) led by Dr. Cheddi Jagan won 18 of 24 elected seats in the House of Assembly in 1953. Six PPP Members of the Assembly were elected to the Executive Council: Dr. Jagan, LFS Burnham, A.Chase, S.King, Dr.J.P.Lachman Singh and Jai Narine Singh. On the 9th October 1953 it was announced in British Guiana that the 1953 constitution was suspended. This was the commencement of the saga to grant Guyana independence but not under the political hegemony of Cheddi Jagan and the PPP.

The Report of the British Guiana Constitutional Commission 1954 would reveal the British colonial discourse on British Guiana and the framework for intervention in the politics of British Guiana in the run up to independence from British colonial domination . The Commission reports:

> "22. At the end of 1952 the population of British Guiana was estimated at about 450,000, of whom 45 percent were East Indian, 36 percent African, 11 percent mixed, 4 percent Amerindian and the remainder European or Chinese."

(Robertson Commission 1954 PG.10)

Faced with an Indo Guianese majority in the population of the colony the Commission's discourse on race and race relations is as follows:

"24. We agree with the description by the Waddington Commission, and confirm from our experience that the Indian element in the population has now shaken off its previous lethargy and is beginning to play a major part in the life of the colony. Education is now eagerly sought by Indian parents for their children; many Indians have important shares in the economic and commercial life of the colony; the rice trade is largely in their hands from production to marketing. Their very success in these spheres has begun to awaken the fears of the African section of the population, and it cannot be denied that since India received her independence in 1947 there has been a marked self-assertiveness amongst Indians in British Guiana. Guianese of African extraction were not afraid to tell us that many Indians in British Guiana looked forward to the day when British Guiana would be a part not of the British Commonwealth but of an East Indian Empire.

The result has been a tendency for racial tension to increase, and we have reluctantly reached the conclusion that the amity 'with which', as the Waddington Report said, 'people of all races live side by side in the villages' existed more in the past; today the relationships are strained; they present an outward appearance which masks feelings of suspicion and distrust. We do not altogether share the confidence of the Waddington Commission that a comprehensive loyalty to British Guiana can be stimulated among peoples of such diverse origins. There is little evidence of a coalescing process of intermarriage between the Indian and African components of the population."

(Robertson Commission 1954 Pg.11)

The Robinson Commission would quote the Waddington Commission as follows:

"Indian aloofness has now given place to a realisation of their permanent place in Guianese life and to a demand for equal participation in it. This claim, reinforced by their growing literacy, leads them to compete for positions which they have not hitherto sought. This challenge from an able and energetic people has stimulated the other races into closing their ranks. Race is a potent difference and is a powerful slogan ready to the hand of unscrupulous men who can use it as a stepping stone to political power. Race, too, is easily identifiable with nationalism, which in recent years has been emergent among all colonial peoples."

(Robertson Commission 1954 Pg. 11)

The first primary reality is then a race based powder keg awaiting the trigger for explosion. The second primary reality for the Robertson Commission is the communist threat to the colonial state posed by the leadership of the PPP in 1953.

> "101. On the evidence as a whole, we have no doubt that there was a very powerful communist influence within the PPP. At the time of the elections at least six of the Party's most prominent leaders specifically Dr. Jagan (General Secretary and Editor of Thunder), Mr. Sydney King (Assistant Secretary), Mr. Rory Westmaas (Junior Vice Chairman), Mr. B.H. Benn (Executive Committee Member and Secretary of the Pioneer Youth League) and Mr. Martin Carter (Executive Committee member) accepted unreservedly the 'classical' communist doctrines of Marx and Lenin: were enthusiastic supporters of the policies and practices of modern communist movements: and contemptuous of European social democratic parties, including the British Labour Party."

(Robertson Commission 1954 Pg. 29)

On the strategy of the hard core communist leadership of the PPP the Robertson Commission states as follows:

> "there is no evidence to show that they were ever prepared even temporarily to abandon or to modify their firm convictions that all British Governments are essentially, if not equally imperialist and capitalist and that no British Government will ever voluntarily concede full self-government to a dependent territory whose population is largely of non-European origin. They did not believe that self-government for British Guiana could be earned in successive steps by revealed capacity for responsible government. On the contrary they believed that a dependent territory can normally expect to win self-government only by violent action little short of revolution. But they thought that, with Great Britain still economically weak and weary of conflict and, as a great colonial power, morally on the defensive, a determined threat of sustained disruption with a strong hint of violence might well be enough to compel a British Government to concede self-government to British Guiana as the only alternative to repression by force."

(Robertson Commission 1954 Pg. 29)

The communist leadership of the PPP is then a clear and present danger to the timetable for constitutional decolonisation of British Guiana. The PPP's grasp on future power was rooted in 1953 in electoral politics and the Robertson Commission notes this and reports as follows:

> "82. With regard to the method of election, it was held by many witnesses that the system whereby a party supported by 51 percent of those who actually voted, and by only 37 percent of the whole electorate, obtained 75 percent of the seats in the House of Assembly was far from satisfactory, and it was suggested that some form of proportional representation should be adopted."

(Robertson Commission 1954 Pg.24)

The conclusions of the Commission would reflect the British agenda in British Guiana from 1953 to 1964. These conclusions are:

> "230. We are satisfied that the setback to orderly constitutional progress in British Guiana was due not to defects in the Constitution but to the fact that those in control of the People's Progressive Party proved themselves to be relentless and unscrupulous in their determination to pervert the authority of Government to their own disruptive and undemocratic ends.

> 231. We are, therefore, driven to the conclusion that so long as the P.P.P. retains its present leadership and policies, there is no way in which any real measure of responsible government can be restored without the certainty that the country will again be subjected to constitutional crisis.

> 232. We have no doubt that British Guiana, with its precarious economy cannot afford another crisis of the kind that developed in 1953 and we can, therefore, see no alternative but to recommend a period of marking time in the advance towards self government.

> 233. We cannot estimate the length of the period which should elapse before the advance towards self government is resumed. Everything will depend upon the extent to which the people of British Guiana, including the leaders of the P.P.P. themselves, can be brought to the realisation that the futile and deliberately disruptive policies for which the P.P.P. at present stands, are no basis for the future constitutional progress of their country."

(Robertson Commission 1954 Pg. 62)

There is then no independence for British Guiana under the leadership of the PPP. Independence is postponed indefinitely as long as the PPP dominates the politics of the colony of British Guiana. The suspension of the constitution in 1953 was in fact the suspension of the process to independence indefinitely until such time as the PPP no longer dominated the politics of British Guiana. On the 9th October 1953 the war was then declared openly and covertly.

Birbalsingh (2007) presented a series of interviews with Guyanese who were involved with the PPP in the period 1950-1992. Moses Bhagwan who joined the PPP in 1957 and left in 1965 states as follows:

"A. After the split in 1955 the party was searching for a role which was similar to the one it played in 1953, as a racially united movement that would appeal to all sections of the population. But from 1957 to 1964 the party failed to re- discover that role, and found instead that it had been degraded into an instrument of service to the Indian section of the population only. That was the context out of which problems emerged with the PYO. The party had decayed in ideological terms, and it produced the contradiction of a Marxist/Leninist leader- Cheddi Jagan- who became a leader only of Indo- Guyanese."

(Birbalsingh 2007 Pgs. 115-116)

Bhagwan continues:

"From the time I joined in 1956 there was always fighting within the party itself, between Indian racist elements and other elements which wanted to preserve the party's multi racial character. Since Indo-Guyanese had become the center of the party, there was an attempt to maintain the party's multi-racial image by bringing Afro-Guyanese into its leadership. Meanwhile, there were Indian elements in the party who were campaigning to make sure that Afro-Guyanese members were not returned at election time."

(Birbalsingh 2007 Page 116)

"In terms of history, Jagan and Burnham reigned over a country that became tormented by ethnic conflicts of a level and intensity that never existed when they were denouncing Indian racism, African racism and British colonialism."

(Birbalsingh 2007 Page 119)

"But Dr. Jagan persevered with his Marxist/Leninist approach believing that if he made the economy right and put poor people into jobs, he could eliminate poverty and all social problems. It is a point of view that I never shared because of the underlying ethnic problem which, I thought, had its own dynamic distinct from the circumstances around it.

In other words, the problem of race would persist in Guyana whether people were rich or poor. It is a major failure of the PPP in its early days, that it did not regard the Indian/African racial problem with due seriousness. I think Dr. Jagan's greatest political contribution was made between 1943 when he returned from America and 1953 when his first Government was dismissed. From then, the impact of Jagan and Burnham, whether individually or jointly has been negative."

(Birbalsingh 2007 Pgs. 119-120)

"Q Did Cheddi really believe he could have won in 1964 even if the elections were held under the PR system.

"A. I think that he was duped by the British Colonial Office into believing that Sandys would not bring in PR. There's a lot of weakness in Cheddi. He had a sense of dependence on white people, and it runs through his whole political life-The Russians, the Americans, the British-they always had a tremendous influence on him."

(Birbalsingh 2007 Page 117)

"He advocated Marxism because he thought it would solve the problems of Guyana, and he believed he could persuade the Americans to accept that."

(Birbalsingh 2007 Page 121)

Bhagwan posits the following:

That Cheddi Jagan failed to grasp the realities of applying Marxist/ Leninist solutions to the problems of the British colony of British Guiana. In both cases Guyana paid the price of these central failures.

Strategically Cheddi Jagan believed that the Americans could be persuaded to enable him to apply Marxist/ Leninist solutions to the problems of Guyana.

That Cheddi Jagan was easily influenced by white people. That Cheddi Jagan believed that solving the problems of Guyana would also solve the race problems of Guyana.

That Cheddi Jagan from the 1957 general elections was in fact an Indian leader who espoused the Marxist/ Leninist political economy.

In Birbalsingh 2007 the interview with Fenton Ramsahoye reveals the following:

> "American intelligence thought that Cheddi Jagan was on the Soviet side in the Cold War, and that Guyana under him would be a security risk, like Cuba was to them. So they fomented disturbances in Guyana in order to destabilize Dr. Jagan's Government.
>
> But the Americans believed that he was being financed by the Soviet Union, and that who paid the piper would call the tune. It is true the party had very strong ties with the Soviet Union. I also think the party was being financed by them and we would not have had to fight for Independence were it not that Cheddi Jagan was considered to be on the side of the Soviet Union in the Cold War.
>
> We would have got Independence at the Constitutional Conference in London in 1962. The reason why the British didn't give us Independence was the security scare that the Americans suffered from.
>
> When we were ministers we were told in correspondence from the Foreign and Colonial Office in the UK that we should not do things to become dependent on the Eastern Bloc. They were hinting that they didn't want us to ally ourselves in any manner or form with the Eastern Bloc, not even trade with them. Whereas the other West Indian countries heeded that warning, we did not. And we paid for it."

(Birbalsingh 2007 Page 123)

Ramsahoye continues:

> "I was at the conference in 1962 when he gave Sandys 'carte blanche'. My advice to Dr. Jagan was that we could win the forthcoming election in 1964. I told him we could get fifty-one percent of the votes. But he must not allow a decision like that to be taken by the British unless they gave us a date for Independence. But I believe that the British had taped our meetings and that Sandys knew the advice that I was tendering to Jagan in the secret conclave with Brindley Benn. So when Sandys wrote his letter, he left out the date for Independence. And Cheddi signed the letter.

(Birbalsingh 2007 Pgs.123-124)

"Q. Cheddi's position was that, not having been given a date for Independence, he could not expect fire and brimstone from the Opposition. He had to take a chance.

A. How could he take a chance when he knew that he was being financed by the Soviets. He would have known, or ought to have known that US and British Intelligence services would have known his business.

Q. So why did Cheddi play into the hands of the British?

A. Because he felt that they could not justify to the world what they were proposing to do. But the truth is that nobody cared, not even the British Labour Party. When they came to power they had no hesitation in passing the necessary PR legislation. The only reason why we didn't win the PR election was because of the civil war when 1300 houses were burnt. The country was divided along racial lines."

(Birbalsingh 2007 Pgs. 124-125)

Ramsahoye who was the Attorney General in the PPP Government of 1961 to 1964 raises the issue of a British covert action designed to result in a change of the electoral system in Guyana for the 1964 elections with no date set for Independence until after the 1964 general elections were held. Was then the civil war that erupted in Guyana in the run up to the general elections of 1964 part of the covert strategy to defeat the PPP in the 1964 general elections? Ramsahoye insists that the PPP could have won the 1964 elections even though it was held under the proportional representation electoral system. For Ramsahoye it was the civil war that destroyed the PPP at the 1964 polls. The next question that arises is: Was the British colonial Massa willing in the run up to the 1964 general elections to give a date for Independence to Cheddi Jagan and the PPP in the period 1961-1964? A third question also arises as to: How were the British covert agencies able to influence/coerce Jagan to sign the said letter of agreement with Sandys without a date for Independence being set in the same letter?

In an interview with Brindley H. Benn founding member of the PPP and part of Jagan's inner circle in the 1960's, Benn states as follows:

"I was aghast at Cheddi signing the document that gave Sandys authority to impose Proportional Representation if he chose to do so. Cheddi had friends in the British Labour Party and they were very kind to him. I think they led him up the garden path to believe that Sandys would never impose Proportional

Representation. Besides Harold Wilson had said in public that Proportional Representation was a rotten system. That's why when Sandys sprung Proportional Representation on him he didn't expect it. Chase, Cheddi, Ramsahoye, a Singhalese gentleman and I were discussing the constitution of various countries when Cheddi was called to a meeting with Sandys. We still carried on our discussion. Then, after about an hour, Cheddi came back with this paper in his hand. You know when you have had a bad school report and you are carrying it to show your father this was how he looked. Proportional Representation was imposed by the British Government before the 1964 British election. Then after the Labour Party won the election and Harold Wilson became Prime Minister, Cheddi went to England to ask him to reverse the decision since Wilson had already said that Proportional Representation was a rotten system. He wasn't even able to see Wilson."

(Birbalsingh 2007 Pgs. 67-68)

Jagan was then alone in the room with the British when he signed the agreement with Sandys and the then Conservative Government. It was left to the Labour Government of Harold Wilson to deliver what was to be the knockout blow to the PPP and Cheddi Jagan in the 1964 general elections in Guyana.

Ashton Chase, founding member of the PPP and part of Jagan's inner circle in the period 1953 to 1964 in his interview states as follows:

"Q. So you are saying the party did what it had to in 1953 and

A. No, I am not saying the party had to do what it did in 1953. The party should not have been guilty of such amateurish displays at the time. It was absolute nonsense to try to establish communism in British Guyana at the time, without the necessary clout, support and foundation, and without having Independence. The thing has to be put in proportion. You couldn't jump straight from colonialism to communism. Those who thought they could, I think, made a colossal error of tactics in the matter. The tactics were hopelessly wrong. And Burnham felt so. He lost credit for that. The extremists in the party took a course of action that provokes the British to react. I think they alarmed the whole Western world. And later the Americans took a position that was so hostile to the PPP, and exercised such influence on the British that there was no hope of establishing communism in the region."

(Birbalsingh 2007 Page 44)

For Chase then it is an issue of tactics in the face of the colonial reality the PPP found itself trapped in. The failure of 1953 for Chase sets the tone for the collapse of Guyana.

Brindley H. Benn in his interview states as follows:

"Q. Describe the 1953 general elections.

A. There were two groups in our party- a leftist or ultra- leftist group consisting of Cheddi and Janet and people like myself, Martin Carter, Rory Westmaas and Sydney King. We didn't call ourselves that, but we knew that another group consisting of people like Jai Narine Singh, Lachmansingh, Hanomansingh, Burnham and Clinton Wong were not interested in the struggle of the working class: they wanted to win seats."

(Birbalsingh 2007 Page 59)

The PPP would then split in 1955 as the two groups listed by Benn parted company. In 1956 the leftist group in the PPP would also split with the departure of Carter, King and Westmaas. The British suspension of the constitution on the 9th October 1953 literally set the cat amongst the pigeons and the PPP fractured repeatedly thereafter. Political instability ensued and the result was a civil war premised on racism and racist hegemony.

Rampersad Tiwari, a civil servant in Guyana during the period 1953-1964 in his interview articulates a position on Cheddi Jagan that focuses on the place of the Indo Caribbean politician in the Caribbean. He states as follows:

"I wonder whether any Indian of Dr. Jagan's ideology, that is with a left-of-center view, would have been allowed to wield political power in Guyana during the Cold War. As a visible minority in the English-speaking Caribbean, with a distinct non- Christian philosophy and culture, Indo-Caribbeans may not be fully acceptable in exercising political power in an Anglo- Saxon driven Caribbean culture."

(Birbalsingh 2007 Pages 105-106)

For Tiwari, Cheddi Jagan was disqualified from leading Guyana to Independence by dint of his race not his Marxist/ Leninist worldview: His worldview simply intensified the handicap of his race.

Rupert Roopnarine, political activist of the Working Peoples Alliance in his interview states as follows:

"In Guyana, the 1961 victory march that was carried out by the PPP from the Corentyne all the way to Georgetown had a similar effect: it was an act of the most extraordinary political insensitivity. I recall my extreme disenchantment when PPP supporters, during the 1961 victory march, spat on Afro- Guyanese bystanders on the roadside.

The 1961 elections simply entrenched the polarisation that had begun in 1957, and produced a situation where victory in democratic elections came to mean the victory of one race over another. It was not a case of one political party securing an electoral victory: it was actually one tribe conquering another. And the conquering tribe behaved toward the vanquished in a way that helped to create conditions for mischief, both internal and external. Thus the PPP by its own conduct in that period, created conditions for its own demise."

(Birbalsingh 2007 Pgs. 157-158)

According to Roopnarine the PPP victory in the 1961 general elections had then placed racist hegemony as the driving force in Guyanese politics. The PPP declared their Indo-Guyanese triumphalism in the march to Georgetown following their 1961 elections victory making it potently clear to all and sundry that Guyana was now faced with a triumphalist PPP Government rooted in a discourse of Indo-Guyanese racist hegemony articulated via a universalist Marxist/Leninist worldview. A volatile contradiction in terms that set the environment and gave space to a race war in the period 1961-1964.

THE EVENTS OF FEBRUARY 1962

In August 1961, general elections held under the 1961 Constitution the PPP led by Cheddi Jagan won 20 of the 35 seats in the Legislative Assembly. The PNC led by Forbes Burnham won 11 seats and the United Force won 4 seats. The report of the Commission of Inquiry into the disturbances in British Guyana in February 1962 (Wynn Parry Report) states:

"There can be no doubt at all that Dr. Jagan looked upon the result of the election as incontrovertible proof of his personal triumph and a complete approval of his policies by the electorate. He had, however, not forgotten the events of 1953 when the government of the United Kingdom had suspended the constitution because it was feared that the party in power in British Guyana was pursuing a course which would lead to a dangerous crisis both in public order and in the economic field by the wholesale imposition of Marxist ideology on the affairs of the country. He therefore proceeded cautiously, limiting his activity to the seeking of foreign aid for his country's development plans,"

(Wynn Parry Report Page 18)

The conclusions of the Wynn Parry Report were as follows:

"We may conclude by briefly setting out our conclusions"

(1) The disturbances of February 16 were not the result of a deliberate plan formulated by any individual or body of individuals to overthrow by force the Government of British Guyana established by law. The riots resulting in the destruction of, damage to, property were clearly not a manifestation of rebellion or civil war.

(2) There was no evidence of the disturbances being the direct result of a racial conflict, though a certain measure of tension between the East Indian and African races which had largely become noticeable acted as a contributory factor.

(3) Political rivalries and the frustrated ambitions of some of Dr. Jagan's erstwhile supporters fostered a sense of resentment and antagonism towards Dr. Jagan and his party. Other factors which contributed to a state of mounting discontent were:

   (a) A feeling of insecurity experienced by the commercial and moneyed classes, because they believed that Dr. Jagan's political convictions were increasingly assuming a Communist pattern.

   (b) A sense of fear that the country would obtain independence under a government with obvious Communist leanings;

   (c) The failure of the Government to remove the grievances of civil servants who were asking for higher salaries and better conditions of service;

   (d) The hostility of Trade Union leaders some of whom, e.g. Ishmael, had personal grievances against Dr. Jagan and his Ministers.

The disturbances were confined to Georgetown where the bulk of Dr. Jagan's political opposition, the civil servants and the trade unionists, are located. (The sugar workers outside Georgetown, about 20,000 in number, it will be recalled, did not strike).

(1) The outburst of February 16, was comparable to an act of spontaneous combustion when some highly fermented substance is subjected to long pressures. The mass of the discontented and idle workers on strike was inexorably driven by the sheer force of bored monotony to find release in rowdyism and rioting. The false rumour of a child's death caused by the deleterious effects of teargas furnished the immediate stimulus to violence.

(2) The rioters were not drawn from one particular race or political party, nor were the victims chosen from any one class. The looters belonged to the category of irresponsible individuals consisting for the most part of hooligans and criminals, who in a moment of excitement and mass hysteria throw away the inhibitions of a civilised society and seize the opportunity of preying upon their fellow citizens.

(3) The police performed their extremely difficult and onerous task to the best of their ability and capacity. If they failed in maintaining law and order on February 16 they cannot be blamed, for in no country is it possible to have available a police force large enough to control a sudden and extraordinary outbreak of violence on such an extensive scale.

(4) The army responded to the call with admirable promptness and handled the situation firmly and effectively without using more force than was absolutely necessary.

(5) In all, 56 premises were destroyed by fire, 87 were damaged of which 66 were also looted. The total loss occasioned has been assessed at BWI $11,405,236, though it is impossible to state the exact figure with any degree of accuracy.

148. One policeman was shot dead by the rioters and 39 more were injured. Of the rioters and looters, four men lost their lives as a result of shooting, and 41 were injured."

(Wynn Parry Report Pgs. 73-74)

It is abundantly clear that by February 1962 the PPP Government lost its hegemony over Georgetown as dominance over Georgetown was keenly contested between British military assets, the urban underclass and the forces of opposition arrayed against Cheddi Jagan and the PPP. The urban criminal insurgency would continue post February 1962 culminating in the 1964 race war in the bauxite belt of Wismar, Christianburg and Mackenzie. Between the period 1962 to 1964 the PPP lost control of the state and security of the state became the responsibility of British military assets in British Guyana. The PPP was then in this period a failed regime ripe for a counter coup waiting to be simply knocked over and this would culminate in the loss of the general elections of December 1964 to a coalition of the Peoples National Congress (PNC) and the United Force (UF).

Report of the Wismar, Christianburg and Mackenzie Commission (the Wismar Report) :

"1. Conclusions:

(a) We have come to the conclusion that the disturbances which took place in the Wismar-Christianburg-Mackenzie area on May 25th 1964 were politically and racially inspired. Although there is a difference of opinion among the security officers who gave evidence before us on the point, the thorough-going destruction of East Indian property, and the fact that the security forces were in no case able to apprehend arsonists, force us to conclude that the destruction, was not 'spontaneous' but was organised, and well organised.

(b) We are of the opinion that the Commissioner of Police, Mr. Owen, acted injudiciously in deciding that until he had received an assessment of the situation from Mr. Neil Isaacs he would not requisition British troops for service at Wismar. In consequence, the arrival of British troops was unnecessarily delayed until most of the damage to life and property had been complete. We are convinced that he had enough information from a number of sources about the extent of the disturbances in the area at least by 10.00am on the 25th May, to justify a requisition for the immediate dispatch of British troops. Had this been done the major portion of the tragedy might not have occurred.

(c) We consider that the Commissioner of Police acted unconstitutionally in not acceding to the request made by the Minister of Home Affairs at 2.00pm on May 25th to requisition British troops for service in the Wismar area.

(g) British troops requisitioned acted promptly and firmly with

the minimum of severity against the population. Their

presence in the area on the 6th and 7th July, 1964 prevented the loss of many more Indian lives.

(k) The recent disturbances in Wismar, Christianburg,

Mackenzie have been examined by your Commissioners in

the context of the wider pattern of planned violence,

murders, arson, bombings, reprisals and counter-reprisals

that characterised life in British Guyana during 1964.

Although the number of deaths caused by violence and the

amount of property destroyed was greater in the rest of the

Colony, Wismar does however, bring the months of violence

into sharp focus.

There within the brief period of 48 hours, a total section of a community was attacked, outraged and subsequently had to be evacuated. Nearly all of their property was maliciously destroyed, while, the majority of their erstwhile friends and neighbours either took part in the destruction or stood idly by."

(Wismar Report 2004 Pages 24-25)

"On the 6th July, 1964, an explosion occurred at Booradia on a launch named 'Sun Chapman' which was taking goods and passengers, the majority of them Africans, from Georgetown to Wismar. About thirty-eight (38) persons perished in this disaster. The echo of the Sun Chapman disaster was immediately felt at Mackenzie when five East Indians were murdered and seven seriously injured. Before the official report of the Sun Chapman tragedy reached the Police and British army, Africans were on the rampage and in the space of two hours, 5.00 to 7.00 pm, more people were killed than on the whole day of the 25th May, 1964."

(Wismar Report 2004 Page 10)

"Following the Sun Chapman disaster the bodies of 35 persons were taken to Mackenzie and 12 others were listed as missing or unidentified. All of these were Africans. The Sun Chapman resulted in five East Indians being murdered at Mackenzie.

(Wismar Report 2004 Page 21)

"In the Sun Chapman disaster 10 persons were injured. Five of these were admitted to the hospital and the other five treated and sent home. Seven other persons were treated for shock when they heard the news of the disaster."

"Two hundred and twenty houses were destroyed. Of those, five belonged to Africans. Three of the five were destroyed either because they were owned by PPP members or by persons who had admitted East Indians during the disturbances.

Stocks, including household furniture and general merchandise, were looted, and what could not be taken away were burnt with the buildings.

The Social Assistance Department compiled statistics relating to the displaced persons from Wismar-Mackenzie area and they were made available to the Commission. The number of families displaced is 744 comprising 1,249 adults and 2,150 children making a total of 3,399 individuals."

(Wismar Report 2004 Page 22)

The questions that arise from the Wismar Report are as follows:
(a) Who organised the race war against Indo-Guyanese in Wismar?
(b) Were they aligned with the opponents of the then PPP Government?
(c) What was the complicity of the political elite in this race war?
(d) Who was responsible for the act of terrorism when the Sun Chapman exploded?
(e) Was the Sun Chapman destroyed in response to the Wismar pogrom?
(f) Was the Sun Chapman destroyed to intensify the pogrom?

Lloyd Best in Birbalsingh (2007) speaks of PPP governance in the period 1961-1964 as follows:

"Guyana was a cauldron in the early 1960's. My first technical task was to help Cheddi Jagan prepare the budget.

We did everything possible and still couldn't find enough money to pay minimum expenditure. Nobody not even the British Government, was prepared to lend Jagan money. He went all over asking for aid and was treated as a pariah. The only revenue he could get was what he could raise in Guyana."

"The budget was the biggest bone of contention."

"Q. This is the budget that caused the long civil service strike in 1962/63?

A.Nicholas Kaldor had come before, in October 1961, and had written the budget which provoked the Black Friday riots in 1962. The Kaldor budget had pushed Cheddi into a corner, and a lot of things that he would normally have been able to do, he could no longer do. The whole budget had been discredited, so we had to go very low key."

"The British and Burnham were in league-we didn't know that then-but the British were trying to move Cheddi; and we didn't want him to give them an excuse for doing so.

Q. The CIA was also active all this time?

A.The CIA was active but we didn't know it. We saw all the manoeuvres in the streets, and we know that Burnham was behind all the riots, but we didn't know the CIA was supporting him. Burnham spoke openly about it.

Q. Burnham spoke openly about what?

A.About anti-Cheddi organisation in the country.

Q. Not about the destabilisation of Cheddi's government by external sources?

A.No Burnham talked about destabilising the government by local forces.

(Birbalsingh 2007 Pages 86-87)

On Jagan's political strategy, Best states as follows:

"He never thought that the US would destabilise him in the way that they did: he never thought that they would support Burnham. He was very naive because he thought that if he could make a convincing case to the US, in terms of economics, welfare, rehabilitation, and so on, they would help. He really thought Kennedy would help."

(Birbalsingh 2007 Page 89)

Best indicates that whilst Jagan refused to deal with the Chairman of Bookers Ltd, he approached Reynolds the US transnational in the bauxite industry seeking to make a deal to fund his budgets which fell through.

According to Best in the period 1961-1964 Jagan made great exertions to make a deal with the President Kennedy towards the survival of his regime.

CHAPTER 6

AMERICAN DECLASSIFIED FILES

The Office of the Historian, US Department of State made public files from the Kennedy presidency dealing with British Guiana 1961-1963. A Special National Intelligence Estimate dated March 21ˢᵗ, 1961 states:

> "2. The politics of British Guiana is determined by the Communist led People's Progressive Party (PPP) of Cheddi Jagan. Jagan is an East Indian, and his party draws its support almost entirely from East Indians, including not only poverty stricken rural and urban workers, but also a considerable number of small businessmen in Georgetown and other centers. Jagan's US born wife, who exercises very strong influence over him, is an acknowledged Communist. She shares with Jagan control of the PPP and is a government minister, several other PPP leaders are believed to be Communists. Jagan himself is not an acknowledged Communist, but his statements and actions over the years bear the marks of the indoctrination and advice the Communists have given him. While there is no Communist party per se in British Guiana, a number of the leaders in the PPP have been members of, or associated with Communist parties or their front groups in the US and the UK.
>
> 3. Moreover, these individual leaders maintain sporadic courier and liaison contacts with the British and US Communists and with Communist Bloc missions in London. Both Jagans have visited Cuba in the past year and have since chosen to identify the PPP with Castro's cause. However, neither the Communist Bloc nor Castro has made any vigorous effort to exploit the British Guiana situation.
>
> 11. How far a Jagan government might go after actual achievement of Independence is obscured by uncertainty about the nature

and extent of his actual commitment to Communist discipline and about the tactical aims of the Bloc with respect to British Guiana.

We consider it more likely that an independent Jagan government would seek to portray itself as an instrument of reformist nationalism which would gradually move in the direction of Castro's Cuba. Such a regime would almost certainly be strongly encouraged and supported by Castro and the Bloc.

13. Before independence, the attitude and actions of the British will bear heavily on the situation in British Guiana. Thus far the British seem to have been motivated chiefly by a desire to see British Guiana independent. They have tried to get along with Jagan and to overlook his Communist associations because he has seemed to them the only man capable of running the country. Since their intervention in 1953 to halt Jagan's first bid for power, they have refrained from actions which would antagonize him; the Governor's veto power has never been used. Even though they retain the capability for controlling Jagan, we believe they will do little to interfere with political developments in British Guiana."

(Foreign Relations 1961-1963 Vol.xii Pgs. 2-3)

For the US intelligence establishment in March 1961 there are two salient realities in British Guiana: (a) the PPP and its Communist leadership and more importantly, (b) the failure of the British to deal with this Communist threat to US interests.

In a memorandum dated August 30th 1961, the Special Assistant (Schlesinger) to President Kennedy wrote the president as follows:

"The State Department feeling about British Guiana (which I share) is that we have no real choice but to feel Jagan out and see what we can do to bring (keep?) him into the western camp.

State accordingly recommends:

(1) That we offer Jagan technical and economic assistance.

(2) That we prepare the way for the admission of an independent British Guiana to the OAS and the Alliance for Progress;

(3) That Jagan be given a friendly reception during his visit to the US in October, including an audience with you.

At the same time, State also recommends (4) a covert program to develop information about, expose and destroy Communists in British Guiana, including, if necessary, the possibility of funding a substitute for Jagan himself, who could command East Indian support.

The idea, in short, is to use the year or two before independence to work to tie Jagan to the political and economic framework of the hemisphere, while at the same time re-insuring against pro-Communist developments by building up anti-Communist clandestine capabilities."

(Foreign Relations 1961-63 Vol.xii Pgs. 6-7)

Memorandum from Schlesinger to President Kennedy dated August 31st, 1961 states:

"I have communicated to Alexis Johnson your assent in principle to points 1-5 on page 2 of Secretary Rusk's memorandum.

I have also communicated to Johnson your particular concern over the covert program and your desire to know more detail before the State Department group goes to London. The present covert program is set forth under Tab. B in the attached file. You will note that the first emphasis is (properly) on intelligence collection, with covert political action to come later. Part ii (if Jagan should turn sour) seems to be pretty feeble, but it is also pretty tentative."

(Foreign Relations 1961-63 Vol. Xii Page 7)

The memorandum establishes that a covert action against the PPP was then approved by President Kennedy on the condition that the President retains oversight over the covert action.

Memorandum of Conversation dated October 25th, 1961 recorded the meeting between Cheddi Jagan and President Kennedy. It is noted that Cheddi Jagan attended this meeting alone. The memorandum states as follows:

"Premier Jagan asked whether the United States would consider as a hostile act a commercial agreement between British Guiana and the communist bloc whereby British Guiana would export bauxite in return for the importation of commodities.

The President pointed out that the United States and its allies were engaged in trade with the communist bloc, thus we would not consider trade per se to have political significance. However, of the nature and the extent of trade between British Guiana and the Soviet bloc were such as to create a condition of dependence of the economy of British Guiana on the Soviet bloc, then this would amount to giving the Soviet Union a political instrument for applying pressure and trying to force damaging concessions to its political interests and goals. Under Secretary Ball emphasized the experience of Guinea in this connection."

(Foreign Relations 1961-63 Vol.xii Pg. 14)

Jagan was then forewarned as Kennedy set the parameters for the PPP Government's engagement with the communist bloc and to heighten the potency of the message the case of Guinea was evoked.

A memorandum from Schlesinger to President Kennedy dated March 8th, 1962 states as follows:

> "The point of these two memoranda is that both State and CIA are under the impression that a firm decision has been taken to get rid of the Jagan Government.
>
> The desired effect is to make sure that nothing is done until you have had a chance to talk with Hugh Fraser."

(Foreign Relations 1961-63 Vol.xii Pg.19)

National Security Action Memorandum No. 135/1 signed by President Kennedy states:

> "No final decision will be taken on our policy toward British Guiana and the Jagan Government until (a) the Secretary of State has a chance to discuss the matter with Lord Hume in Geneva, and (b) Hugh Fraser completes his on-the-spot survey in British Guiana for the Colonial Office.
>
> The questions we must answer before we reach our decision include the following:
>
> (1) Can Great Britain be persuaded to delay independence for a year?
>
> (2) If Great Britain refuses to delay the date of independence, would a new election before independence be possible? If so, would Jagan win or lose? If he lost, what are the alternatives?
>
> (3) What are the possibilities and limitations of United States action in the situation?"

(Foreign Relations 1961-1963 Vol.xii Pg.21)

This action memorandum sets the tone for US action in British Guiana in 1962 towards the political demise of Cheddi Jagan and the PPP. Clearly the strategy calls for a delay in the granting of independence to British Guiana within a time frame that allows for a general election to be held with the defeat of the PPP in the said general elections. To effect this a viable alternative to Cheddi Jagan and the PPP had to be created.

A paper prepared in the Department of State dated the 15th of March 1962 states:

> "c. A vocal section of the US public, several Members of Congress and US labor unions are strongly opposed to working with Jagan. We have received since Jagan's visit 113 Congressional letters and 2,400 public letters critical of a policy of working with him. A high level effort would be required to obtain public support for such a policy. We would need to prevent private Americans, e.g. individuals, labor unions, large companies having investments in British Guiana, and right wing groups (such as the Christian Anti-Communist Crusade) from intervening in British Guiana contrary to this policy."

(Foreign Relations 1961-63 Vol. Xii Pg.23)

What is noteworthy is not the price the Kennedy presidency would pay politically for embracing Jagan. But the fact that a series of interests in US civil society were in action mode to remove the PPP Government in March 1962. In March 1962 the covert actors of note were not then US Government covert agencies but public forces arrayed against the PPP. The paper is then pointing to the reality that there is a need for strategic order in the assault on the PPP Government and that the risk existed that these non-governmental actions can in fact scuttle presidential strategy. To effect order then Jagan must not be embraced by the Kennedy presidency.

Memorandum of Conversation dated March 17th 1962, reports on the meeting held with Hugh Fraser, British Parliamentary Under Secretary of State for Colonies. The memorandum states as follows:

> "Mr. Fraser stated that the racial tension between Africans and East Indians in the colony was no central problem.
>
> Mr. Fraser felt that Jagan was a nice man but he was surrounded by a visibly sinister group of advisors. He thought it likely that the PPP would win another elections since there was no clear alternative to the Jagan leadership. He thought that the United States was now unpopular with the leaders of all the parties. The United States had promised to send a mission to British Guiana

but had not done so. Mr. Fraser emphasized his feeling that a delay in British Guiana's independence would not help matters. He did not believe that the Jagan regime was Communist. Mr. Fraser explained that the independence conference to be held in May would discuss two things, a date for British Guiana's independence and the means for achieving it.

In response to a question, Mr. Fraser did not believe that there was an alternate Indian leader within the PPP who could command support equal to Jagan. Rai had been spoken of in this connection but Fraser seriously doubted whether he had the capacity to lead the PPP.

In response to a question, Mr. Fraser expressed the opinion that independence would come possibly at the end of 1962 but more probably in early 1963. He emphasized strongly that it would be madness to attempt to delay independence and maintain British Guiana's colonial status with British bayonets. He felt the situation would not improve and delaying independence would make things worse. Mr. Johnson suggested the advisability of discussions between the US and UK about a political program. Mr. Fraser did not respond.

Mr. Fraser felt that neither Bookers nor Alcan would wish to get involved in British Guiana's politics. Bookers probably considered Jagan to be the best leader of the lot. Any attempt to dump Jagan or to manipulate the political molecules in the situation would be tricky and apt to be counterproductive. If proportional representation became part of the British Guiana constitution this might help in affecting the outcome of a new election. He stressed, however, that such a solution could not be imposed either by the United States or the United Kingdom. We must manoeuvre British Guianese opinion into wanting some kind of adjustment in the present political machinery."

(Foreign Relations 1961-63 Vol. Xii PGS.26-28)

Fraser's position is one which thrashes the danger that the US presidency sees in the PPP government led by Cheddi Jagan. In a condescending manner that reeks of colonialist arrogance Fraser makes it clear that he has not bought into the courses of action formulated by the Kennedy administration to neutralise the threat perceived in British Guiana. The inevitable conclusion that arose from the meeting is that there were two threats connected to British Guiana: Cheddi Jagan and the PPP and the intransigence of members of the government of the United Kingdom in 1962. Together both elements influenced actions that ultimately destroyed Guyana as a sustainable social order.

The nature of the game being played by the British in British Guiana is indicated by Fraser's statement as follows:

> "Mr. Fraser felt nevertheless that all elements were shocked by the racial factor in recent riots. He pointed out that Jagan could easily have called in the Indian cane cutters from the field to attack the African rioters. The violence in Georgetown had been directed mainly against Indian shops. The demonstrations had begun as a non-racial, public protest against Jagan's budget. The causes of the rioting would be determined by the Commonwealth Commission of Inquiry which had recently been announced."

> "In discussing the Commonwealth Commission of Inquiry, Mr. Fraser emphasized that its terms of reference were deliberately being kept narrow. Jagan had initially asked for a United Nations Commission which would have placed the problem squarely into a cold war situation. Mr. Fraser had talked him out of this and obtained his agreement to a commission appointed by the United Kingdom.

(Foreign Relations 1961-1963 Vol.xii Pg.27)

The Wynn Parry Report denied that there was a racist assault upon Indian's in the Georgetown riot of 1962. Fraser told the US Government officials that there was a racist agenda. Fraser indicated that the Wynn Parry Report was manufactured to serve British colonial interests and that Jagan was persuaded by Fraser to accept the agenda of the British. But the agenda of the British was premised on the ability of the British to resist the US presidential agenda. The lesson of this is the influence wielded by a British conservative politician on Cheddi Jagan.

A memorandum for the Special Group dated June 13th, 1962 is not declassified. The existence of the memorandum proves that on June 13th a special group that governed the covert operation in British Guiana was in existence and operational.

Memorandum from the President's Special Assistant for National Security Affairs to President Kennedy dated July 13th, 1962 states as follows:

> "These documents seem to me to demonstrate that Jagan will indeed go the way of Castro, if he is not prevented. He would be weaker than Castro, because he is even more inefficient, but he would also probably be more easily controlled from Mexico.

But while the papers make a clear case against supporting Jagan, or even trying to sustain peaceful coexistence with him, the case for the proposed tactics to be used in opposing him is not so clear. In particular, I think it is unproven that CIA knows how to manipulate an election in British Guiana without a backfire.

My immediate suggestion is that when you have read this, we should have a pretty searching meeting on the details of the tactical plans, in which you can cross-examine those who are really responsible for their development. I do not think the Secretary of State should go to the British Ambassador with the proposed talking paper until we are a little more sure of our capabilities and intentions."

(Foreign Relations 1961-1963 Vol. xii Pg.7)

Memorandum from the President's Special Assistant (Schlesinger) to the President's Special Assistant (Dungan) dated July 19th 1962 states:

"In short, I agree that there is no future in Jagan; and that the Burnham risk is less than the Jagan risk; but the CIA plan makes me nervous.

I would suggest that you bear down hard on two points:

(1) Does CIA think that they can carry out a really covert operation i.e. an operation which, whatever suspicions Jagan might have, will leave no visible traces which he can cite before the world, whether he wins or loses, as evidence of US intervention.

(2) If we lose, what then? The present suggestions are pretty bleak-especially when our chances of winning are probably less than 50-50."

(Foreign Relations 1961-1963 Vol. xii Pgs.7-8)

The uncertainty of the outcome of the covert operation necessitated the full court press to bend the Conservative Government of the UK to the will of President Kennedy.

The memorandum of record dated June 21st, 1962 reported on a White House meeting on British Guiana which included President Kennedy. The memorandum states:

"6. This meeting clarified the significant extent to which British Guiana has become a major policy issue between the United States and Great Britain."

(Foreign Relations 1961-1963 Vol. xii Pg.20)

President Kennedy is now piling on the pressure on the government of the UK as he deems British Guiana a major policy issue between the UK and the US.

A telegram from the Department of State to the Embassy in the United Kingdom dated June 21st, 1963 states:

> "Our fundamental position is that the UK must not leave behind in the Western Hemisphere a country with a Communist Government in control. Independence of British Guiana with a government led by PPP is unacceptable to US. Our objective in London is to get HMG to take effective action to remove Jagan Government prior to independence. As you know there has been long series high-level exchanges this subject. Last fall Macmillan agreed to this objective but he has now reverted to view UK should wash its hands of British Guiana by granting early independence, leaving the mess on our doorstep.
>
> I hope you will let it be known to Alec Home and the Prime Minister that President and I intend to focus on this subject while in England. I think it most important that we involve Alec Home. This is not just a colonial problem but one with the highest foreign policy implications.
>
> I also ask your views on what might be done with labor leaders. George Brown while in Washington seemed to sympathize with our position, but Patrick Gordon Walker was less receptive. Would you advise frank talks with Labor leaders. If so, by whom? What we wish to avoid is Labor's committing itself publicly to early independence to British Guiana from ignorance of true facts and in effort to needle government. This of course would make it extremely difficult for them to reverse course once they come to power."

(Foreign Relations 1961-1963 Vol. xii Pg.21)

President Kennedy on a visit to the UK would meet with the Prime Minister of the UK at Birch Grove one of the topics on the agenda was British Guiana. This meeting was held on June 30th 1963 and President Kennedy would lead the assault on the UK government to bend its will to conform to the US agenda for British Guiana. It is at Birch Grove on the 30th June 1963 the then conservative government dumped Cheddi Jagan and surrendered to President Kennedy.

The report on Birch Grove, England, June 30th 1963 is as follows:

"Mr. Sandys then spoke and confirmed the Secretary's account of the conversations which had been held in London. He said he thought that, theoretically, there were four courses open (1) To muddle on as we are now doing, which he thought should be rejected as a choice; (2) To move forward by granting British Guiana independence now (he said that although this would be a move forward it obviously presented grave problems); (3) To suspend the constitution and institute direct colonial rule (he said this would be a move backward politically); (4) To establish a Burnham-D'Aguiar government and then grant British Guiana independence.

He said we had to be careful that Jagan should not be put in a position where he would ask for dissolution and new elections, because he would certainly win again. Under the present constitution he had the right to ask for dissolution, and the Governor would have to grant it.

Mr. Sandys said he thought the best solution was that of a Burnham-D'Aguiar government to which the UK would grant independence."

(Foreign Relations 1961-1963 Vol. xii Pg.22-23)

It is Duncan Sandys who persuaded Cheddi Jagan to sign the document permitting the UK government to change the electoral system in June 30th 1963 at Birch Grove indicated that the Macmillan government of the UK had in fact surrendered and accepted the Kennedy strategy to remove Jagan and the PPP from political power in British Guiana. In June 30th 1963 Sandys accepted the need to remove Jagan and the PPP and then persuaded Jagan to surrender thereafter.

Memorandum of Conversation dated February 19th, 1964 contains a note from the official historian which states:

"121 A Constitutional Conference in London in October 1963, the major British Guiana party leaders asked British Colonial Secretary Sandys to devise a constitution, 'since they were unable to agree among themselves'. Sandys then decreed a new registration and general election under proportional representation for a single house legislature. Jagan was furious at being outsmarted."

(Foreign Relations 1964-1968 Vol. xxxii)

If this is the method/strategy used by Duncan Sandys in October 1963 to change the electoral system in British Guiana why didn't Jagan call immediately for dissolution and new elections before the change of the electoral system? Was it because of realities not spoken of? Such as the powerlessness of a failed PPP government that owed its existence to the British military presence in British Guiana?

The Johnson presidency that resulted from the assassination of President Kennedy does not change the policy of the late President on British Guiana. In fact the Johnson presidency raises the pressure on the British government whilst it indicates to the Labour Party then in opposition the role expected of them. A Memorandum of Conversation dated February 19th, 1964 records a meeting with Patrick Gordon Walker then the Labour shadow Foreign Minister. The memorandum states as follows:

> "4. Labour would like to find a way to give independence to British Guiana without affronting or injuring the US. Britain of course cannot afford to appear as an agent of the US. The way in which the Douglas-Home government was trying to do this was completely unacceptable to the people of British Guiana because it makes the entire country into one constituency.
>
> Some other form of proportional representation might well be considered by Labour.
>
> Mr. Gordon Walker thought the US exaggerated the menace of Jagan. There was a limit to what he could do, in view of the racial division in British Guiana; for example, he could hardly have complete control of a situation where the capital of the country was against him."
>
> (Foreign Relations 1964-1968 Vol. xxxii)

What is clearly apparent is that the leadership of the Labour Party has accepted the US agenda to remove Jagan in the 1964 general elections. There is then no dispute over the change of the electoral system to proportional representation. Gordon Walker would make a most noteworthy statement in the conversation. He said:

> "However; if a way could be found for the US to put its troops into British Guiana, the Labor Party would not object. Britain did not want to keep its troops there indefinitely. Britain has no real reason of its own to stay. Furthermore its troops were spread too thin. One battalion now in British Guiana was not enough."
>
> (Foreign Relations 1964-1968 Vol. xxxii)

The leadership of the Labour Party is then making it clear that they would in fact aid and abet a US military incursion into British Guiana. They were in fact ready to hand over British Guiana to the US.

Research Memorandum from the Deputy Director of Intelligence and Research to the Acting Secretary of State dated May 12th, 1964 states as follows:

> "In an effort to prevent the holding of a UK imposed proportional representation election, expected to be held late this year, the Jagan regime has been resorting to intimidation and violence. What began some 12 weeks ago as a strike by the pro- Jagan sugar workers' has developed into a campaign of beatings, bombings, and arson in which 19 persons have been killed and more than a million dollars worth of property and sugar cane have been burned. This violence has exacerbated the racial tensions between the majority East Indians and the minority Negroes to such an extent that some officials fear that the situation may get out of hand. Contributing to this concern has been the agitation of activists in the Jagan regime, who have attacked not only members of the competing sugar workers union but also the opposition parties, which are composed mainly of Negroes and other non-Indians. Local police have uncovered arms buried by members of Jagan's Youth Organization.
>
> As the Jagan regime grows more desperate its extremist elements may well be tempted to undertake more ambitious acts of terrorism. Such acts could provoke the threatened Negro minority into large scale retaliation."

(Foreign Relations 1964-1968 Vol. xxxii)

How then does the US Government respond to this Jagan/PPP inspired instability? A Telegram from the Department of State to the Consulate General in British Guiana dated May 13th, 1964 states as follows:

> "1. We concur with guidance to Burnham not to resort to counter violence and that he can be assured that if PPP makes effort to take over country by force the US Gov't will not stand by and see opposition crushed by terror, and Carlson's comments on arms to Burnham.
>
> 2. We are now exploring possibility of giving counterterrorist training to selected members of opposition. While this will not have any immediate positive effect on containing violence, it may give boost to opposition. We will inform you when final decisions and plans are made."

(Foreign Relations 1964-1968 Vol. xxxii)

The US Government has then committed itself to train and possibly arm a militia led by Burnham. It is then a multi pronged assault on Jagan and the PPP Government to end Jagan and PPP political hegemony. The violence of 1964 opens a window of opportunity for the assault on Jagan and the PPP and this is the declaration of a state of emergency which obviated the need for the British suspension of the constitution and the return to direct rule in order to change the electoral system and to then hold general elections under the new electoral system.

A Memorandum from the Deputy Director of Plans of the Central Intelligence Agency (Helms) to the President's Special Assistant for National Security Affairs dated May 22nd, 1964 states as follows:

> "The Governor has urged both Cheddi and Janet Jagan to end the strike on the sugar estates and to give him the necessary advice of the Council of Ministers to declare a state of emergency, as reported in my memorandum of 21 May. The Governor has reported that Premier Jagan would be prepared to give him the advice of his Ministers on either 22 or 23 May; he said the legal documents were ready for the emergency order, but they were still a few decisions yet to be made.

(Foreign Relations 1964-1968 Vol. xxxii)

A Memorandum from Gordon Chase of the National Security Council Staff to the President's Special Assistant for National Security Affairs (Bundy) dated June 13th, 1964 states:

> "1. Attached to Georgetown's 422 which reports that the Governor of BG has taken over the emergency powers from the Council of Ministers and has started to pick up some of the people who are suspected of being responsible for the recent violence. This action by the Governor does not detract from the other responsibilities of the Ministers, which remain intact."

(Foreign Relations 1964-1968 Vol. xxxii No.382)

A note from the Editor states as follows:

> "A June 12 memorandum to Bundy reported that a number of prominent PPP leaders were scheduled for immediate arrest under the secret and about-to-be invoked order-in-council emergency regulations, which permitted the detention of persons suspected of being involved in terrorist activity."

(Foreign Relations 1964-1968 Vol. xxxii No. 382)

The race war of 1964 especially in the Wismar- Christianburg and Mackenzie area was then the reason for the pressure applied to Jagan to surrender to the Governor by vesting emergency powers in the Governor. The race war of 1964 aided the covert strategy to remove Jagan and the PPP from state power. This does not mean that the race war was the product of the agenda of the US and its allies in British Guiana. The race war was in fact the most potent reason for Britain to postpone the general elections and pressure the PPP and the allies of the US to form a government of national unity thereby creating an environment that stymied the US covert agenda.

A Memorandum from the Deputy Director for Plans of the Central Intelligence Agency (Helms) to the President's Special Assistant for National Security Affairs (Bundy) dated July 17, 1964 states as follows:

> "2. The British maintained that the principal threat to elections comes from the deteriorating security situation. They suggested that even with one division peace and order could not be guaranteed. The situation in Georgetown is particularly critical in that violence there could force the postponement of elections. The British urged that Forbes Burnham, leader of the People's National Congress (PNC), be counselled to exercise all possible restraint on his supporters in Georgetown. The noted that the London papers played up the killing of Indian children, omitting African deaths and arson."

(Foreign Relations 1964-1968 Vol. xxxii No. 385)

The Memorandum indicates that the British knew that the US was running Burnham's agenda and expected the US to reign in Burnham's covert agenda to destabilise the PPP Government. The question that arises is: who was running Jagan and the PPP's agenda?

An Action Memorandum from the Assistant Secretary of State for European Affairs (Tyler) to the Secretary of State Rusk dated July 31, 1964 states as follows:

> "Duncan Sandys has written to you (Tab. B) stating that he believes order and security in British Guiana can only be restored through an all party coalition government. He asks for our support in bringing about such a coalition."

(Foreign Affairs 1964-1968 Vol. xxxii No.387)

An editorial note states:

> "The attached July 30 message from Sandys states that the British were not certain they would be able to restrain racial violence

157

sufficiently to hold elections and that they were satisfied that the only method of restoring order and security was to bring about a temporary all-Party coalition to bridge the period to the elections."

(Foreign Affairs 1964-1968 Vol. xxxii No.387)

An editorial note to a Message from the Secretary of State (Rusk) to the British Colonial Secretary (Sandys) dated August 4, 1964 states:

"In a personal message to Rusk, attached to an August 17 covering note from the British Embassy, Sandy's deputy, Sir Hilton Poynton, reported that the risk of violence was diminished and the case for a temporary coalition was therefore less strong. Poynton stated that he was sure Sandy's would agree, upon his return from holiday, that the idea should not be pursued under these circumstances. If, however, violence were to set in again at the pitch it reached in June and July, a temporary coalition might be reconsidered."

(Foreign Relations 1964-1968 Vol. xxxii No.388)

The English strategy then had the desired effect. Reduce the social violence and we drop the issue of an all party coalition government which would indefinitely postpone general elections.

A Memorandum from the Director of the Office of the Commonwealth and Northern Europe Affairs (Shullaw) to the Assistant Secretary of State for European Affairs (Tyler) dated October 27, 1964 states:

"Several weeks after the Anglo-US consultations in July 1964 violence in BG came to a virtual halt with the end of the sugar workers strike, and the beginning of the election campaign.

(Foreign Relations 1964-1968 Vol. xxxii No.396)

The race war came and it ceased when it jeopardised a political agenda or agendas.

A Memorandum from Gordon Chase of the National Security Council Staff to the President's Special Assistant for National Security Affairs (Bundy) dated October 17, 1964 states:

"1. The election prospects still look good. One of the things we are concentrated on is ensuring that the opposition parties turn out to vote on election day: to this end the CIA, in a deniable and discreet way, is providing financial incentives to party workers who are charged with the responsibility of getting out the vote. Another thing worth concentrating on is the job of ensuring that intimidation, threats and violence do not hamper the conduct of the BG elections;

2. With respect to the impact on the BG situation of the Labor victory, State feels that the election was sufficiently close so that Labor will be chary of tampering with the present course of events in BG."

(Foreign Relations 1964-1968 Vol. xxxii Vol. 393)

The anxiety of the Johnson Administration involves the outcome of the December 1964 general elections in British Guiana and the course of actions by the Labour Government headed by Harold Wilson that replaced the Conservative government of the United Kingdom in October 1964.

In a Memorandum of Conversation dated October 27, 1964 Patrick Gordon Walker the Foreign Secretary of the Labour Government meets with the US Secretary of State. The memorandum reports as follows:

"With respect to British Guiana, the Foreign Secretary gave the assurance that his Government would proceed with the elections as scheduled. The Foreign Secretary said he had a very unfavorable opinion of Burnham who is a thoroughly unreliable person. Regardless of the outcome, the election will provide no answer to the problem of racial conflict and therefore there is little prospect of early independence emerging from it."

"(Foreign Relations 1964-1968 Vol. xxxii No.397)

In A Memorandum of Conversation dated December 7, 1964 Prime Minister Wilson in a meeting with President Johnson reports as follows:

"Mr. Wilson said that he wanted to talk to the President about British Guiana. He had told Jagan that who ever wins in BG, the UK would not grant BG independence as there would be a blood bath if it did so. He thought that if both Burnham and Jagan (the latter of whom he described as a naive Trotskyite) were out of BG it would be so much better. He didn't think a government could be entrusted to either of them and the UK rather felt that the US placed excessive trust in Burnham who was just as bad in his own way as Jagan was in his."

(Foreign Relations 1964-1968 Vol. xxxii No.399)

The Labour Government led by Harold Wilson accepted the strategy laid out by its predecessor Conservative government and marched in lockstep with the agenda of the Johnson presidency of the USA. This agenda was the creation of the Kennedy presidency.

The general elections held on the 7th December 1964, saw the PPP winning 24 seats, the PNC winning 22 seats and the United Force winning 7 seats. The Governor invited Forbes Burnham to form the government despite the fact that the PPP won the largest number of seats. The PNC led by Forbes Burnham and the United Force led by Peter D'Aguiar would form a coalition government with 29 seats in the Assembly. The US covert and overt agendas attained their objectives but the US agenda for British Guiana was not exhausted. The potent reality was that the next general elections was under the threat of the failure of proportional representation as an electoral system to hold back the tidal wave of the Indo-Guyanese demographic majority in support of the PPP at the polls due some time in the future. In the 1964 general elections and thereafter the issues were paradoxically dual as a political party that owed its existence to a race vote was led by persons espousing classic orthodox Marxist-Leninist discourse, an ironical paradox that destroyed Guyana.

It is fitting to end this section of the deconstruction of the declassified American files with a Memorandum from Gordon Chase of the National Security Council Staff to the President's Special Assistant for National Security Affairs (Bundy) dated July 14, 1965. The Memorandum states as follows:

"In response to your question, here are some reasons why the announcement of a Constitutional Conference seems a good thing. 1. Since we can in no way be assured that the British will stay in BG for 5 to 10 years, it is probably better to get the British out of BG sooner rather than later.

(a) With the British in BG and the East Indian population growing, there is always the chance that the British will change the rules of the game (e.g. coalition, a new election). In this regard, it is probably true that Jagan feels he still has a chance so long as the British are around. With the British gone, Jagan himself may decide to bug out.

(b) With the British gone, it is highly likely that Burnham will do what is necessary to ensure that Jagan does not get back into power on the wings of a growing East Indian population (e.g. import West Indian Africans, establish literacy tests for voters-these would hurt the PPP).

(c) The chances for violence probably won't increase significantly with independence. Generally speaking, the East Indians are timid compared to the Africans and, without the British to protect them

they might be even more timid. Also, it is conceivable that a British
military presence could be maintained even after independence."

(Foreign Relations 1964-1968 Vol. xxxii No. 411)

The US administration is assured that Burnham would do all in his power
to keep Jagan and the PPP out of state power. To realise this the British must
now grant independence to Guyana under Burnham's leadership in order for
him to be free from British interference. What Burnham has in his favour is
not only US support but the timidity of the Indo-Guyanese.

A Memorandum from the Deputy Director for Operations of the Central
Intelligence Agency (Helms) to the President's Special Assistant for National
Security (Bundy) dated August 6, 1965 states:

> "3. The security situation in the country remains disturbed and
> Jagan is believed to be directing arson and sabotage activities,
> attempting to increase these to such an extent that the British
> Government will be forced to delay the independence conference.
> The leadership of the Guiana Agricultural Workers' Union, which
> is loyal to Jagan, plans a major strike effort on the sugar estates
> during August and September. This could lead to racial violence,
> and it may be Jagan's intention to utilize the strike for this purpose.
> Local security forces continue to be less than adequate, and the
> presence of 1300 British troops is still required to insure internal
> security.
>
> 1.   The [less than one line of source text not declassified] program
>   in British Guiana has three objectives:
>
> a.to obtain intelligence on the PPP's capabilities and intentions,
> particularly Jagan's plans in the immediate future;
>
> b.to keep Burnham and D'Aguiar working together in the coalition
> government, and to keep their parties organized in support of the
> coalition government and prepared for a quick election if one
> should be necessary; and
>
> c.to counter Jagan's efforts to gain control of organized labor
> in British Guiana. [1paragraph (8 lines of source text) not
> declassified].

(Foreign Relations 1964-1968 Vol. xxxii No.43)

Jagan is then in August 1965 a clear and present danger to US interests.
The covert operation to ensure that Jagan never again wins a general election

in Guyana continues, the pressing reality is to prop up the Burnham/D'Aguiar coalition and to mount an effective covert/ overt operation against Jagan.

A Memorandum from Gordon Chase of the National Security Council Staff to the President's Special Assistant for National Security Affairs (Bundy) dated October 5, 1965 states:

> "4. East Indians. Del said that we are so far getting nowhere with respect to building up an alternative East Indian party. He went on to say, however, that the situation is still very fluid and that we should properly wait until after independence before we get to work on this problem in earnest . The big hope is that we can locate an alternative East Indian leader; so far no one of any stature appears to be on the horizon. A lesser hope is that Burnham will, by sensible and progressive policies, be able to win the East Indians over to his side. Burnham, however, is not all confident that he can ever translate East Indian acceptance of his regime into East Indian votes. Neither is Del. Del added that even if the East Indian cannot be wooed away from Jagan, Burnham will do whatever is necessary to win the election in 1968. This could take the form of importing Negroes from other Caribbean countries or, in a pinch establishing literacy tests for Guianese voters. Literacy tests would hurt the East Indian population more than the Negro population."

(Foreign Relations 1964-1968 Vol. xxxii No.415)

The meeting was between Gordon Chase and Del Carson. Del Carson was the Consular General of the US Embassy in British Guiana in 1965. This is then a clear statement of the US discourse of the East Indian problem in British Guiana in 1965. The Indo Guyanese refuse to abandon Jagan politically in spite of US efforts to wean them away from Jagan. The solidarity of the Indo voting bloc in its support of Jagan then demands victory for Burnham by any means necessary in the upcoming general elections. The victim is then the aggressor thereby exonerating imperialist aggression.

A Telegram from the Ambassador to Guyana (Carlson) to the Department of State dated July 15, 1966 states:

> "6.Best estimates available indicate that the domestic non-East Indian voting population in 1968-1969 will still exceed the East Indian electorate by five to eight thousand. No provision is made in these estimates for new immigrants. Absentee voters probably number between ten and fifteen thousand, with the non-East Indian in the majority. Balanced against this apparent margin in favour of the government, is the fact that the government could

easily lose the votes of as many as ten thousand of its nominal supporters. They would be the dissatisfied and the disgruntled who might well refuse to go to the poll or in some cases conceivably even vote for the PPP. Facing a contest such as this, a man as astute as Burnham, will probably want to enter the game with at least a few aces. (In 1964 the PPP received 109,000 votes, the coalition parties a total of 126,000; the total vote was 238,530 out of 247,495 registered. The projected registration in 1968-69 is estimated at 284,387).

(Foreign Relations 1964-1968 Vol. xxxii No. 419)

US Ambassador Carlson did the arithmetic and it is clearly apparent that a Burnham/ PNC victory in 1968 has to be achieved via massive electoral fraud. In Document 419 Carlson would state on Burnham's agenda as follows:

"8. Burnham had confided to close colleagues that he intends to remain in power indefinitely-if at all possible by constitutional means. However, if necessary, he is prepared to employ unorthodox methods to achieve his aims. In these circumstances, probably the best that can be hoped for at this time is that he might respond to guidelines and thus take the most effective and least objectionable course to attain his goals."

(Foreign Relations 1964-1968 Vol. xxxii No.419)

The US government is then forewarned that Burnham intends to hold on to power by any means necessary and as this serves US interests in Guyana then so be it.

A Memorandum prepared for the 303 Committee dated March 17, 1967 states:

"SUBJECT

Support to Anti-Jagan Political Parties in Guyana

1.   Summary

It is established US Government policy that Cheddi Jagan, East Indian Marxist leader of the pro-Communist People's Progressive Party (PPP) in Guyana, will not be permitted to take over the government of an independent Guyana. Jagan has the electoral support of the East Indians, who are approximately 50% of the total population of Guyana. It is believed that Jagan has a good chance of coming to power in the next elections unless steps are taken to prevent this.

Prime Minister Forbes Burnham, leader of the majority People's National Congress (PNC) in the coalition, is aware of the problem, and has stated that he is fully prepared to utilize the electoral machinery at his disposal to ensure his own re- election. Burnham has initiated steps for electoral registration of Guyanese at home and abroad, and has requested financial assistance [less than one line of source text not declassified] for the PNC campaign. It is recommended that he and his party be provided with covert support in order to assure his victory at the polls. At the same time, it is believed that support to Peter D'Aguiar and his United Front (UF) the minority party in the coalition government, is also essential in order to offset Jagan's solidly entrenched East Indian electoral support. It is recommended that the 303 Committee approve the courses of action outlined in this paper at a cost of [less than 1 line of source text not declassified]."

(Foreign Relations 1964-1968 Vol. xxxii No.421)

An editorial note to the text quoted above states:

"131 According to an April 10 memorandum for the record, the 303 Committee approved this proposal at its April 7 meeting. [Text not declassified] emphasized during the Committee's discussion the importance of starting early in the implementation of the proposal."

(Foreign Relations 1964-1968 Vol. xxxii No.421)

It must be noted that on March 17, 1967 Guyana was an independent state and the US methodology to realise its anti-Jagan agenda has changed dramatically.

A 303 Committee has been reactivated to drive the anti-Jagan agenda in Guyana and the US is not hindered by the need to be wary of a colonial overlord in Guyana in 1967. Document 421 states:

"6. Relationship to Previous 303 Committee Actions

Action to remove Jagan from power in British Guiana was considered by the Special Group during the period 6 April 1961- 23 May 1963. [less than 1 line of source text not declassified] financial support to British Guiana Trades Union Council during the strikes of 1962 and 1963 was approved. The Special Group did not approve other political action against Jagan during that period because of British Government concern. Since early 1963, political action operations in Guyana have not been the subject of

Special Group consideration."

(Foreign Relations 1964-1968 Vol. xxxii No.421)

No Special Group was involved in the covert action leading up to the 1964 general elections in Guyana. To ensure maximum security this covert action was the responsibility of US covert agencies. The independence of Guyana in 1966 changed the operational terrain increasing the effectiveness of covert operations. Document 421 continues:

> "[less than 1 line of source text not declassified] will continue to monitor the Guyana situation to permit identification and evaluation of other courses of action should Jagan depart from his current strategy or should it appear that he is likely to win an election despite our best efforts to prevent this. These courses of action are outlined in Tab C."

(Foreign Relations 1964-1968 Vol. xxxii No. 421)

Tab C was not declassified. The existence of Tab C indicates the willingness to remove Jagan and the PPP from power should they win the 1968 general elections. The impetus was then on Burnham to win the 1968 general elections by any means necessary.

A Memorandum from the Deputy Director for Coordination of the Bureau of Intelligence and Research (Trueheart) to the Director (Hughes) and Deputy Director (Denney) dated December 6, 1967 reveals part of the US case against Jagan as follows:

> "Committee approval was grounded in the belief that as Prime Minister Jagan would be an instrument of Communist influence in Latin America. The [less than 1 line of source text not declassified] paper embodying the proposal noted that during Jagan's years (1961-4) as head of the government, some 50 PPP youth trained in Cuba in guerrilla warfare, a 'Guyana Liberation Army' was organized and equipped largely with Cuban weapons, and $3,000,000 of Soviet Bloc funds entered Guyana for the support of the PPP. A paper also stated that some 90 PPP youths were currently being trained (? educated?) in Bloc countries and that in Guyana Jagan's Accabre College was training Guyanan Youth in Marxist thought."

(Foreign Relations 1964-1968 Vol. xxxii No. 423)

The US evidence to support its action against Jagan consists of the creation of a Cuban trained and armed PPP militia, the creation of Accabre College for the insemination of Marxist discourse towards the creation of a PPP Marxist cadre, financial support from the Soviet Bloc countries and the education of a PPP elite in Soviet Bloc countries. In December 1967 this evidence demands that the US ensures that Jagan and the PPP do not rule Guyana.

A Memorandum prepared for the 303 Committee dated November 21, 1968 states:

> "This report notes that the elections have been set for 16 December 1968, describes progress in the elections campaigns of the People's National Congress (PNC), led by Prime Minister Forbes Burnham and the United Force (UF), led by Peter D'Aguiar, notes the outcome of the national census and voter registration effort in Guyana and describes the problems facing Burnham stemming from his having padded the registration lists of the United Kingdom excessively in an attempt to win an outright majority in the elections. This report also notes the security implications arising from Peter D'Aguiar having become aware of this padding and his efforts to counter it. This progress report also states that somewhat under half of the funds approved for this activity for fiscal year 1969 were obligated by mid-November 1968."

> "7. Future plans [less than 1 line of source text not declassified] will continue to provide financial support and electoral guidance to the PNC and the UF for their campaigns in Guyana and overseas. To date, however, Burnham has not responded in the manner desired to US advice to avoid an overly large false registration and to US urging to plan for the formation of another coalition government after the elections. He feels that his own pride, self-respect and competence as a leader are called into question when he is urged to continue his cooperation with Peter D'Aguiar, whom he hates. Racial considerations are most likely a significant ingredient in Burnham's attitude. Thus we have no assurance that he will accept our guidance in this regard. Peter D'Aguiar also is an extremely difficult person to deal with and so far has rejected our attempts to persuade him to take a more moderate and flexible line toward Burnham. However, D'Aguiar despises Burnham passionately and has a paranoid streak in him; this combination may well induce him to take attitudes and to pursue courses of action that a better balanced man would avoid."

(Foreign Relations 1964-1968 Vol. xxxii No. 439)

The US is fully aware of the electoral fraud Burnham is involved in to steal an outright electoral majority in the 1968 general elections. The US is concerned about the sloppy nature of Burnham's electoral fraud and the rift that has become public between D'Aguiar and Burnham. D'Aguiar is the major concern of the US as his action is deemed injurious to the security situation. It is than apparent that Burnham is the only candidate embraced by the US to keep Jagan out of state power. Burnham's electoral fraud that ensures a PNC majority solves the problem for the US as both Jagan and D'Aguiar are relegated to the wilderness of opposition politics in Guyana after 1968. In addition it commits the US to further engagement with Burnham in the future to shore up his regime militarily, economically and with covert support to pre-empt the Jagan threat.

Document 441 an Editorial Note states:

> "The People's National Congress (PNC) of Prime Minister Burnham won 30 of the 53 seats in Parliament in the December 16 elections. Burnham's PNC won 50.7 percent of the domestic vote and a heavy majority of the overseas which raised his total to 55.8 percent of the registered voters. The United Force (UF) Party of Portuguese businessman Peter D'Aguiar emerged from the elections with only 4 seats in Parliament. Jagan's Peoples Progressive Party (PPP) won only 19 seats. Ambassador Carlson reported that Burnham 'was somewhat disappointed at not making greater inroads into East Indian community [Jagan got almost all of their votes] in view his four year record of peace, stability and economic progress'."

(Foreign Relations 1964-1968 Vol. xxxii No.441)

The electoral fraud is then palpable in the results of the general elections of 1968 but the said fraud served US interests in Guyana. It was Burnham's primary strength a strength conjured up by Jagan. This power of Burnham was never organic but the product of an abysmal failure of Cheddi Jagan to live in the real world. Jagan's denial fed Burnham's megalomania to epic proportions to the detriment of the people and the state of Guyana.

CHAPTER 7

THE BRITISH DECLASSIFIED FILES

On the 9th October 1953 the British colonial overlord suspended the constitution of the colony of British Guiana. The statement of the colonial overlord made in British Guiana stated as follows:

> "Her Majesty's Government have decided that the Constitution of British Guiana must be suspended to prevent communist subversion of the Government and a dangerous crisis both in public order and in economic affairs."

> (Document 44 The Suspension of the British Guiana Constitution-1953)

The PPP having won the April 1953 general elections formed the government. The said government was removed in October 1953 and until its defeat in the general elections in 1964 the British failed to assault the communist subversion of the PPP thereby banishing it from the electoral politics of British Guiana. The files show that in the period from 1953 to 1964 the British failed to establish an intelligence structure in Guyana to do battle with the PPP. Document No.74 Telegram (No. 166) from the Governor of British Guiana to the Secretary of State dated 23rd October 1953 states:

> "Our police intelligence service needs strengthening and reorganisation, while our bureau of public information has lost the confidence of the Press and public.

> 2. I consider that we require a top flight intelligence and propaganda service in an independent supervisory and coordination organisation being fed by and assisting similar services in the above fields."

There is no intelligence structure to deal with the said communist subversion in 1953. Where then was the evidence of communist subversion to merit suspension of the constitution in October 1953? Document 150: Notes of the Colonial Office on possible answer to question asked of the Secretary of State in the British Parliament dated 24th November 1953 states:

> "3. The Governor, however, never actually recommended the suspension of the Constitution.
>
> 4. It was on the basis of documents listed above, plus a letter from Sir Stephen Luke, plus the various reports received on the developing sugar strike (and in particular the attempt to start a general strike on 21st September) which led the Secretary of State to decide on 23rd September that the Constitution should be suspended. The decision was sent to the Governor on 24th September.
>
> 5. The Governor never replied to this telegram as such, but he clearly accepted the decision and acted promptly on it."

(Document 150 The Suspension of the British Guiana Constitution-1953)

The decision to act was then a knee jerk reaction to perceived threats to British economic interests in Guyana and specifically to Booker's interests. There was then an attempt to pressure Jagan to obey the British script for independence for Guyana. There was no attempt to destroy Jagan politically. The British strategy was then to coerce Jagan by fomenting a split in the PPP in 1953 and by detaining the leaders of the extremist wing of the PPP. British strategy was not based on covert knowledge of Jagan's agenda and they were simply shooting in the dark which encouraged extremism and forced the entry of the US to protect its hemispheric interests in Guyana. The tragedy of Guyana from October 1953 to 1964 was then the product of British incompetence that gave space to US, PPP, PNC and UF extremism. Successive British governments talked up a storm, painted pictures of the dangers of the US path adopted but failed to commit the resources to engage with Jagan in keeping with their repeated outbursts of his communist inclinations and his invitation to Cuban and Soviet interests to subvert Guyana. Successive British governments bumbled through, suffering with an acute case of wanting to hurriedly leave a colony that was of no value whilst labouring with the angst of post- empire withdrawal syndrome most acutely seen in successive Labour and Conservative governments from 1945 to 1966. The British surrendered to the Kennedy and Johnson US presidencies and Guyana paid the price for British incompetence.

Document 58 Internal Colonial Office note to Sir T. Lloyd from P. Rogers dated 16 October 1953 states:

> "Today's article in the Times reinforces doubts I have been feeling over the past two or three days about the way the Governor is allowing the situation to develop in British Guiana. I cannot, for example understand why it was only two days after his broadcast that a search was carried out of PPP headquarters. It is clear that many dangerous documents were burnt in that period. Nor does it seem to me, as far as one can judge from here, reasonable in present circumstances to allow PPP supporters free scope e.g. to enter sugar estates and encourage strikes. Once we have entered into open conflict with the PPP and taken the first and decisive step, it seems to me that the right course is to go hard at it and try to smash the Party completely. At present the Governor merely seems to me to be presenting them with an admirable rallying cry and giving them too much scope to proclaim it."

(Document 58 The Suspension of the British Guiana Constitution-1953)

Rogers aptly describes the failure of Governor Savage to prosecute a war declared on Jagan and the PPP on the 9th October 1953. The war declared was never prosecuted as it was simply an action to break a strike that threatened British interests and the British colonial state in Guyana did not have the assets, the resources, the will to prosecute the war on Jagan and the PPP in Guyana.

Document 67 Telegram (No.155) from Governor Savage to the Colonial Secretary dated 20 October 1953 states:

> "it is now clear that PPP extremists are determined to continue to encourage sugar workers to strike and to encourage intimidation. As this may lead to public disorders, I have decided that extremist leaders, including Janet Jagan and King, be detained under Emergency Order as we have not yet got sufficient evidence to prefer charges under ordinary law. I hope this action will deter ordinary rank and file in the party."

(Document 67 The Suspension of the British Guiana Constitution-1953)

Governor Savage intends to detain PPP extremist leaders including Janet Jagan for continuing to pose threats to British interests in spite of the suspension of the constitution on the 9th October 1953. There is no evidence to prosecute PPP extremists under law hence their detention must be under

Emergency Order. The British having declared war on the PPP has no evidence to prosecute PPP leaders in a court of law. The British have then no assets in the PPP and have failed to utilise the Emergency Order to collect intelligence on the activities of the PPP, a potent example of utter British incompetence.

Document 71 Telegram (No. 160) from the Governor of British Guiana to the Secretary of State dated 22nd October 1953 states:

> "2.For your information great difficulty is being experienced in obtaining sufficient evidence to prefer charges as agents are unwilling, through fear of intimidation, to make written statements or to give evidence in court and we are unwilling to disclose source of information for security reasons."

> (Document 71 The Suspension of the British Guiana Constitution-1953)

Janet Jagan was never detained as was the case with Cheddi Jagan. Covert agents are not placed to testify in court and to make sworn statements. Covert agents supply intelligence which drives intervention and pre-emptive acts to destroy organisations and individuals under attack. The British simply had informants who gave information after the fact which is useless in a covert war. This is but one reason for the intervention of the US in the war on Jagan.

Finally there is the gross incompetence of the Secretary of State for the Colonies, Oliver Lyttelton, in 1953. Document 72 Telegram (No. 164) from Governor Savage to the Colonial Secretary dated 23 October 1953 states:

> "6. Only alternative as I see it is to detain persons named in paragraph 4, together with approximately eight others, at Atkinson Field under military guard in the hope that complete removal of the leaders will paralyse the organisation and enable us to counter with propaganda and possibly to obtain further evidence to charge any of these persons in a court, but I am advised that in view of the records and behaviour and actions of the persons in the past and of the deterioration in the situation, their detention would be justified under Section 13(1)(c) of the Emergency Order to prevent them from acting in any manner prejudicial to public safety, order or defence.

> 7.Neither I nor my advisers are of the opinion that it is any good depending on a split in the party to solve the problem, even partly."

> (Document 72 The Suspension of the British Guiana Constitution-1953)

The Secretary of State for the Colonies has then politicised the war thereby seeking to implement a strategy of appeasement in a terrain of declared war on Jagan and the PPP. The Colonial Secretary does not want the leadership of the PPP detained and the strategy is to wait for the implosion of the PPP as the chasm between Jagan and Burnham is supposed to implode the PPP. But the implosion when it comes worsens the situation as it places race violence on the agenda driven by the desire for racist hegemony. It is then apparent that the Colonial Secretary insisted that Janet Jagan must not be detained during the emergency in 1953.

Document 13 Letter from Henry Seaford, General Manager of Bookers Companies in British Guiana, to Jock Campbell, Managing Director of Bookers Group of Companies dated 8th September 1953 states:

> "What is worrying me and my colleagues today is that the present situation can only be dealt with effectively by the Colonial Office and from our conversations with the powers- that- be, it is clear that they do not understand the position. What the majority of the Ministers is trying to do is to cause chaos in the colony, then go to the Colonial Office and say that it is because they do not have complete control, that these things are happening. Their aim is to get rid of all white officials and make life so unpleasant for other whites that they will get out. Schools are to be taught communism and those Masters that don't agree will be fired. Can you imagine what this colony will be like in 5 years time if this sort of thing continues. Unless something drastic is done, Bookers will cease to exist as a large firm in 5 years."

(Document 13 The Suspension of the British Guiana Constitution-1953)

For Seaford communism is the whipping boy, the problem is independence and the end of white colonial racist hegemony. It is then a double headed appeal to pressure a Conservative Government in 1953 headed by Winston Churchill. The appeal to the race, the end of empire and the angst of losing the colony bit by bit with the red veneer moved Churchill to action on the 9th October 1953. Action that was so flawed that it set the colony on a downward spiral to racial violence that it is yet to recover from.

Document 60 Letter from the Proportional Representation Society to the Secretary of State for the Colonies dated 17 October 1953 points out that under an electoral system of proportional representation the PPP would have won 13 seats and the remaining 11 seats to the forces opposed to the PPP. An entirely different political dynamic would have been unleashed in the colony in 1953, apparently a political dynamic that successive British governments did not want because the general elections of 1957 and 1961 were under the said first pass the post electoral system which manufactured a majority for the PPP fanning the flames of anti-PPP agitation and racial violence. PPP victory in the general elections of 1961 would place on the agenda independence for the colony under PPP leadership thereby engendering US governmental paranoia and their resorting to covert activity.

Document 20 Text of reply from Lord Home to Dean Rusk dated 26 February 1962 states:

> "You say that it is not possible for you 'to put up with an independent British Guiana under Jagan' and that 'Jagan should not accede to power again'. How would you suggest that this can be done in a democracy? And even if a device can be found, it would almost certainly be transparent and in such circumstances if democratic processes are to be allowed, it will be extremely hard to provide a reasonable prospect that any successor regime will be more stable and more mature.
>
> So I would say to you that we cannot now go back on the course we have set ourselves of bringing these dependent territories to self-government. Nor is it any good deluding ourselves that we can now set aside a single territory such as British Guiana for some sort of special treatment."

(Document 20 The British Declassified Files on British Guiana 1958-1963)

A reply to the then Secretary of State (Dean Rusk) that reeks of arrogant colonial imperialism seeped in denial. Home is literally calling out the US to pursue a unilateral action to protect its interests in the colony and by extension the Western Hemisphere. Home insists that the British Government has no intention to change the formula devised for moving colonies to newly independent states. That the US alarm over an independent Guyana under the rule of Jagan and the PPP and the volatile race mix of the social order do not merit special attention, a specific strategy from the British Colonial overlord. Home deploys the red herring of the need for the British to be transparent and democratic in the process and the futile brain dead discourse of the incompetence of those politicians in the colony arrayed against Jagan. The then British government simply did not care as in their worldview British Guiana was overshadowed by other colonial events in the British Empire as Kenya and the Middle East.

Document 31 Note from Hugh Fraser to Lord Home dated 20 March 1962 was Fraser's report of a meeting with then US President John F. Kennedy on British Guiana. He states:

"The objects of my talks were:

(i) To tone down any excitement caused by the Rusk/Home exchange of letters;

(ii) To get the Americans to accept our policy of a fairly swift withdrawal from B.G. as the best; and

(iii) To endeavour to change the American attitude in two fashions:-

(a) To damp down the importance of British Guiana; and

(b) To abandon their present policy of boycotting the Jagan Government and reneging on the various pledges of aid which the Americans made to Jagan during his visit to Washington. I think I have made it clear to them that over the next ten years the Portuguese will remain a minority and the Africans will become one, and that therefore their policy must be whilst helping minorities to look to the Indians as the centre of power to concentrate on weaning Jagan and the moderates away from the communist apparatus. This is run, I think, by Mrs. Jagan, and I hope I have made it clear that a line can be drawn between these types of international communists and what I would call the anti-colonial type of communist.

(7) Having, I think, sold the ideas to the Americans that British Guiana was really now more their responsibility than ours and would increasingly become more so."

(Document 31 The British Declassified Files on British Guiana 1958- 1963)

Fraser expects the US President to support British Guiana with aid. He actively sought to convince the US President that Cheddi Jagan was not a hardcore communist but where is the British covert intelligence to support this political discourse? There was none. Fraser sought to convince the US President that British Guiana was not a primary threat to US interests in the Western Hemisphere. But whilst attempting to sell the US this bill of goods the British gave Jagan three manufactured majorities in the general elections of 1953, 1957 and 1961.

Finally Fraser abdicated the British colonial overlord's responsibility for the management of the colony of British Guiana he indicated that British Guiana was a US problem as the British wanted a clean and fast break from the colony. Britain abdicated its responsibility but yet played hard to get when the US President demanded that the British government implement the US agenda. The British played a nasty game with US Presidents Kennedy and Johnson and Guyana paid the ultimate price for British colonial imperialist arrogance refusing to accept that they were now a second class imperial power at best in the post World War 2 era. The British stoked a fracturing of the PPP along racial lines in the post October 9, 1953 scenario but refused in two subsequent general elections to change an electoral system that hardened the racial divide by manufacturing majorities for the Indo dominated PPP. Fraser reveals that it was the British government's position that the future of the colony of British Guiana lay in the dominance of the Indo majority and the US must live with that. But the US had no problem with Indian hegemony what they had a problem with is Jagan's leadership of the Indian hegemony. The British then were seeking to shore up their economic interests by accepting Indian hegemony failing to see the resistance to Indian hegemony that was on the cards within the colony and that the US covert operation to remove Jagan would enhance the battle for racist hegemony to the point of ethnic cleansing. One explanation for British incompetence in the handling of this minefield is that they simply did not care.

Document 43 Note from Sir Ralph Grey, Governor of British Guiana, to R.W. Piper of the Colonial Office, London dated 25 September 1962 states:

> "9. What is worrying about all this is the story of ministerial antipathy for Americans. The Americans have made a thorough muddle of things here-if it had not been for Melby it would have been even worse. It is ironical that American functionaries (again other than Melby) should be so critical of what Britain has done or has not done here when it is they who by their own defects have so greatly contributed to the unhappy state in which the country now is. Their efforts to influence the course of the events are the reverse of skilful. I have written to warn Melby privately on his return that unless they are much more adroit they will, as Searwar volunteered this morning, 'worsen the situation here irretrievably' – not only for themselves, but for us also."

(Document 43 The British Declassified Files on British Guiana 1958- 1963)

Governor Grey is either in denial or is brain dead, possibly both. The US covert plan cares nothing about the attitude of PPP ministers of government to the US. The US President is at war with Jagan and the PPP and by extension the colonial overlord of British Guiana. The US President has one single aim to destroy Jagan politically and if that means shattering the Guyanese social order so be it. A collapsed Guyanese social order favours US interventions then and after Guyana's independence to make war on Jagan. The US then successfully defended their interests in Guyana and the British before Guyanese independence in 1966 was the reluctant vassal of the US in Guyana.

Document 8 Annex: Background Note on British Guiana for the Kennedy-Macmillan meeting planned for Washington in April 1961- prepared by the Colonial Office dated 29 March 1961 states:

> "11.Publicity was given some time ago to the reported offer of economic aid to British Guiana from Cuba. The terms of the proposition have never been made precise but they relate primarily to the exploitation of British Guiana timber for export to Cuba. Any such arrangement would require the sanction of H.M.G. which would have to balance the difficulty of denying outside aid to British Guiana when the West was not providing as much development money as British Guiana Ministers claim is needed, against obvious objections. Such information as we have however suggests that the proposition partakes more of trade than aid. Our thinking is that we should probe further to see whether there would be any real advantage for British Guiana. If so we should probably not seek to veto it. At the moment the matter is still being considered by the Departments concerned in Whitehall."

(Document 8 The British Declassified Files on British Guiana 1958- 1963)

Document 50 Memorandum prepared by the American department of the British Foreign Office dated 29 November 1962 states:

> "and it is to be hoped that the Americans will be left in no doubt of the economic problems of British Guiana and of the consequent danger of her turning to the Eastern Bloc for aid. The Soviet Trade Mission is due in British Guiana on December 4."

(Document 50 The British Declassified Files on British Guiana 1958- 1963)

It is obvious that in 1962 the British Government is playing chicken with a US President, John Kennedy, engaged in a bitter cold war engagement with the Soviet Union and Cuba with the flashpoints of the Bay of Pigs fiasco in April 1961 to the Cuban missile crisis of October 1962. The British are now insisting to the US President that given his failure to grant the aid he promised to Jagan the British have moved to allow Cuban and Soviet trade links with British Guiana. Post empire colonial arrogance at its best for which Guyana paid handsomely. The nature and gravity of the engagement of the Castro brothers with the US in revolutionary Cuba enables understanding of the suicidal nature of the action of a second rate ex- colonial power calling out the US President in the early 1960's over American policy in British Guiana. But what was dismally stupid is to call out the US President by allowing a Cuban and Soviet presence in British Guiana this sent all the wrong messages to the US President. The British are then welcoming a Soviet and Cuban presence in the colony at the time in which it is clearly admitted that the quality of internal security in the colony is poor at best in reality non- existent. Moreover internal security for the colony is in the hands of Jagan and the PPP Government.

Document 51 Background Document prepared for the British Prime Minister Harold Macmillan for his meeting with President Kennedy in December 1962 dated December 10, 1962 states:

> "16. It is accepted that the forces available for internal security should be strengthened. This was shown necessary by the disturbances of February 1962. The British authorities consider that the most effective way of doing this would be to expand the Police Force. But the British Guiana Government will not support this method and they are responsible for internal security. They want an army, primarily for internal security duties. Two Israeli officers have been in British Guiana on an invitation from Dr. Jagan and have drawn up a proposed scheme on Nahal lines. The Colonial Secretary has recently decided to pursue the idea of expanding the Police Force. It is clear that the British Government will have to meet the cost of expansion, whatever form this took."

(Document 51 The British Declassified Files on British Guiana 1958-1963)

Jagan's agenda is to create an army loyal to him packed with PPP assets to wage war on his political enemies. The political realties of Guyana translates this into racist Indian hegemony and the methodology adopted by Jagan is the Lee Kuan Yew model of Singapore where the Israelis were used to create an ethnic Chinese dominated army in post colonial Singapore.

Document 39 Memorandum from R.H.G. Edmonds to N.J.A. Cheetham dated 17 May 1962 states:

> "and that the Americans have now dropped their objections to our plans for strengthening the Special Branch in Georgetown."

(Document 39 The British Declassified Files on British Guiana
1958- 1963)

It is then evident that the Americans were against the expansion of the
surveillance capacity in the colony because said capacity was under the daily
management and control of the PPP Government and could be used against
the US covert operations in the colony. The US agreed to the British plan on
the expectation that the intelligence gathering activities of Special Branch
would be structured to deny sensitive intelligence to the PPP Government.

British de-classified file CO 1031/4495 contains an undated letter signed
by Cheddi Jagan, Forbes Burnham and Peter D'Aguiar addressed to the
Secretary of State for the colonies which states as follows:

> "At your request we have made further efforts to resolve the
> differences between us on the constitutional issues which require
> to be settled before British Guiana secures independence, in
> particular, the electoral system, the voting age, and the question
> whether fresh elections should be held before independence.
>
> We regret to have to report to you that we have not succeeded
> in reaching agreement; and we have reluctantly come to the
> conclusion that there is no prospect of an agreed solution. Another
> adjournment of the Conference for further discussions between
> ourselves would therefore serve no useful purpose and would
> result only in further delaying British Guiana's independence and
> in continued uncertainty in the country.
>
> In these circumstances we are agreed to ask the British Government
> to settle on their authority all outstanding constitutional issues
> and we undertake to accept their decisions."

(CO 1031/4495)

A Telegram dated 1st November 1963 from the Secretary of State for the
Colonies to British Guiana states:

> "British Guiana Conference
>
> The Conference ended yesterday when Colonial Secretary gave his
> decision.
>
> Main decisions are as follows:-
>
> (a)Constitution must provide the strongest safeguards to protect
> minorities;

(b)electoral system will be revised so that whole country forms a single constituency and seats are allotted in proportion to votes cast for each party (i.e. party list systems);

(c)voting age will remain as at present (21 years);

(d)fresh elections on the new basis will be held as soon as possible, under supervision of a special commissioner from outside British Guiana appointed by British Government;

(e)after these elections, British Government will convene a conference to settle any recurring constitutional issues and to fix a date for independence;

(f)documents to implement these decisions will be made available in draft to the leaders before receiving final approval;

(g)additional security forces (i.e. to replace British troops) will be raised locally before independence under direction of the Governor who will endeavour to ensure that recruits are not drawn predominantly from any one racial group.

2.Jagan received these decisions with undisguised dissatisfaction. He has shown signs of reversing out of his prior undertaking to accept them, but has not so far committed himself to any course of action."

(CO 1031/4495)

It is revealed in CO 1031/4495 that the letter signed by the three political leaders was received by the Colonial Secretary on the morning of the 25th October 1963. Jagan therefore gave the momentum to Duncan Sandys Colonial Secretary who then moved to implement the US strategy to remove Jagan from political dominance by changing the electoral system. Burnham and D'Aguiar kept to the agenda that the US set for them and Jagan collapsed under the pressure exerted by Duncan Sandys. Jagan failed to know that Sandys was also under intense US pressure and was forced to capitulate to the US agenda. On the 31st October 1963 the US agenda attained hegemony over the British and the politics of British Guiana.

The issue then is not why Jagan signed the letter of abdication but the reality is that he was seduced by the white colonial overlord confirming his servility to his white colonial Massa. From 1953 to 1963 the white colonial Massa played Jagan convincing him that he was the political leader fit and able to lead Guyana to Independence and in return he was obligated to modify his Marxist-Leninist rhetoric and actions. They played this game with Jagan through two general elections, 1957 and 1961, and successive outbreaks of race violence to destroy Jagan on the 31st October 1963, a date that was strategically vital to the political interests of the Conservative Government of the day a date that owes its genesis to developments in British politics, US politics and ultimately political developments in British Guiana.

In October 1963 Alec Douglas Home replaced Harold Macmillan as Prime Minister of Britain. Alec Douglas Home was intimately involved in the ongoing war between successive US Presidents and Conservative British governments over the politics of Jagan and British Guiana. Alec Douglas Home drew a line under British ambivalence over Jagan and the politics of British Guiana. In October 1964 general elections were called and the Labour Party headed by Harold Wilson replaced the Conservative Party with a majority of 4 seats in the House of Commons.

A CIA Declassified file dated 6th December 1963 titled "Special Report Cross Currents in British Guiana" states:

> "The PPP, nevertheless, has gone quite far in trying to supplant private trading and distributing facilities in order to make the economy ever more dependent on bloc goods. During the strike, for example, the government imported and distributed fuel and food-stuffs from Cuba and the bloc and tried to curb private sales until these imports were sold. Another link to the bloc is Guyana Import Export (GIMPEX), a PPP firm which has become the colony's trading agency with the bloc as well as a channel for foreign Communist financial support of the party itself. Cuban funds, paid to GIMPEX, were loaned both to the government and the PPP's publishing firm. According to another report, funds for PPP salaries and expenses are funnelled to Janet Jagan from GIMPEX via this publishing company."

(Cross Currents in British Guiana December 1963)

A CIA Declassified file dated 20 November 1964 titled "Special Report British Guiana Approaches a Critical Election" states:

> "The PPP has a considerable capability to oppose the government with force and violence. In addition to the militants in its youth organisation, it also controls the so-called Guyana Liberation Army, which is cadred with Cuban-trained personnel. If the PPP elects to conduct a campaign of terror, the police may need backstopping from British troops more or less indefinitely."

(British Guiana Approaches a Critical Election 20 November 1964)

The critical change in the politics of British Guiana in 1963 and 1964 was Jagan's dance with the Cuban agenda since 1959 of engaging with the West. Jagan's embrace of revolutionary Cuba had then finally alienated the British ruling elite thereby shooting himself in the foot and Guyana in the head.

Declassified file CO 1035/173 contains reports from the Security Liaison Officer for British Guiana to MI5/ Security Intelligence Agency, London, England. The reports that are declassified give a glimpse of the covert war that was being waged in 1963-1964 in British Guiana between Cuban intelligence, the PPP and Jagan and MI5. What is of primary importance is the fact that the Security Liaison Officer (SLO) was based in Trinidad and Tobago and he visited British Guiana. At this time Trinidad and Tobago was an independent nation. This reality also indicates that the MI5 operation in Guiana was under deep cover and the Governor was on a need to know basis. Given the fact that under internal self government Janet Jagan was the Minister of Home Affairs responsible for internal security of the colony heightened the need for strict organisational integrity of the covert operation. The SLO reported to MI5 London and the Security Intelligence Adviser released what was cleared from the reports to the Colonial Office. It is highly likely that the SLO did not meet with the covert assets and operations in British Guiana his role was simply to visit British Guiana, meet with the Governor, the Commissioner of Police, the Head of Special Branch and the Ministry of Home Affairs. His was the public face of MI5 in British Guiana.

The extract from the SLO's letter of the 20th August 1963 and his visit to British Guiana states:

> "He mentioned, specifically, that he had received no information of any significance regarding the activities of Clinton Lloyd ADLUM, the Cuban Intelligence Office ostensibly representing ALIMPEK in Georgetown.

> On the other hand, Martin lost little time in explaining his own difficulties to me, he is short of well placed agents in the PPP, and is, in any case inhibited from directing his effort against the party from which the Government he is serving is drawn."

(CO 1035/173)

In August 1963 there is then a Cuban Intelligence Officer based in British Guiana placed in a structure that was created by the Jagan government to trade with Cuba and the Soviet Bloc. The Governor is in the dark about this Cuban Intelligence Officer because he is out of the loop and Martin the Head of Special Branch admits that Special Branch is also out of the loop. In 1963

Cuban Intelligence was the vassal of the Soviet KGB which meant that the Cuban intelligence officer was pursuing a KGB agenda in addition to Fidel Castro's agenda. The Castro brothers, Fidel and Raul at this time were clearly linked to the KGB. British Guiana in August 1963 was then a hot spot in the Cold War in the Caribbean. Jagan's blunder would then be his undoing when Alec Douglas Home became the Prime Minister of Britain in October 1963.

An extract from the SLO's report on his visit to British Guiana from 23-26 September 1963 states:

> "UF allegations of Moscow payments to the PPP

> Although the Police Investigation into allegations made by the United Force (UF) that the PPP was receiving funds from Moscow has not yet been completed, there seems to be no doubt that the bank documents which the UF cited as evidence of these payments are forgeries. The culprit is believed to be one Anne Abraham, a UF supporter who is a junior employee of Barclays Bank and the daughter of the Permanent Secretary to the Premier, and against whom the Police have made a holding charge of conspiracy to commit a seditious libel. Arising from this investigation, the Police obtained information on the basis of which searches were carried out at the house of Senator Ann Jardim, UF, and also at Peter D'Aguiar's office on the 13th and 18th September, where Thermofax copies were found of a number of documents, all of which, it has been proved, form part of a single file held in the Premier's office. Some of the documents involved, including one graded SECRET, emanated from the Governor's office, but these were properly on the Premier's file and there is no question of the Governor's office being concerned in the leakage. It had not been decided before I left British Guiana whether D'Aguiar would be charged under the Official Secrets Acts, but it seems likely that this will be done shortly."

(CO 1035/173)

Clearly this was an attempt to knock D'Aguiar out of political contention thereby derailing the US agenda to remove Jagan. Forged documents that were designed to cause panic and chaos were a specialty tool of the KGB in the prosecution of the Cold War. The KGB via the Cubans and other assets in British Guiana passed the forged documents knowing fully well that undisciplined D'Aguiar would go public with them without first passing them to his US covert minder. The forged documents were passed to D'Aguiar and the police were informed of this with the intention to have D'Aguiar charged with a felony in turn implicating the Permanent Secretary and his daughter destroying his credibility and integrity as a civil servant providing material for the PPP propaganda machine. Jagan was then no victim of US imperialism but a willing and active participant in a Cold War battleground. The US was then forced by these actions to pre-empt a conviction of D'Aguiar before the general elections in 1964. The said Permanent Secretary to the Premier, Arthur Abraham, was subsequently moved to the Ministry of Works and Hydraulics. Arthur Abraham was also Secretary to the Governor of the colony Ralph Grey. Arthur Abraham was killed along with some of his children when his home was bombed.

An extract from the report of the SLO on his visit to British Guiana from the 24-29 August 1964 states:

"POLICE

5 It is difficult to judge how serious the consequences may be of the discovery by the Police of a P.N.C. terrorist network, responsible for recent bomb outrages in Georgetown, and the maltreatment during interrogation by the Police of a key figure in the network, one Emmanuel FAIRBAIRN, who has been charged with the murder of Michael FORDE (killed in the bomb attack on PPP headquarters) and in whose house a considerable quantity of arms, ammunition and explosives was found, at the beginning of August.

On the instructions of the Governor, who was not informed of what had been going on until some days after FAIRBAIRN'S interrogation, the Commissioner appointed his Deputy and a Superintendent to enquire into the allegations that FAIRBAIRN had been maltreated."

(CO 1035/173)

From the report it is clear that the Police had their own agendas and the Governor was cut out of the loop. Were the expatriate officers in charge of the Police and Special Branch in control of these two bodies? It is apparent that the Governor, the Commissioner of Police and the Head of Special Branch were cut out of the loop, not in control or were claiming plausible denial. In all three realities the beating put down on Fairbairn during his interrogation was an attempt to implicate Burnham as being an active part of a terrorist network thereby damaging his political relevance if not destroying it. Again this was an action seeking to derail the US agenda to destroy Jagan's hold on state power on the path to Independence for British Guiana. The SLO continues:

"There can be little doubt that BURNHAM is seriously perturbed by all this, for he cannot be sure how much those arrested and detained have disclosed and how far they may have implicated him."

(CO 1035/173)

For the SLO Burnham is then involved in the terrorist network and is now at risk of being publicly implicated. Burnham is clearly not a British asset as the language of the SLO conjures up images of joy in Burnham's apprehension with the threat of public disclosure of his terrorist acts. This is another instance of the indiscipline of Burnham and the price the US paid for its agenda having to once again intervene and clean up after him. This meant that individuals in the structures were rewarded handsomely to make the problem go away before the general elections of 1964. The SLO continues:

"8. I saw Major Mineef, M.I.O., on the last day of my visit and I have arranged with the Army and Police that he should go over to Paramaribo as soon as possible to discuss with my Dutch liaison contact, Major Maoville, the tactical use of information he gave me about the illegal entry of arms into British Guiana from Suriname."

(CO 1035/173)

It is noteworthy that reports from the SLO on his visits to British Guiana made for the period September 1964 to September 1965 are not declassified. The period leading up to the 1964 elections and thereafter until 1965 are locked up and I expect for a very long time to come. This is the most potent indication of the intensity of the cold war that raged in British Guiana in this period. All the players were active in Guyana the KGB, the DGI of Cuba, various US covert agencies one of which was the CIA and MI5 of Britain and Venezuelan intelligence. In the reality of this intense covert war Jagan, Burnham and D'Aguiar and the Governor were then the public faces of the covert war but they were in the actual prosecution of the cold war second string players, the B team. The final extract from the file is from a report by the SLO on his visit to British Guiana from 18th to 22nd October 1965. In this report Sonny Ramphal Attorney General in the PNC/UF coalition government headed by Burnham is again requesting a SLO be present in Guyana on a full time basis rather than visiting from Trinidad. MI5 is not supportive of Ramphal's request. The SLO in his report on the meeting he had with Ramphal reported on Ramphal's meeting with Barrow of Barbados as follows:

"He told me, first of all, of the C.F.T.A. meeting attended by Barrow, Barbados, Bird, Antigua, and an observer from St.Vincent in addition to the British Guiana team. C.F.T.A. had started as a political stunt to do down Trinidad (both Burnham and Barrow detested Williams) and now the problem was to turn it into a workable proposition. The Barbados team had done their homework and nearly managed to push through a basis of agreement highly favourable to Barbados, but inimical to British Guiana's interests.

Barrow was determined to use the veto provided for in the draft agreement to prevent Trinidad from joining C.F.T.A., but Ramphal felt that, if the issue ever arose, British Guiana, could, if it wished, force Barrow to give way."

(CO 1035/173)

So much for Caribbean unity and integration at its finest.

Declassified file CO 1035/194 reveals the existence of the PPP Accabre College and the fact that there was an intelligence asset/ assets present in the college. The undated report was created from various intelligence reports. The first course put on at the college was held from 21st January 1963 to 8 March 1963. The cover for the College was the training of agricultural experts and the education of the members of the Progressive Youth Organisation (PYO) of the PPP. The College was located at Success, East Coast, Demerara. The principal of the College was George David. The intake of students for the first course was 25 students, five were female and eight were Africans. Paid up membership in the PPP and PPP satellite organisations was compulsory to be considered for entry into the College. Janet Jagan gave the opening address and the list of visiting lecturers to the College during the first three weeks of the course were: Dr. and Mrs. Jagan, Brindley and Mrs. Benn, Kelshall of Trinidad, Bhagwan, Felix Mentore, Laurence Mann, George Bowman, Chase, L.S.H. Singh, Victor Downer and Chandisingh. The report also indicated the presence of four white men who taught at the college but presented no information on the identity of them. The Special Branch would name the four white men in a report dated 6th April 1963 as follows: Phillip Reno of the USA who arrived in the colony on the 11th January 1963; Una Godrey and Sam Muizac of the USA who arrived in the colony on the 26th January 1963; Craig Stephen Vincent of the USA who arrived in the colony on the 2nd March 1963 and Douglas H. Vincent of the USA who arrived in the colony on the 9th March 1963. The Special Branch was informed by a source in the US Consulate that the four named US citizens were members of the US Communist Party.

Governor Ralph Grey in a letter to R.W. Piper of the Colonial Office dated 8th April 1963 would state:

> "My attention having been drawn to certain named Americans whose curious activities were mentioned in the 'Daily Chronicle', I asked about them. It seems that all four are members of the US Communist Party and that two of them have been here since January! Why was I not told of this earlier I just cannot think! It maybe that these are the 'Europeans' mentioned in the Accabre College report."

(CO 1035/194)

The Governor and Special Branch are out of the intelligence loop and on a need to know basis. Piper replies to the letter of 8th April 1963 stating:

> "Martin went on to point out that the British Guiana Special Branch was not intended to be more than (in your own words) a good Special Branch from the point of view of a reputable government of British Guiana, and to suggest that we look to other sources for more delicate intelligence."

(CO 1035/194)

Morton is the MI5 Security Intelligence Adviser (SIA) for British Guiana. Morton is telling the Governor do not go where he has no clearance to go. The Governor has then to depend on the SLO for British Guiana to inform him on what he the Governor needs to know. This is then a most potent indicator of the intensity of the covert war in the colony in 1963.

The prime lesson of this historical event is the fact that Jagan was in fact a part of the cold war engagement raging in the colony in 1963. Jagan was no victim he was an operative in the war and he was doing everything in his power to win this cold war engagement utilising any and all assets supplied by the Soviet Bloc and Cuba. Jagan fought a war and he lost, it was that simple, and he died never publicly admitting that he fought a cold war and to this day the PPP continues to peddle the discourse of victimhood at the hands of US imperialism. Jagan fought a cold war engagement that he could not win. He was then used by the KGB and the Cubans and Guyana paid for it. Power is always amoral. The analysis of historical events via notions of morality and right and wrong is a discourse of power.

The Governor of British Guiana in a letter dated 15th August 1963 states:

"In your letter of July 30, you asked that I keep you posted about the Cubans who came in the tanker 'Cuba' and did not leave when the others did.

But what I am told amounts to very little-and certainly not as much as would justify tying up eight policemen on a surveillance team. I find it hard to believe that these men could stay so many weeks in a strange country and do so little. The three pilots want to the P.Y.O. rally at Wakenaam last weekend and had not returned when I asked about them yesterday. But there must be more to them than has so far emerged from Police reports."

(CO 1035/194)

This is another instance in the covert war of 1963 in the colony of British Guiana in this case Cuban tourists who attended a PPP rally.

A letter by Fenton Ramsahoye then Attorney General dated 29th April 1964 to the Commissioner of Police states:

"With respect to the raids which culminated in the finding of arms and ammunition at Triumph East Coast, Demerara, I shall be grateful if you will answer the following questions for me:-

1.What are the manes of the members of the Force who found the items?

2.When were the items actually found?

3.If the items were found on different occasions, what items were found each time?

4.If the arms and ammunition were recovered as a result of information received, when was the information received?"

The Deputy Commissioner of Police replied on the 30th April 1964 as follows:

"1.It is not in the public interest to disclose the manes of the members of the Force concerned.

2.During the weekend 24th-26th April, 1964.

3.It is not in the public interest to provide this detail.

4.The information was received over a period of time and inquiries and investigations over some three weeks resulted in the finding of these arms and ammunition."

(C) 1035/194)

Ramsahoye's questions as an Acting Minister of Home Affairs are strange if the US position that the arms cache belonged to the PPP's PYO is not considered. Why does a Minister of Home Affairs want to know the names of the police personnel who discovered the arms cache and the nature and timing of the information that alerted the police to the arms cache. The PPP Minister was looking to ferret out a police informer or a covert asset of the Americans, the British or both within the PYO. The PPP Minister wanted the names of the police officers to mark, monitor and surveil these officers hoping to find the leak or to exact revenge upon them in some form. The questions Ramsahoye posed were an attempt to prosecute the covert war using the state against the enemies of the PPP.

An extract from the minutes of a meeting of the Joint Intelligence Committee (JIC) on the 9th July 1964 states:

> "While the general rate of incidents remained steady, a significant development was the increased use of firearms and explosives. Some 9-10, no licensed shotguns were known to exist, mainly in Indian hands: a few automatic weapons had been found by the security authorities and it was thought that they had come from Cuba or Venezuela. Although there was no proof, it seemed probable that many of the incidents were not spontaneous, but were the result of deliberate action, particularly by Dr. Jagan's party, for political motives."

(CO 1035/194)

There is no proof to implicate the PPP in deliberate personal attacks of a racial or non racial nature. The probable evidence of activities to wage a covert war by Jagan and the PPP is legion.

Colonel A.W. Cowper of the Defence Intelligence Staff visited the colony from 29th June 1964 to 1st July 1964 and reported as follows:

> "5.Incidents A steady rate of incidents between Africans and Indians continues principally in the coastal strips of WCD and ECD and in the vicinity of the bauxite mine at Mackenzie. The incidents are mainly murder by shooting or slashing with knives, setting fire to houses, the throwing of petrol bombs and the use of homemade explosives. Increasing use is being made of shotguns. During the four months up to mid-June some 1300 incidents had taken place. By 1 July there had been more than 60 murders.
>
> 8. There is no firm evidence available that terrorism is being organised by political leaders but it is believed that the ruling

Indian-dominated People's Progressive Party (PPP) under Jagan is generating unrest through its allied Pioneer Youth Organisation (PYO) in order to:-

a. Focus international attention on British Guiana in support of anti-colonialism.

b. Delay the proposed elections under the popular Proportional Representation system.

c. Show that the recent arrests of political leaders have not reduced terrorism and that such terrorism is therefore 'spontaneous'.

21. Although some useful results are being produced in SB headquarters, there is no doubt that Special Branch is failing in the task of producing effective information on the direction and organisation behind the present waves of terrorism. Neither is information being produced on which Security Force operations can be mounted against the terrorists and arsonists. Valuable opportunities are being lost by the inability of Special Branch to carry out prompt and effective interrogation of suspects and arrested persons."

(CO 1035/195)

From the declassified files it is apparent that the overt British colonial state did not have a clue as to what was driving the racial violence in the run up to the 1964 general elections. The PPP government sought to relentlessly block attempts to expand Special Branch's human capacity through the importation of British officers. The Governor of the Colony and the Colonial Office ensured that Special Branch was inadequate to the task at hand with logistic blockades to attempts to fill the human intelligence void. MI5 did not want Special Branch polluting the covert waters of the colony and indicated this to both the Governor of the colony and the Colonial Office. The military force to the colony was then left out in the cold as their presence was political to pressure Jagan to accept the reality that a general election under proportional representation in 1964 was a given. The racial violence was then irrelevant in fact it was in Britain's favour as long as British colonial personnel were not targeted. The covert war between the PPP, its allies, the US and Britain now drove the daily politics of the colony.

On the 10th July 1964 the Garrison Commander for British Guiana sent a signal to the Commander British forces Caribbean area. The signal states:

"1. The general security situation since my last report has remained unchanged. It is usually the case that week ends are disturbed and mid week quieter. Tension is very high in the coastal area, there is much misery and fear.

4.Amongst negro population much political capital is being made that launch explosion was PPP inspired. There is no direct evidence of this and there is theory that explosives were on launch when leaving Georgetown and being moved to Mackenzie for African use in bombs for industrial sabotage. Reports indicate groups of Africans from Mackenzie coming North at week end to stir up trouble Georgetown and Buxton. Some dead come from latter place."

(CO 1035/195)

The garrison commander in British Guiana simply does not know who bombed the ferry and the theory he reports is seriously flawed. Explosives hidden on the ferry in order to attack US interests in the bauxite mines point to Jagan and his allies not the allies of the US. Then there is the possibility of racist renegade interests on both sides. For the explosives to explode on their own, spontaneous combustion, either they were so degraded to do so or were badly constituted with detonators in place. The nature of the blast that destroyed the ferry does not support this position. It is apparent that the British Guiana Garrison commander does not have a clue as to what went down. Clearly the bombing of Freedom House, GIMPEX and the ferry are linked. The Sun Chapman was bombed on the 6th July 1964.

Major Nicholson as head of the military interrogation team visited British Guiana. Nicholson was in the colony from 11th July to 12th August 1964. During his stay in the colony 30 persons were interrogated and a report on the visit states:

"…. but had been unable to elicit any information giving an insight into the PYO Organisation."

(CO 1035/195)

Nicholson failed to collect the intelligence to finger the PYO. The question arises of the quality of the persons interrogated and hence the effectiveness of the sweeps that detained said persons. Sweeps meant to send messages to political actors and unsupported by intelligence would pick up an operative of quality haphazardly and by chance. Again further proof that there was no desire to engage with the covert war and its covert assets.

Fairbain was interrogated by Nicholson and the report states:

"During the interrogation by Major Nicholson, Fairbain confessed to being responsible for placing the bomb under Freedom House.

He also gave the names of the two people responsible for the bomb at GIMPEX."

(CO 1035/195)

What actions are launched as a result of the Fairbain confession are not revealed in the files. In fact in these files specific reports are expunged, destroyed even, In 2008 the covert war in the colony remains an official secret confirming that there was in fact a covert war in the colony.

A report dated 11th August 1964 by the military intelligence officer G1 states:

> "We still have a fair amount of explosives about and there have been odd attempts at rather amateurish bomb attacks on houses in the area. We are continuing to round up illegal arms and getting a fair amount of information to help us. At the same time we are collecting intelligence on possible terrorist aims and hope to carry out one or two operations in the near future."

(CO 1035/195)

In the aftermath of the bombings of the Sun Chapman, Freedom House and GIMPEX the availability of intelligence and assaults on terrorist activities indicate a changed operational reality. The covert war has now switched to enabling general elections in 1964. The messages have been sent Jagan and his enemies have surrendered to the hegemony of the US. The British overt state is now in play as the means to have a change of government via credible general elections must happen in 1964 by any means necessary.

The report of the G1 Officer for the colony states:

> "and it is even more noticeable that although the East Indian population in general seems to be very anxious that the present quiet period should continue, the African population are confident and almost arrogant, mainly due, I think, to the fact that the Indians have recently had their arms withdrawn. This withdrawal of arms, the formation of the Home Guards, the end of the sugar strike and a recent reward scheme which has been announced with fairly generous rewards for passage of information, all help in getting to grips with the IS situation."

(CO 1035/195)

Three bombings between July and early August 1964 have resulted in the disarming of a race, the surrender of its political leadership, the end of terrorist acts and the hunting down of recalcitrant mavericks bent on prosecuting a race war inimical to the interests of the US and Britain. From the files it is apparent that the strategy applied overtly and covertly was towards the surrender of a race and the throttling of its political leadership. The abiding lesson was not the ways and means utilised to achieve said outcome but the manner in which the race targeted aided and abetted this strategy and enabled the hegemony of the agenda.

The lesson of the entire engagement is the inherent flaw of a strategy that attempted to mask the quest for racist Indo-Guyanese hegemony with Marxist-Leninist clothes at the height of the Cold War in the Caribbean. The masses of Guyana saw the drive for Indian hegemony over the state and reacted to this drive given their race persuasion. Jagan then gave Burnham a pressing reason to leave the PPP and an excuse for leaving the PPP. Jagan without Burnham lost the multi racial base of the PPP as there was no African leader of the PPP able to challenge Burnham's leadership of the African masses now opposed to the PPP. The PPP was then destined to be alienated from Georgetown and Mackenzie/Wismar with Buxton becoming the heart of African engagement with the PPP for hegemony over the Guyanese state. The East and West coasts of Demerara would in this scenario become the battlegrounds in which the tit for tat of race war manifested itself in a futile challenge to PPP hegemony in these regions of Guyana. These areas would become the heart of PPP engagement with the African support base of the PNC.

Indo Guyanese in a majority position then failed miserably to translate this majority into domination of the state in Guyana in the post 1964 scenario. This was the direct result of the failure of Jagan to understand the realities that impacted his quest for hegemony and to respond to said realities in a strategic manner. There was then a pressing need to abandon a failed worldview and hold on to power by any means necessary. Force Burnham to quit the PPP on the sole ground of his insatiable desire for personal aggrandisement. Marginalise D'Aguiar as an arch conservative that does not want independence for Guyana. Have both the Americans and the British destroy Burnham for you. The British and Americans cared little about racist Indian hegemony in Guyana and PPP hegemony for as long as it was devoid of Marxist-Leninist taint. Jagan would continue to use the discourse of Indian racist hegemony and Marxist-Leninist discourse interchangeably as the weapons of choice in the political wars of Guyana. For this failure of strategy by Jagan, Guyana paid the ultimate price. Jagan refused to abandon Marxist-Leninist discourse and gambled on retention of power because he believed that Marxist- Leninist methodology was the means to make him great, the father of the modern, developed Guyanese nation. To abandon Marxist- Leninist discourse would be to abandon his means to immortality and greatness. He lived in constant hope that he would be given the means to prove his greatness and he would be given the opportunity once again in the aftermath of the collapse of the Soviet Union. This was the only crisis of his worldview and he solved this by dying.

Declassified file CO 968/750 deals with the deployment of the British military in British Guiana. A report dated April 1962 states:

"2.The TOP SECRET Security Plan covers all foreseeable emergencies which might arise in BRITISH GUIANA. The plan covers the breakdown in one or more services. This plan has been limited in distribution to H.E Governor, War Office, 1E Anglian and 2nd Infantry Brigade.

16 February

7 a.The riots were in fact settled by the use of 1 Rifle Company and the arrival of R.N.Frigates. No doubt the arrival and rumours of arrival of reinforcements did much to settle the town. The arson was obviously planned and was not as a result of a sudden decision.

b.Looting

In general the looting was not malicious and people who looted are normally law abiding people. The temptation, however was too great and in many cases goods were given away by the shop owners themselves. There were rumours that some people set fire to their own shops."

"and there are I believe a number of serving Policemen who should be dismissed as a result of inefficiency during the riots. Some of the administrative staff of the Police force threatened to strike during the riots and had to be addressed by the Commissioner of Police. Lastly, the Police were fired on by the crowd and this may have a tendency to weaken the morale of the Police during the next riot."

"11.The reinforcements for the increase in the Police force should be Indian. The African, unfortunately, despises people of small stature and the present high standards for the Police of 5'8" cannot be achieved by many Indians. The Commissioner of Police told me that a small Indian could not keep control in the town."

"17.a.It will be seen that the PPP obtained their majority on a racial vote and under the present system of encouraging racial support, the PPP must stay in power unless proportional representation is accepted, PPP are unlikely to sponsor this."

"UF

They have made a great effort to overthrow the Government and failed, and I believe have shot their bolt. However, there are desperate elements in the Party who might do anything to achieve continuation of Colonial rule."

(CO 968/750)

The report was written by K.R.S. Trevor, Brigadier Commander 2 Inf. Brigade GP. Trevor reveals the existence of a top secret military plan to handle any contingencies in British Guiana but Trevor does not list the threats that the military plan was formulated to address. Trevor describes the riots of 16 February 1962 and the apparent ease with which they were quelled with the intervention of the British military. Moreover Trevor insists that it was the political party the United Force in opposition to the ruling PPP that was responsible for the riots in an attempt to overthrow the then government. Trevor also indicated the commonality of the position amongst British officials that the electoral system has to be changed in order to remove the PPP from power via general elections. In addition, Trevor revealed the fact that the Police force was not only understaffed, lacking in leadership and in need of purging but that it was now politicised and racially polarised. Trevor calls for a deliberate recruitment policy of recruiting Indo Guyanese to the Police force to offset the dominance of the Afro Guyanese. Given the propensity for racial violence Trevor describes then a minefield.

In Appendix B to the report of the Brigadier Commander, Trevor states:

> "It is particularly important to watch for signs of pronounced animosity between Africans and Indians particularly in country areas where Indians predominate, and in areas where African and Indian villages are in close proximity to each other and where racial feelings is liable to erupt on a local level, subsequently spreading to other districts.
>
> The East Bank Demerara, East Coast Demerara and Coventry areas are danger spots. The Indians in these areas are fanatical supporters of the PPP and or Dr. Jagan and any attempt at violence towards him or indeed to any of the PPP's Ministers would provoke an immediate reaction."

(CO 968/750)

Trevor therefore expects that the torrent of racial violence would flow from the rural areas dominated by Indo Guyanese. The riots of 1962 were confined to Georgetown while these said Indo dominated rural areas remained inactive. Trevor is then expecting further assaults on the PPP Government and an Indo Guyanese backlash expressed via heightened race war.

In a telegram dated 8th May 1963 the Governor of British Guiana reports to the Secretary of State as follows.

> "Premier immediately advised me to declare State of Emergency tonight. For mechanical rather than tactical reasons I was able to persuade him to defer it until tomorrow.
>
> 3.Premier has asked that Whirlwind brought close to Georgetown forthwith. With support of Commissioner and Garrison Commander I ask that this be done."

(CO 968/750)

By May 1963 the cycle of 1962 had returned but the lesson of May 1963 is the support the Governor and the colonial military apparatus is affording Cheddi Jagan of the PPP. It is apparent that the military agenda was the retention of British hegemony and was not formulated to destabilise the PPP government thereby fomenting social instability that would be inevitably expressed in race war. The British would deal with the Jagan political juggernaut by simply changing the electoral system and with the military assets of the British colonial empire deployed and active in the colony Jagan simply had no choice but to acquiesce. Jagan in his call for a State of Emergency in May 1963 strengthened the hand of the British to impose a settlement on the electoral system in October 1963. The ultimate question then is whether US destabilisation was the means used to precipitate the British military intervention from 1962 onwards? The picture that is emerging is much more complex than this simplistic explanation.

The Governor of British Guiana by way of a telegram via the Ministry of Defence dated 5th June 1963 informs the Secretary of State as follows:

> "Still generally quiet but still very tense everywhere. There has been a worsening of inter-racial feeling on West Coast Demerara with African and Indians drawing apart ready for battle even though Police AND Coldstream Platoon have so far kept the battle from being joined.
>
> 2.Georgetown is quiet. Coldstream patrolling again this evening. Chief Justice has told Commissioner of Police that incidents reported in paragraph 2 of my telegram No.277 were politically

directed by Opposition in an endeavour to bring administration of justice to a halt.

5.Mine Workers Union at Mackenzie have withdrawn skeleton staff from essential services. Company urgently requested armed guard for senior staff operating station. Police and small company (50) of BGVF embodied yesterday will be busy on both sides of river where there were some incendiarism attempted last night and 2 shops looted. 1 Officer and 9 other ranks of Coldstream have therefore been despatched by road, cause of withdrawal of skeleton staff seems to be local and due to second eleven in Union attempting to show their paces while first eleven are at the TUC Congress in Georgetown.

6.Unfortunately Robert Willis has come entirely unstuck with BG TUC largely due to influence of Burnham. Congress has today vilified him as a Communist determined only to aid Jagan and after abusing British TUC they have demanded his recall.

7.Expectations that Secretary of State will visit Georgetown has caused both Government and TUC to harden respective attitudes. Burnham seems determined to produce as chaotic a state of affairs as possible for Mr. Sandy's edification. Willis is bitter against him. Earlier Mr. Sandy's can come the better.

9.First Shell barge with replenishment stocks berths at Ramsburg tonight. Second is probably entering harbour tonight. On Ministerial advice I have had to make order under Trade Ordinance 1958 imposing import control of petroleum products. This can only be to protect Governments' Cuban Trade but thought it better to leave Oil Companies to make fuss than to try to talk with my Ministers out of it.

11.GAWU is making much inroads in MPCA membership that sugar producers may have to consider which Union they are to recognise in future."

(CO 968/750)

The telegram indicates the nature and terrain of the war against the then PPP Government that was expressed on the ground as race war in a battle for racist hegemony in a British colony, lunacy at its most potent. The PPP dominated union the GAWU is challenging the hegemony of the MPCA in the sugar belt of the colony. The MPCA is led by an Indo-Guyanese opposed to Jagan but the war for hegemony would be expressed manifestly as an

Indo-Afro race war on the ground. In the face of union activism against his government which commenced in 1962 Jagan would move to fracture his most active and effective opposition by challenging the MPCA for control of his natural voter base: the Indo-Guyanese of the cane belt.

Political actions for and against the PPP government in the Guyanese context were interpreted on the basis of racist hegemony nothing else and could not be interpreted any other way given the racist social order hence the salient relevance of Fanon and not Marx to understanding the Guyanese social order in 1963. What must be noted in the telegram is the level of intensity and racist aggression that was being manifested in Mackenzie the primary urban center of the bauxite belt. The Governor was duty bound to protect the expatriate lives and the property of the multinational corporation that controlled the bauxite industry at that time. The inadequacy of the police at hand led to the placement of 50 British Guyana Volunteer Force personnel as the base of policing in Mackenzie. It is apparent in the said telegram that Mackenzie was already a flashpoint in the race war of 1963 and the Indo Guyanese minority in Mackenzie were already under racist attack.

The British Guyana Trade Union Congress was in 1963 leading the charge against the PPP Government and the Governor insists that Burnham was calling the shots. Furthermore the PPP was willingly involved in the war for racist hegemony in a British colony. The PPP unlike the discourse of Indo victimhood propagated since 1964 were prosecuting a war that intensified the nature of the engagement with them to the point where their political defeat became easier. The PPP strategies adopted in this war they prosecuted did not match the reality of the topography of the war. This war was being fought in a British colony where the British Governor ruled supreme backed up by a British military presence that British hegemony was rooted in and by extension unchallenged. The PPP is then importing fuel from Cuba against the express wishes of the multi national energy companies that monopolise fuel supplies and distribution in the colony and expects the British police and military to protect said fuel. This is lunacy at its highest only possible in the schizophrenic mind of the colonised.

R.W. Piper in writing to Thomas dated 13th June 1963 states:

> "The military are called in to aid the civil power only when the police cannot cope. The Governor says (personal No.214) that Jagan is trying to get deterrent and repressive action by the military and quite probably unjustified shooting that Garrison Commander very properly would not give. The Americans have been stressing the need for an early policy decision and have been prophesying violence. I suspect that they are behind the course of

events over recent days and have been advising the TUC to behave disorderly so as to press HM Government to an early decision. So far the police have maintained control. The army have not been called upon to maintain law and order, although military patrols were arranged last night."

(CO 968/750)

Piper reveals the British rules of engagement which meant that the first line of defence was the colonial police structure both the Police force and the Volunteer force. When this first line collapses leading to a clear and present danger to British hegemony then the British military intervenes as a strike force towards reinserting the police structure. Piper is also of the view that the Americans are engaged in covert activity through the TUC to force the British to make a decision on the methodology to be utilised to get rid of the PPP as the dominant political force in Guyanese politics in 1963. There is then an Anglo-American power play in the mix and this impacts the response of the British to events on the ground rendering power relations and strategies even more complex and at times arcane and brazenly ineffective.

A telegram to the Secretary of State from the Governor via the Ministry of Defence dated 3rd July 1963 states:

"Since my SITREP275 was despatched there have been two serious incidents and several minor incidents on East Coast.

2.Disorderly crowds in Georgetown this afternoon. Some invaded law courts and had to be dispersed with tear-smoke. Crowds of African youth beat an Indian to death. Many personal assaults and robberies. 47 injured reported to hospitals. 15 arrests. This clutching at excuses for not having a meeting designed to end an agonising inter-racial situation is unhappy and suggests that Burnham may still be hoping for violence to work some good for his cause if he can avoid being openly associated with it."

(CO 968/750)

In this telegram both the East Coast Demerara and Georgetown burn hot simultaneously necessitating the British military to intervene in the East Coast allowing the police contingent in Georgetown to be bolstered. Two flash points two different agendas, strategies and operatives one pro PPP the other anti PPP. The Governor has expressed openly Burnham's role in precipitating violence but the obvious is not stated that it is a war for hegemony prosecuted via the instrument of racist terror and violence.

By way of a telegram dated 3rd July 1963 the Chief of Defence Staff states:

> "Situation in British Guiana is deteriorating. If, as now seems likely, trouble spreads on East Coast and incidents develop on West Coast. Governor, British Guiana considers that reinforcements will be needed immediately."

(CO 968/750)

A telegram to the Secretary of State from the Governor dated 5th July 1963 states:

> "2.Prospects of early solution to industrial problem are dim. But even when we have got that settled we shall have continued tension for a long time and although it is unsatisfactory to use soldiers in a Police role we shall have to give our Police a rest soon and we have no quick means of expanding the Force.

(CO 968/750)

When faced with a war for racist hegemony the Governor recognises the major limitation of the Police force. The immediate solution therefore is to increase the size of the British military in the colony and to expand the interventions of the military into the terrain of race war and terrorism.

A telegram dated 5th July 1963 from the Governor to the Secretary of State recognises the geographic expansion of the race war in July 1963. The Governor states:

> "having regard to prevalence of incidents of violence in both East and West Demerara and now in Mackenzie area, as well as in the city of Georgetown, and to the fact that British Guiana Police Force have been at full stretch for many weeks, there are sound military reasons for requesting the despatch of the remainder of second battalion Green Jackets."

(CO 968/750)

Questions of the efficacy of the Police are then paramount. What must be noted is that the Police as created to serve British hegemony and it was deliberately underdeveloped, politicised and made to serve a racist agenda. In the run up to independence the Police was called upon to play a role it was never designed for, hence the handwringing.

A telegram dated 6th July 1963 from the CBFCA to the Ministry of Defence for specifically the Chiefs of Defence Staff states:

"I would however stress most strongly the urgent need to strengthen the police. Troops are being used constantly on patrol and policing duties largely because of inadequacies in the police force beyond the control of excellent commissioner. Even an additional 20 good officers sent quickly provided that this was associated with an extension of local recruits to broaden the racial base of the police in line with your policy for the security forces after independence, could have a major effect. Without such action the force faces a serious risk of increasing racial partiality and subsequent demoralisation such as would immediately complicate an eventual return to normal and the disengagement of military forces."

(CO 968/750)

Prophetic words. The immediate and sole agenda was the removal of the PPP from power and in this scenario the structures of the politicised, racist police force served this agenda. The racist agenda of Burnham and the PNC was handed a gift by the colonial Massa of a police force that continued serving racist hegemony after independence.

A telegram dated 8th July 1963 from the Force British Guiana to the War Office states:

"1. Situation. General Situation quiet.

Isolated incidents ECD and Rose Hall. Picketing at Mackenzie prevented return to work. Reports of possible arms movement in ECD tonight. Majority of workers returned to work."

(CO 968/750)

A telegram from Force British Guiana to the War Office dated 17th July 1963 states:

"Sit. A. 350 workers from Albion Sugar Estate on strike over incentive pay. Some picketing. Otherwise NTR. Extensive patrolling continues."

(CO 968/750)

A telegram from the Force British Guiana to the War Office dated 18th July 1963 states:

"1. Situation. Generally quiet. Industrial strife at LBI when 200 field workers refused to work after pay argument. Expect return tomorrow. At Albion 820 workers withdrew membership of MPCA. Some number took up menacing attitude at 1100 local time and is still there. Shift due at 1400 local time did not report. One platoon is standing by.

1. Otherwise NTR."

(CO 968/750)

A Telegram dated 20ᵗʰ July 1963 from Force British Guiana to the War Office states:

> "1.Situation. ECD. Six fields of sugar cane burnt at LBI night 19/20 July. Two wooden bridges were destroyed, with firm evidence of sabotage to prevent fire-fighters reaching the fire.
>
> 2.Berbice strike at Albion continues.
>
> 3.Otherwise no change from pervious SITREP."

(CO 968/750)

The sections quoted from Situation Reports above indicate the level of engagement in the cane belt, the heartland of PPP voter support. In addition developments in this rural cane growing economy were closely monitored by the British military and the application of British military resources was the highest outside of Georgetown.

In a document dated 23ʳᵈ July 1963 the Governor of British Guiana made the following comments:

> "6.There were inter-racial incidents on the West Coast of Demerara on July 8, 9 and 10 and extensive damage was done to African provision farms on July 13 (for which retaliation may be expected in due course). On July 9/10, there were deliberate explosions on East Bank, Demerara, and at Bartica. There were anti-personnel bomb incidents on July 12 and 13 (including, on July 13, one in which an Indian killed himself when attempting to throw an Army-type grenade at the house of a political opponent). There was then a cessation of violence for a week. On July 31 there were four dynamite explosions at the Rice Marketing Board Wharf, where a Russian ship was discharging. Since then there have been no further serious incidents, inter- racial tension is reported to be easing, and a series of strikes on the sugar estates has been ended, although industrial trouble still threatens at the Rice Marketing Board. On purely military grounds, therefore, the situation may well be such that the Battalion of reinforcements could be withdrawn and with it the justification for the Brigade Headquarters would disappear."

(CO 968/750)

Brigadier Trevor wrote an assessment of the situation in British Guiana dated 23rd July 1963 stating as follows:

> "b.Possible trouble areas based on the present situation and in the light of past experiences are as follows:-
>
> Georgetown, Atkinson and Mackenzie, East Coast and Berbice: LBI, Blairmont, Rose Hall West Coast: La Grange, Leonora, Uitvluigt.
>
> (1)The trouble areas can be divided into four i.e. (a)Georgetown (b)Atkinson and Mackenzie (c)East Coast and Berbice (d)West Coast.
>
> (2)These areas have the following numbers of troops at the present time:-
>
> (a)Georgetown 7 platoons
>
> (b)Atkinson and Mackenzie 4 platoons
>
> (c)East Coast and Berbice 2 platoons
>
> (d)West Coast 1 platoon"

(CO 968/750)

The reports of both the Governor and the Brigadier indicate two operational theatres of the insurgency Georgetown and Demerara/ Berbice. Both areas are the preserves of the anti PPP and pro PPP forces respectively and are dominated by specific race groups. The Afro Guyanese dominated Georgetown and the Indo Guyanese dominated Demerara and Berbice. It is then an organised insurgency in a battle for racist hegemony with the prime target being not the British colonial overlord but Afro and Indo Guyanese and primarily the PPP government headed by Cheddi Jagan.

A telegram from Force British Guiana dated 30th July 1963 to the War Office states:

> "1.Mackenzie. Seven attempts at arson occurred between 300345Z and 300700Z on both sides of river Demerara at Mackenzie and Wismar. All were on Indian houses. Only slight damage done."

(CO 968/750)

By the 30th July 1963 it was obvious that a new front in the racist insurgency was being opened at Mackenzie/ Wismar. The attacks were on

Indo-Guyanese, the race minority in the area, on both sides of the Demerara River stretching an already limited British military presence in the area. This was cold, calculated terrorism exploiting a minority in difficult terrain with the smallest British military contingent in the entire colony. The message sent was clear but did the British military respond to the threat?

In a telegram dated 9th August 1963 the Ministry of Defence gave advance information to the CBFCA as follows:

> "The Chiefs of Staff today considered reference and decided that the present strength of the garrison in British Guiana should be maintained. It is expected that this will be for at least another 6 to 9 months."

(CO 968/750)

This was a decision that was made contrary to the position of the Governor and the Brigadier who both called for a reduction of the British military contingent. It is apparent that the course of action the Secretary of State for the colonies would adopt in the constitution consultation in October 1963 was already set. The military was to keep its deployed strength in response to the backlash expected from the PPP.

A telegram dated 11th August 1963 from the Governor to the Secretary of State states:

> "Sitrep. All quiet save for damage to an Indian shop in Wismar (opposite Mackenzie) by Molotov cocktail. This may have been no more than Saturday-night hooliganism but Ministers are perturbed about the Mackenzie area and Commissioner of Police will personally investigate on 12th."

(CO 968/750)

The signals are forthcoming from Mackenzie/ Wismar and the Governor in his mad agenda to halve the troop size of the British military contingent is trivialising the signals from Mackenzie/ Wismar. But the decision to maintain present troop size has not been relayed to the Governor on the 11th August 1963 as he is not in that loop since that loop involves the players in the power relation with the US President and his staff. The Secretary of State informed the Governor via telegram on the 12th August 1963 of the said decision.

The Declassified file CO 968/751 reports on the issue of internal security in British Guiana from the standpoint of the British military force in the colony for the period 1963/1964.

A telegram dated 13th August 1963 from Force British Guiana to the War Office states:

"1.Sit Report. Quiet all areas. NTR.

2.Dispositions. 1 platoon of 2nd Company Grenadier Guards now complete at Mackenzie in view of unconfirmed reports of possible trouble there on 15 August."

(CO 968/751)

The expanding level of terrorist activity is then clearly apparent to Force British Guiana and in response the troop level is now one platoon at Mackenzie.

On the 18th August 1963 the CBFCA in a telegram to the Ministry of Defence states the rules of engagement binding on the British military in British Guiana. The telegram states as follows:

"Following instructions regarding use of force have been issued.

a.Principle of minimum force to be observed.

b.If exercising right of hot pursuit a shot may be fired across bows of offender to make her heave to.

c.Force may only be used under following conditions.

(1)In retaliation if the force is fired upon first.

(2)In self defence if force is in danger of being overwhelmed.

(3)In defence of British property which cannot be safeguarded by other means.

(4)To frustrate illegal acts of force in British waters."

(CO 968/751)

The rules of engagement issued in August 1963 clearly placed the Guyana police as the primary instrument to deal with terrorism in the colony. The British military would intervene when the police fail to subdue and especially if urgent action was demanded in a situation of threat, clear and present danger to British property and lives of expatriates. Hence Georgetown, the sugar industry and its expatriates owned by Booker and DEMBA the bauxite mining multi-national corporation were the primary points of protection afforded by the British military in the colony. The anti- PPP terrorist order of battle was formulated in response to these rules of engagement but with the decision made by the Secretary of State in October 1963 to change the electoral system the pro-PPP terrorist agenda in the cane belt now targeted

Booker plant, equipment, infrastructure and expatriates. This then forced a priority British military response in Demerara and Berbice.

A telegram dated 19th August 1963 from Force British Guiana to the War Office reports as follows:

> "1.Situation. Mackenzie. 4 minor incidents entailing no casualties and little damage occurred on night of 18 August.
>
> 2.Albion. 60 percent strike on Sugar Estate this morning for guarantee of minimum work. No incidents.

(CO 968/751)

A telegram dated 20th August 1963 from Force British Guiana to War Office states:

> "1.Situation. Industrial disputes resulting in partial strikes on sugar estates Albion, Ida Cornelia, Lenore, and go slow at Versailles. No Incidents."

(CO 968/751)

The PPP engagement with the Booker sugar industry continues in 1963. This engagement is in fact a cover for terrorist operations against Booker plant and equipment, cane crops and expatriate and other personnel. This is a PPP rooted terrorist operation/insurgency. At the same time a racist, terrorist insurgency of low level intensity continues at Mackenzie and Wismar. The threat to DEMBA is limited obviating the need for British military intervention. It is a racist assault on the property and persons of the minority Indo Guyanese population which puts the Police in play but excludes the British military given their rules of engagement. Clearly the Mackenzie/ Wismar operation is rooted in the PNC but with the decision of the Secretary of State in October 1963 to change the electoral system this terrorist insurgency was no longer in the political interest of the PNC. The reality is that the Mackenzie/Wismar racist terrorist insurgency was allowed to grow in strength as the Police failed to destroy this terrorist cell.

A telegram dated 22nd August 1963 from the Governor to the Secretary of State states:

> "In past three days there have been various minor strikes on sugar estates on various pretexts but it is clear that all arises out of action by Harry Lall designed to build up for his GAWU claim for recognition by Sugar Producers Association. No estates had to stop grinding. All strikes are off again but it is interesting that

Harry Lall has been able to get men to prejudice their chances of bonus.

3.Police have established that loss of sloop was due to attempted theft of vessel in order to get gasoline. Three men slightly drunk succeeded in blowing up sloop and one was trapped in engine room.

4.Cubans have returned from Berbice. They inspected sawmills on Berbice and may be genuinely concerned with proposed sleeper contract.

9.Local press tomorrow is likely to have sensational material resulting from Press conference given by Janet Jagan to expose as bogus various bank documents showing money for PPP from Russia which D'Aguiar and Senator Ann Jardim have been flourishing in America. For once Mrs. Jagan seems to have more right of the matter than her opponents and United Force look like coming badly unstuck."

(CO 968/751)

A telegram dated 26th August 1963 from Force British Guiana to War Office states:

"1.Situation. One case of suspected arson at Anns Grove (East Coast Demerara) in early hours of 26th August."

(CO 968/751)

A telegram dated 29th August 1963 from Force British Guiana to War Office states:

"SIT. 1300 out of 2000 sugar workers at La Bonne Intention (ECD) out on strike. Some intimidation of blacklegs. Situation under control of police.

2.Locations at 291545Z

A.2 Grenadier Guards. 1 company Mackenzie 2 companies Georgetown. Inkerman company ECD (less 1 platoon Rosehall). HQ company Georgetown (less Reece platoon Takama).

B.2 Green Jackets. A company Atkinson (less one platoon Mackenzie). Company Atkinson. D company WCD (less Reece platoon Georgetown)."

(CO 968/751)

Posted at Mackenzie there are 1 company of the Grenadier Guards and 1 platoon of the Green Jackets. Given the rules of engagement this force has no role in rooting out the terrorist cell operating in the Mackenzie/Wismar area.

The Governor of British Guiana wrote to R.W. Piper dated 31ˢᵗ August 1963 stating as follows:

> "If, as the PNC so commonly alleges, the PPP were planning a civil war and the wide use of arms, Janet Jagan would hardly wish to have another battalion of troops here to spoil the fun. Owen has never thought there was anything in the PNC story of a PPP intention to use arms at least for some time after a 'solution' had been imposed that was very much against them and they had been driven into active opposition. But it would seem that they are not expecting that 'for at least another six months'.
>
> On the other hand, Owen says that the United Force are getting increasingly despondent and increasingly desperate. He feels that they are the party that want watching as regards violence. At PNC constituency meetings (remarks at which must become public knowledge) it has been increasingly argued recently that the PNC have nothing in common with the United Force. The UF people who hoped for a united opposition that would topple the PPP are now feeling more and more isolated and are realizing that they have nothing to hope for from Burnham. If Owen is right in this (and it reflects a view that I have stated in other papers), there are others who had better do some fresh thinking."

(CO 968/751)

For the Governor the villain of the piece is the United Force political party. He insists that there is no organic link with the PNC and the hope of an alliance in the aftermath of the next general elections to remove the PPP from power is remote. History shows the inaccuracies of the Governor's analysis for he failed to understand that without an alliance with the United Force Burnham was doomed once again to the futility and powerlessness of opposition politics. A coalition with the PPP would not afford Burnham the power he craved and lusted after neither would Burnham's handlers in Washington accept such an alliance with the PPP. The hatred that the UF had for the PPP meant that they were doomed to accept the role of willing handmaiden to Burnham's acquisition of state power in 1964 to then fade away in the politics of Guiana as Burnham established his personal hegemony by stealing every single general election thereafter during his lifetime. Such was the power the Washington elites wielded in the politics of Guiana.

A telegram dated 2ⁿᵈ September 1963 from the Force British Guiana to the War Office states:

> "1.Situation. Redeployment now complete. Final location as follows:
>
> A.2 Grenadier Guards. 1 Company WCD. 2 Company Georgetown. 3Company Georgetown (less MT platoon at Atkinson). Inkerman Company ECD (less 10 platoon at Rosehall). HQ Company Atkinson.
>
> B. 2Green Jackets A. Company Atkinson (less 2 platoon at Mackenzie). C.Company Atkinson. D company Atkinson. HQ Company Atkinson."

(CO 968/751)

The two battalions that comprise the British military in the colony have been redeployed with an emphasis on East and West Coast Demerara and Georgetown. There is now only a platoon of Green Jackets at Mackenzie down from a company. The terrorist cell has been given room to play with disastrous effect in the future.

A telegram dated 26ᵗʰ September 1963 from Force British Guiana to the War Office states:

> "1.SIT. Civil labour unrest continues but there have been no incidents of violence.
>
> 2.Mil forces not involved.

(CO 968/751)

The PPP agenda of engagement in the cane belt is ongoing providing the means for terrorist activity in response to the major event of October 1963 the decision to change the electoral system for the 1964 general elections announced by the Secretary of State for the colonies.

A telegram dated 22ⁿᵈ October 1963 from the Ministry of Defence to the CBFCA states:

> "British Guiana Constitutional Conference opened in London today. Agreement unlikely and conference will probably break down at end of this week or early next. In this event HMG may have to impose a solution and this may involve suspending constitution.

2.Internal security situation could arise very suddenly though Colonial Office state that Governor is confident he can maintain law and order with present garrison."

(CO 968/751)

A confidential annex to the minutes of the meeting of the Chiefs of Staff on the 22ⁿᵈ October 1963 states.

"Mr J. D. HIGHAM (Colonial Office) said that the Conference had opened that morning. It was virtually certain that no agreement would be reached and, if this was the case, HMG would be forced to impose a solution, as forecast by the Secretary of State, the Conference, would probably breakdown at the end of this week or at the beginning of next.

The main constituent of the imposed solution was likely to be a complicated system of proportional representation which would redress the racial balance. It was likely that, faced with this situation, the Prime Minister (Jagan) would resign. If he did not do so, it would be necessary to remove him and this could be done only by suspending the Constitution."

(CO 968/751)

On the morning of the commencement of the British Guiana Constitutional Conference Higham already expected the opportunity to impose the change in the electoral system was forthcoming.

A telegram dated 27ᵗʰ November 1963 from CBFCA to the Ministry of Defence states:

"The recommendations in this paper are strongly supported.

2.After consultation with garrison commander I consider that a light aircraft flight capability should be established at the earliest opportunity if necessary by charter.

3.Capability is required whether or not garrison remaining at present strength."

(CO 968/751)

The War Office would subsequently deny this request insisting that the British military charter civilian aircraft then existing in the colony.

A report dated 29ᵗʰ October 1963 on the issue of light aircraft states:

"5.The likely areas for military IS operations are spread in a T shaped area. The distance along the coast is 170 miles and inland along the DEMERARA RIVER is 50 miles. Examples of road/track travel time (1/4 ton land rover).

a.GEORGETOWN to CORENTYNE (a new likely trouble area which we are reconnoitring now). Single trip 8-10 hours-Round trip two days-8 daylight hours for reconnaissance makes a three day reconnaissance necessary. (By air the same task can be done in 4 to 5 hours-allowing for touchdowns to contact local police and administration).

b.GEORGETOWN to MACKENZIE (where we have an outpost platoon) single trip 6 hours-Round trip two days. (By air the same task takes two hours)."

(CO 968/751)

The capacity to airlift a military strike force into Mackenzie to enable speedy intervention did not exist in the colony. In the absence of the British military platoon stationed in Mackenzie the area was then solely under the protection of the police and the volunteer force. The quickest route to move manpower to the Mackenzie/Wismar area was then via the river and the response time via this route enabled the terrorist cell to run riot in the face of the inability of the police to ensure the peace. A disaster waiting to happen which did happen in 1964.

A telegram dated 1st January 1964 by the Governor to the Secretary of State states:

> "2.Garrison Commander's Military appreciation is that even if Ministers seek to create tense security situation through obstructing implementation of Secretary of State's settlements, the nine platoons of Second Battalion Grenadier Guards could adequately contain any such situation likely on present showing of political parties. He is strengthened in this view by Commissioners report that police are thoroughly rested and are in excellent heart.
>
> 3.Unhappily such political trends as have manifested themselves since London Conference and towards increased racialism. PPP tactics seem to be (despite vaunted multi-racialism and presence of non-Indians in Ministerial and other high places) to rally Indian support by working on Indian fears of domination of Negroes and Portuguese and particularly by Burnham. Assaults on Indians during 1963 disturbances and particularly sexual assaults on Indian women (which were greatly exaggerated in public allegations of numbers and of gravity) undoubtedly consolidated Indian support for PPP even though many Indians felt and still

feel that Jagan's policies are objectionable. It may be that PPP will deliberately seek to provoke further inter-racial clashes. Such a possibility even more than obstruction of Hucks, etc. Would create need for presence throughout Coast lands of Security Forces additional to Police.

7.Our local joint assessment is thus that there is no security need for relief of Green Jackets by BUFFS.

(CO 968/751)

The Governor recognises that anti Indo violence serves the political interest of the PPP in having the majority race, the Indo Guyanese, line up as a voting bloc behind the PPP. The perpetrators of anti Indo violence are then serving the political interests of the PPP. One expects that in areas where Indos are in a minority position, such racist violence and terror would take place. But what is the reality of Demerara and Berbice where the Indos dominate, the heartland of the PPP? But in the midst of this anti PPP hand wringing, the Governor indicates the position of the military, police and administrative structure of the colony that the military force in the colony can now be halved.

A telegram dated 3rd January 1964 from the Secretary of State to the Governor states:

> "Because of other commitments, the Green Jackets will not (not) be replaced on withdrawal as originally planned."

(CO 968/751)

A telegram dated 20th January 1964 from Force British Guiana to the War Office states:

> "1.Routine redeployment completed. Headquarters 2 Grenadier Guards Georgetown. Number 1 Company Georgetown with platoon at Diamond. Number 2 Company ECD with platoon at Port Mourant. Number 3 Company Georgetown. Inkerman Company Atkinson. Reece platoon at WCD Leonora.
>
> 2.Five cases of arson during period 11 to 19 Jan. These cases seemingly unconnected. Platoon at Leonora assisted in quelling fire in store there."

(CO 968/751)

The military is now one battalion in size and there was no platoon based at Mackenzie. The PPP assault on the Booker sugar empire is accelerating to keep the British gaze fixed on protecting British economic interests. The Indo minority of Mackenzie/Wismar would pay the ultimate price for this. They would soon become collateral damage and political assets for the PPP.

A telegram dated 23rd January 1964 from Force British Guiana to the War Office states:

> "1.Similar incendiary material in three arson cases reported in our G/381 of 20th January suggest some form of guidance in incendiarism is being given out probably leaving choice of location and use to any local group with grievance.
>
> 2.Cases of cane firing on night 22/23 January."

(CO 968/751)

A telegram dated 23rd January 1964 from Force BG to the War Office states:

> "Cases of cane firings continue otherwise NTR."

(CO 968/751)

The battle in the cane belt has the gaze of the British military fixed.

A telegram dated 7th February 1964 from the Governor to the Secretary of State states:

> "PPP 'Freedom March' has fortunately gone thus far without any major incident.
>
> 5.Commissioner of Police today stressed to Janet Jagan as Minister of Home Affairs that if PPP bring large numbers of Indians into Georgetown on 9th February, police will have to concentrate here and will be unable to protect individual Indians in their homes.
>
> But not only is neither Mr. Jagan nor Burnham to be trusted but possibility of inadvertent occasion for widespread violence is considerable.
>
> 9.There was a small explosion of an electrically detonated device at East Riumveldt on night of 5th."

(CO 968/751)

The race tension abounds but the technological sophistication of the terrorist attacks is intensifying.

A telegram dated 27th February 1964 from Force British Guiana to the War Office states:

"1.Strikes continue. One further cane fire. Abortive dynamite attempt at one sugar factory."

(CO 968/751)

The attacks are now escalating the targets chosen and the technology utilised and the target is the Booker sugar empire. The escalating nature of the attacks flow with the changeover of the battalion of British military force in the colony as the Queen's Own Buffs are replacing the Grenadier Guards.

A telegram of 17th March 1964 from Force British Guiana to the War Office states:

"1.GAWU inspired strikes on estates continue. Further incidents on or near estates include use of tear gas by Police.

2.Command of garrison Battalion passed to Queens Own Buffs on 16th March. 1 Queens Own Buffs platoons now also at Leonora and Versailles.

(CO 968/751)

The assault on the Booker empire has forced the deployment of two additional platoons in the cane belt. Mackenzie/Wismar is no longer of strategic importance as there is no apparent threat to DEMBA. The British military presence is withdrawn as all assets are mobilised to protect British interests in the cane belt. DEMBA is also irrelevant to the PPP driven insurgency against the Booker empire. The PNC terrorist cell in Mackenzie would now move to unleash its strategy of race cleansing.

A telegram dated 4th April 1964 from Force British Guiana to Ministry of Defence states:

"No indication that Sugar Estate Workers Strike is yet nearing an end. Incidents continue.

2.At request of police one Queen's Own Buffs have deloused or destroyed seven home made bombs in approx. two weeks. Types now being found are more sophisticated and include one with timing mechanism."

(CO 968/751)

A telegram dated 29th April 1964 from the Governor to the Secretary of State states:

"Gradual spread of racial incidents from West Coast Demerara to other coastal areas continues. No change in military dispositions. Reconnaissance platoon One Queen's Own Buffs being sent

Skeldon on Corentyne Coast today on trip of short duration in attempt to restore spirit of estate staffs since ambush and murder of expatriate in that area on 25th April."

(CO 968/751)

The ultimate assault on the white colonial structure takes place on 25th April 1964 with the murder of an expatriate on a sugar estate. The murder takes place on the Corentyne Coast at Skeldon. The attack does not take place on the Demerara Coast where the British military presence is at its highest outside of Georgetown. The terrorists are seeking out soft targets and Mackenzie beckons.

A telegram dated 6th May 1964 from Force British Guiana to Ministry of Defence (Army) states:

> "There has been a general abatement of incidents in whole coastal area during last four days. There may be various reasons for this on West Coast such as tiredness and dispiritedness on part of various groups behind terrorism because of lack of tangible results, vigorous police action and Governor's visit but as the slackening off is general on whole coast it is more possible because violence is no longer politically expedient. Militarily the lull is looked on as the probable end of a phase and period during which reappraisal and replacement may take place rather than the end of provocation and terrorism. The next 14 days or more may confirm or discount this view. In the meanwhile Army patrols continue at same intensity especially to areas where troops are not normally stationed such as East Bank Berbici (Berbice) and Springlands on Corentyne. No relaxation or thinning out on coast will take place although some field training and leave expeditions would be welcome."

(CO 968/751)

Within the stipulated 14 days an orgy of racist violence and terrorism would be unleashed not only in the coastal belt but at Wismar left naked as the British were absent from the area. The British response would be qualitatively different increasing its military effectiveness and for the first time under the state of emergency declared they began the process of hunting and interdicting the terrorist cells. The British military focus has then dramatically changed in 1964 and the general elections were held as carded in 1964 in spite of the violence and the declaration of a state of emergency.

The declassified file CO 968/752 deals with internal security and the British military in the colony from 1964-66. A telegram dated 15th May 1964 from CBFCA to MOD UK states:

"In view of continuing violence and on advise of Governor regret that notice for one company 1 Devon and Dorset must remain at 72 hours."

(CO 968/752)

A telegram dated 20th May 1964 from the Ministry of Defence, UK to CBFCA states:

"I must give firm warning of strong possibility of necessity to declare state of emergency within next two to three days. This will almost certainly be accompanied by request for immediate despatch to British Guiana of additional company to reinforce British troops and for remainder of battalion to be placed in readiness to follow at short notice."

(CO 968/752)

A telegram dated 21st May 1964 from British Guiana to the Secretary of State states:

"Commissioner of Police has now advised the Minister for Home Affairs that he no longer sees reasonable prospect of the police being able to contain the security situation by their own resources and their normal powers. He has advised the Minister in writing to advise me to declare a state of emergency and to request the aid of the military to control the situation.

2. The Premier has now notified me that the will be advising me to declare a state of emergency tomorrow or on Saturday."

(CO 968/752)

A telegram dated 21st May 1964 from Force British Guiana to CBFCA states:

"Last night WCD bad with increased racialism which had spread to ECD.

I have said firmly that without emergency powers troops can do no more than at present. Therefore full Emergency Regulations must be enacted.

Message just received 2 police shot and wounded WCD and their weapons taken by assailants."

(CO 968/752)

The violence escalates the police indicate that they cannot maintain the peace and a state of emergency must be declared to empower the British military to now become the premier agency responsible for internal security of the colony. The garrison commander makes it clear to the Governor that they want a full state of emergency handing all power for security to the military which is nothing less than capitulation of the PPP government and the Governor was acceptable to the British military.

A telegram dated 23rd May 1964 from the Secretary of State to British Guiana informs the acting Governor that one company of British troops was despatched to the colony and another was on 24 hours notice.

A telegram dated 25th May 1964 from British Guiana to the Secretary of State states:

> "Serious rioting, house burning and two Indian deaths at Wismar today have necessitated the despatch of a platoon of the Devon and Dorsets to the area this afternoon. Mackenzie special police and the Mackenzie company of the Volunteer Force have all been called out but it may be necessary to send further army reinforcements.
>
> 2.The two Indians were killed during an attack by the majority negroes on the minority Indians. This may have a chain reaction on the Demerara East Coast and at Corentyne and Port Mourant in Indian majority areas. This in turn increases the danger to Georgetown where negroes might take reprisals and where the situation is already inflammable. Buxton is likewise very tense."

(CO 968/752)

A telegram dated 26th May 1964 from CBFCA to MOD UK states:

> "Serious rioting broke out today at Wismar, opposite Mackenzie on Demerara resulting in death of 2 Indians with 33 wounded 70 houses burnt.
>
> 3.Spread of danger areas and inadequacy of communications make balance of BN essential."

(CO 968/752)

The simultaneous terrorist assaults in the cane belt and at Wismar have stretched the capabilities of the British military to the limits of its capability. This would provoke a response from the British Government to ensure such a reality never re-occurs from 1964 to independence for Guyana in 1966. The PPP and PNC driven racist- terrorism in May 1964 would place Guyana under a state of emergency, place the British military in absolute control which enabled the general elections of November 1964 to be held and the placing of the PPP into opposition until 1992. At minimum the PPP driven racist terrorism was a gift to the British agenda which empowered the British agenda.

A telegram dated 27th May 1964 from CFBC to MOD UK states:

> "1. Understand from Governor that order in council is likely to be made tomorrow giving him power to make and apply emergency regulations in his discretion without the need to obtain advice of a recalcitrant council of ministers. Orders existence to be secret initially.
>
> 2. Strongly recommend this be done as at present Garrison Commander has more responsibility than power. His right to impose curfew, ban processions, arrest on suspicion has been and may be withheld, limited or delayed by Ministers. Moreover fact of this is kept confidential and army's image as well as effectiveness may become impaired if this continues.
>
> 3. Main object of order is to allow arrest and detention without trial of instigation of violence if Ministers refuse to advise this in all appropriate cases."

(CO 968/752)

In the wake of Wismar on the 25th May 1964 where there was no state of emergency in place and on 27th May 1964 there was need for an order in council which in effect suspends the power of the PPP government over internal security. PPP political agendas involved terrorist assaults in the cane belt and the use of internal self rule to enable the PPP driven terrorist agenda. The PPP dual agendas failed miserably to attain its ends but what it did was facilitate the British agenda to banish the PPP to the opposition benches in the politics of Guyana.

A telegram dated 29th May 1964 from CBFCA to MOD, UK states:

> "Sufficient troops are deployed in British Guiana at the moment to control the present situation providing rapid movement to any sudden flare up can be ensured.
>
> 2. There is however, since Wismar, less chance of avoiding racial conflict which may well result in widespread disturbances along the whole coast and in the mining areas. It is possible, the same time there will be increasing acts of terrorism against the white population.

217

3.In such circumstances the police are likely to remain loyal and effective where supported by even small numbers of troops but the BGVF must be discounted except for certain static guard duties.

4.To maintain law and order in this situation it is estimated up to 36 platoons would be required. The equivalent of a small brigade headquarters would also be essential.

5.Some warning may be expected of any organised uprising but the volatile temperament of the people could lead to local outbreaks of increasing frequency and scope which could develop into the situation being considered. This would take days rather than hours."

(CO 968/752)

The British military in May 1964 has then to be empowered and outfitted to deal with the terrorist threat to British hegemony over the colony. The order in council, an increase in manpower deployed in the colony and a flight of helicopters were what the military demanded. They got all three and the terrorist threat melted away.

The Commander British Forces Caribbean Area (CBFCA) to the Chief of Defence Staff dated 2nd June 1964 via a report states:

"1.Present Disturbances. A partial strike of Sugar Estate Workers began in February 1964, in support of the claim of GAWU, a PPP sponsored union, to represent these workers as the official bargaining agent in the industry in place of the MPCA. Incidents began with firing of cane fields and gradually increased until widespread racial violence was in evidence on the West Coast Demerara (WCD), and at Wismar, a village on the opposite bank of the Demerara to the Bauxite Works at Mackenzie. Destruction of houses by fires, use of explosives and firearms, and the occasional ambush have occurred. Other incidents have taken place on the East Coast Demerara (ECD) and the Corentyne, including the ambush and murder of an expatriate estate manager at Skeldon. There are now definite reasons to fear increased racial violence between Africans and Indians which can no longer be related to the inter union dispute. On two or three occasions Police have been fired on."

(CO 968/752)

The CBFCA describes the terrain of the racist terrorist violence devoid of pointing fingers at the political operatives and parties of the colony. He describes what is devoid of considerations of the struggle for hegemony that drive it.

> "6.The rank and file of the police are primarily African, and although up to now have carried out their duties satisfactorily, in the event of major racial conflict there is no doubt concerning their reliability. They are likely to remain loyal and effective where supported by even small numbers of troops.
>
> 7.If racial conflict occurs along the whole coastline it would not be possible for the Police to contain it and the military would have to assume operational responsibility.
>
> 8.British Guiana Volunteer Force. The BGVF is organised on similar lines to a British Territorial Battalion and has a strength of approximately 600 all ranks when fully embodied. Two rifle companies are stationed in Georgetown, one in New Amsterdam, one in Mackenzie, and one further company is being trained on WCD.
>
> 9.The force is primarily African, is poorly led, and it is not considered that it can be relied upon to perform its duties effectively if faced with a major situation of racial violence. Their value even in the internal security situation obtaining at present, must be discounted except for certain static guard duties."

(CO 968/752)

The British removed the single platoon of British military at Mackenzie in spite of racist attacks preceding this withdrawal at both Mackenzie and Wismar. The events at Wismar commencing 25th May 1964 were unleashed in a security environment in which the police and volunteer force would both respond without British military support. A situation at Wismar was then enabled by British military strategy that created a list of priorities meriting British military presence and intervention. Wismar was not one such priority. The analysis of the CBFCA in its accuracy convicts the British of classic white colonial callousness driven by an imperialist agenda.

> "13.Most of the population is situated on the coastal belt, and in Georgetown and New Amsterdam. The rural and coastal areas are mainly populated by the East Indians, and villages adjoin each other closely along the WCD, ECD, West Bank Demerara (WBD), East Bank Demerara (EBD), West Coast Berbice (WCB), East Coast Berbice (ECB), and the Corentyne Coast. There are however a considerable number of Africans in these areas and in quite a few cases a predominantly Indian village is next door to one with an

African majority. These areas are usually the main trouble spots. Georgetown is predominantly African. Populated areas removed from the coast the mining towns of Mackenzie, approximately 70 miles up the Demerara, Kakwani approximately 100 miles up the Berbice, and Matthews Ridge in the North West District approximately 70 miles up the Kaituma. These mining towns are mainly African with small European colonies and in the past there have been minor incidents of unrest and civil disturbance."

(CO 968/752)

Both the PPP and PNC driven racist terrorist agendas have then specific operational theatres that are mutually exclusive, which means that in these theatres of operation race minorities are the specific targets. The British concentrated on specific theatres where their interests were under clear and present danger hence concentration in Georgetown and East and West Coast Demerara. Minorities outside of these major operational theatres of the British had to rely on the colonial police.

"15. In the past the Guianese have been a basically friendly people with little or no racial animosity. Although poor they are easy going and generally contented. The Africans are lazy and live mainly in the urban areas and the comparatively industrious Indians are employed in sugar estates and rice farms. The Guianese African is tough, reckless and he has no settled stake in society. The West Indian capacity for personal violence and disregard for human life is latent throughout the community. Both races are volatile and can be completely unpredictable.

16. Politicians in recent years have encouraged inter racial feeling for their own political ends. Life has been unsettled and minor incidents prevalent for a long time. Rumours are rife and fear widespread.

17. Neither the East Indian or the African is considered to be of great moral or physical courage when confronted by British troops, nor is it considered that this has been altered radically recently.

(CO 968/752)

The racism of the British military officer is expected but it is also strategic as it masks the covert operations in a cold war battle zone that is the colony in 1964. In the case of British Guiana in 1964 the Indo Guyanese are the majority of the population and endowed with characteristics which make them fit to rule the colony to independence and thereafter but they are still inferior to the white man. The Afro Guyanese are unregenerate sub humans unfit to rule and are a minority of the population. From 1953 to 1962 the Indo Trinbagonian is unfit to rule, an unregenerate sub human species that must be relegated to the opposition benches of the politics of Trinidad and Tobago. The Indo Trinbagonian is also then a minority of the population of Trinidad and Tobago.

The presence of Jagan, the PPP and the American agenda to remove the PPP from power trumps the British choice of the Indo Guyanese as the race to carry the colony to independence. Independence for the colony in 1966 under a PNC government was then the most potent indicator for the British that the sun had finally set on their empire in the Western Hemisphere. British weakness and subservience to US hegemony would place a minority race in power from 1964-1992 and Eric Williams of Trinidad and Tobago would never forget this lesson on US hegemony until his death.

"Possible Terrorist Organisation.

20. There have been reports lately of arms caches and military training being carried out clandestinely. Furthermore 'Students' to Cuba are suspected to have been trained in terrorist activity before returning home. In the past month information on this subject has become more common although the majority of this intelligence is uncorroborated. The Police have many suspicions but little or no evidence and the identity of the leaders if any is obscure."

(CO 968/752)

There is no intelligence at the operational level of the internal security structure. In a cold war battle zone with the presence of Cubans on the ground in the colony at minimum MI5 is operational. But only the Prime Minister of Britain is privy to MI5 operational assets, resources and operations, the British military, the colonial governor and the colonial office are on a strict need to know basis. To date MI5 has failed to declassify its files on its operations in the Caribbean. The military officer is then speaking from military intelligence, police and special branch realities in 1964 in the colony. His grasp of reality is then incomplete, even flawed. Military intelligence, the police and special branch had then no assets within the PPP, PNC and racist supremacist groups to garner an understanding of the reality. Furthermore these state agencies were heavily limited in their operational resources given the covert agencies operating in the colony, both those of Britain and the US.

"Probable Development

32.It is considered that there is now less chance of avoiding racial conflict which may well result in widespread disturbances along the whole coast and in the interior. It is possible that at the same time, there will be increasing acts of terrorism against the white population. This could lead to the worst case of a general breakdown of law and order with the races in conflict."

(CO 968/752)

Visions of the Kenyan apocalypse with the slaughter of the minority whites by the savages of the colony. A vision that was flawed as it never came to pass. A product of a racist British military officer or is it an attempt to pump resources into the conflict to bolster this officers career?

A telegram dated 13th June 1964 from CBFCA to the Ministry of Defence, UK states:

"No reaction at moment to detention of known trouble makers."

(CO 968/752)

A telegram dated 23rd June from Force British Guiana to Secretary of State reports as follows:

"1.Main incidents during period 20th to 22nd June were:-

(A)West Coast Demerara. Relatively quiet with approximately eight incidents including shooting at civilians, stoning, arson.

(B)East Coast Demerara. Violence increasing especially in area of Mahaicony. 52 incidents including in shooting at civilians, stoning, assaults, and of explosives. One African seriously injured at Beterverwagting on 20th June. Five Africans fired at Mahaicony on 21st June and two now in hospital. Indian woman and child shot dead at Dochfour. Portuguese man shot dead behind Golden Grove. Automatic weapon used by six Indians to kill African at Perth on 22nd June. 14 houses burnt in Perth same night. Second African body found nearby. Crowds of Indians at Beehive and Annandale bent on mischief dispersed. Shot fired at Police land rover at Perth.

3.Assessment. Latest incidents East Coast Demerara indicate organised violence with planned terrorist attacks by PYO and direct encouragement by PYO of retaliatory methods. Now increased possibility that Africans may react Buxton, Georgetown and at Mackenzie where Indians have been returning over last (? Few days omitted)."

(CO 968/752)

The PYO or Progressive Youth Organisation is an arm of the PPP in 1964. The description of the nature of the racist terrorist actions in East Coast Demerara (ECD) is but one instance that the discourse of the Indo Guyanese victim and victimhood in the colony from 1962-1964 was created to maintain the solidarity of the voting bloc and to appeal to external supporters. This discourse has in fact tainted analyses of the events of 1953 to 1964 in British Guiana produced by Guyanese, Guyanese abroad and non Guyanese analysts. The discourse of the Indo Guyanese victim/victimhood masks especially the racist terrorist actions of Indo Guyanese especially in Mahaicony. The victim was not Indo or Afro Guyanese it was the social order of Guyana which emerged from 1962-1964 mortally wounded with independence in 1966.

The minutes of a meeting of the Chiefs of Staff reports on the situation in British Guiana. The minutes state as follows:

> "Sir Richard Hull said that to meet the emergency in British Guiana the resident garrison (Queen's Own Buffs) had been reinforced by an infantry battalion (1 Devon and Dorset), a battery of the Spearhead Unit (20 Medium Regiment, RA) and two Wessex and three Alonette helicopters; in addition, individual reinforcements had been despatched to augment the garrison, headquarters and others being held at 72 hours notice in the United Kingdom.
>
> British forces had taken over operational command and control of several troublesome areas including East and West Coast Demerara to enable the Police to re-train and re-organise. Arrangements had been made to retain the two infantry battalions in British Guiana until after the elections which were programmed to take place in November 1964;
>
> In January 1962 (2) the Chiefs of Staff had considered that the need for British forces to be held in British Guiana would soon lapse; the present situation, however, did not support this view and he was perturbed by indications that even more British troops might be required in British Guiana."

(CO 968/752)

The garrison commanders of Force BG have been given the military contingent and the helicopters requested in a move to end the race war and racist terrorism in the colony. For the first time since military intervention in 1962 the British have configured Force BG to deal with an insurgency. But Hull is now wary that the situation is accelerating and Britain might be engulfed in a quagmire of racist terrorism. The British at this juncture must have an exit strategy this exit strategy therefore hinged on the successful staging of credible general elections at the end of 1964, removing the PPP from power, breaking the PPP's terrorist insurgency whilst rapidly declaring a date for independence and exiting the colony.

It was not in Burnham's favour to embark on the agenda of racist terrorism after the October 1963 decision to change the electoral system. By October 1963, Burnham got what he always demanded of the British it was his duty now to defeat the PPP at the upcoming polls. The attacks at Wismar did not serve Burnham's political interest nor did the bombing of the river vessel the Sun Chapman in 1964. Anti Indo terrorist attacks served the PPP's agenda to solidify its Indo Guyanese voting bloc. What is then apparent is that there were racist supremacist groups within all races who were bent on an orgy of blood letting to cleanse specific pieces of Guyanese geography. They were then anarchists with no concern for a national political agenda as they saw race as nation and nation as tribe. The agenda was racist hegemony etched on the landscape of Guyana expressed in terms of apartheid and John Crow segregation. Whilst the PPP, the PNC and the UF gave succour and space to these racist hegemonists the anarchists were out of their political control. Today in Guyana the racist hegemonist anarchists are back but with a new twist they now work for Venezuelan and Colombian illicit drug traffickers.

A telegram from Force BG to MOD Army and CBFCA dated 22nd July states:

"General.

Number of African assaults on Indians including shooting of 4 East Indians one a woman at Xeskideven East Coast Demerara.

2.Main incidents.

a.Mackenzie Wismar, African store set on fire. Slight damage.

b.West Coast Demerara. Three Africans seriously wounded by 9mm and shotgun fire at Leonora. Three incidents Arson. Slight damage. One African assaulted. Slight damage.

c.East Coast Demerara. Ten arson incidents. Four successful. Six slight damage. Six explosions. Three untraced. Two slight damage to African houses. One slight damage to Indian house. One East Indian chopped to death by masked men and two East Indian women seriously injured at Victoria.

3.Air operations.

Patrols and Recces carried out to West Coast Berbice. Wessex and one Alonette unserviceable.

5.General Assessment

No violent reprisals after PPP buildings explosion but slight increase in assaults on Indians in coastal areas."

(CO 968/752)

The engagement between the races is based on race cleansing. Houses are fire bombed and many persons are beaten and chopped. The weaponry is predominantly an accelerant such as gasoline and crude methods of application of the accelerant. The attacks on the person are personal and in your face most times with cutlasses. Most important there are marauding groups/group of attackers. The attacks then are to force specific race minorities in specific geographic spaces to flee to leave, to race cleanse these areas. Separation that then supports segregation and apartheid. The strategy employed to effect race cleansing mutes the effectiveness of the British military as the battle is not against the military but against races and political parties and their activists and supporters. The British military is then near panic as they are charged with enabling the general elections of 1964 the lynch pin of the British exit strategy.

A telegram from the Governor to the Secretary of State dated 18th July 1964 states:

> "(c)I have decided, but not yet announced , that all firearms other than pistols will be withdrawn from all the coastal districts lying between the Essequibo and Corentyne Rivers (including Georgetown) and up the Demerara River to Mackenzie/ Wismar. An announcement would be made on Monday 20th July. An amnesty on a colony-wide basis for the surrender of unlawful arms will run from 22nd July to 27th July inclusive. Pistols are not being withdrawn because:
>
> (a)there have been few incidents involving the use of pistols, and
>
> (b)the relatively few pistols possessed by the public are largely in the hands of more responsible persons for genuine self defence purposes.
>
> It has been known for some time that the withdrawal of arms, particularly shotguns, might ease the military problem and the Army have been pressing for it. There will arise a risk of law-abiding people being attacked by terrorists possessed of unlawful

arms which does not exist to the same extent when the law-abiding folk are known to be armed. There will also be opposition from sections of the public, particularly East Indians (who will fear African cutlasses). I have consulted all three political leaders, D'Aguiar will probably not complain and I hope that Burnham's opposition has also been overcome. Jagan will criticise.

3.I would also emphasise that too much must not be expected from the arms withdrawal although it should be helpful. Many more deaths have resulted from other causes than from the use of firearms. I propose also to endeavour to tighten up drastically on the use and possession of explosives.

4.Please do not assume that the above measures will substantially relieve pressure on the troops or remove the potential need for reinforcements. I see these measures as helpful not fundamental in our bitter inter-party, inter-racial conflict. I must stress that we may need more troops if we are to be able to keep order sufficiently well to justify holding an election in 1964."

(CO 968/752)

The Governor has then revealed the political realities of an Army in a near state of panic calling for a measure that the Governor fears would put the elites of the colony in harm's way. This indicates that British colonial hegemony has in fact collapsed under the assault of a black on black race war. In addition the Governor insists that given the nature of this black on black race war the measure would amount to little if anything. The British military placed in a political wasteland is then agitating to save its image of invincibility so tarnished in other hotspots of a colonial empire in collapse.

A telegram dated 5th September 1964 from Force BG to CBFCA and MOD Army indicates that the black on black race war is abating as the British military presence has limited the field of operations. The next move is now towards the election campaign. A telegram from Force BG to CBFCA and MOD Army dated 12th September 1964 shows that the hot spots especially the coastal areas of Demerara, Berbice and Corentyne have all gone dead. Unlike Kenya and Aden this was never a war of liberation to remove the British colonial overlord this was a black on black war for racist hegemony in the aftermath of the granting of independence.

A telegram dated 13th September 1964 from Force BG to CBFCA and MOD Army states:

"1.a.All areas remain quiet.

b. Two minor incidents arson of East Indian houses on West Coast Berbice.

2. Mahaicony. Police patrol arrested Yanki Persaud and one other East Indian. Both wanted men and believed leaders of Mahaicony terrorist gangs.

5. General Assessment. No change anticipated in present calm situation."

(CO 968/752)

By the 13th September 1964 Force BG can now move to accomplish its primary task to hold the peace that affords a credible December 1964 general elections.

A telegram from CBFCA to MOD UK dated 30th December 1964 states:

"My understanding is that Governor has recommended to Colonial Office that he exercises his emergency powers only on advice of Ministers instead of at his own discretion. This is not quite the same as handing over responsibility for internal security.

2. Am advised that Burnham has agreed that emergency powers will remain in force for present and that Governor has stated to Garrison Commander that if new Government makes any major abuse of powers after relaxation the Governor will re-assume powers.

3. There is no intention of rescinding Order Number 2. This gives troops protection from civil proceedings unless with consent of Governor.

5. Garrison Commander will continue to receive instructions for UK troops solely from Governor."

(CO 968/752)

From December 1964 to independence on 20th May 1966 Burnham needs the British military to afford him the space to put his security apparatus in play to ensure his hegemony with independence. He therefore supports the continued presence of Force BG and the emergency powers until such time that he sees fit for the removal of both. The British Governor is then exposing the PNC/ UF Government to daily internal security affairs to wean them eventually handing this over and exiting from the colony. The exit strategy is now in phase 2 in December 1964.

A telegram dated 24th July 1965 to MOD UK from CBFCA states:

"Have had discussions with Governor and Force BG. Future intentions of PPP are not clear but several good indications that large scale strike of sugar workers will occur about mid- September. If this takes place intimidation of non strikers and racial violence will follow. Period before and after constitutional conference also potentially dangerous.

2.Garrison at present two battalion strength and mobility can handle and foreseeable situation. Reduction to one battalion with emergency reinforcement from UK would be adequate to restore order but request for reinforcement unlikely until serious violence has occurred.

3.Present activities of military, BGVF and SSU and security precautions being taken by Government and on estates keeps temperature down, gives confidence to inhabitants and discourages communal acts of lawlessness. Any reduction in these measures or numbers of troops resulting from withdrawal of one battalion would lower confidence, tempting troublemakers to act and allow no mobile reserves.

4.Consider best contribution Army can make in assisting BG to Independence is to ensure as far as possible peaceful conditions in country. With less than present strength no assurance of achieving this can be given."

(CO 968/752)

Force BG has attained goal 1 and is now insisting that a reduction in its strength would jeopardise goal 2 to independence. What is noteworthy is the glowing terms in which Force BG speaks of Burnham's moves to ensure peace in the sugar belt Force BG's primary strategic focus. Burnham is then satisfying the wishes of his masters moving to getting rid of the British to then reveal his secret agenda for his hegemony over Guyana not PNC, not Afro Guyanese his personal hegemony. All races were welcome as long as you recognised and served Burnham's hegemony.

CO 1031/4757 is a declassified file containing the monthly intelligence report to the Secretary of State for the Colonies by the Governor of British Guiana. This monthly report consisted of the Governor's personal report, the report of the intelligence committee and the monthly report of the head of the Special Branch. The monthly report of the intelligence committee was made available to the PPP Government but the rest of the monthly report contained reports not made available to the then PPP Government as they were the subjects of surveillance of the said agencies which generated these reports.

The intelligence report dated 11th February 1963 states:

> "13.From time to time I have reported my anxiety about the large number of firearms in the country and my attempts to get my Ministers to realise that licenses should not be handed out to all and sundry on any paltry excuse.
>
> It seems that in December last a senior Police Officer interviewed Kelshall about the .455 colt automatic that had been seized from Toolsie Persaud (who was mentioned in my Personal Despatch No.11 of May, 1962)."

(CO 1031/4757)

The PPP was then legally arming their supporters and activists. A handwritten note on the left side of the report on Toolsie Persaud states:

> "As a young PYO member who was prevented from leaving for 'study' in Cuba because he was wanted by the police for attempted murder."

(CO 1031/4757)

As early as 1962 the PYO was then under surveillance especially with reference to the students sent to Cuba and back to the colony.

The intelligence report dated 11th April 1963 states:

> "2.The long continuing labour troubles at the Rice Marketing Board are in outward form the struggle between two unions for sole recognition by the Board, but in reality they are a struggle between those who sympathise with the PPP and those who do not. They flared in violence towards dusk on Friday, April 5. Large crowds assembled outside the Rice Marketing Board. The nucleus were workers claiming that they had been locked out and demanding their pay for the week but they attracted others, including many who are aptly described by the Commissioner of Police as 'layabouts'. The crowd were aroused when Mrs. Jagan sent her car to the Board with packages for the Russian ship alongside, loading rice for Cuba. In the event the captain of the Russian ship refused to accept the packages. When the car returned with the packages in it, the crowd insisted that the parcels should be examined lest they contained guns, and, in spite of police attempts to prevent them, the crowd stoned the car and seized and opened the packages. Having been thus aroused, the crowd later over-turned and set fire

to the car of the leader of the pro-PPP union. Police already on the scene were reinforced but were heavily attacked after darkness fell, and it became necessary to use tear smoke. The crowd were further incensed by the continued loading of the Russian ship by black-leg labour brought in by the Chairman Senator Mooner Khan, but neither the Premier nor Senator the Hon. Claude Christian, the Acting Minister for Trade and Industry, would agree that loading should cease. In fact the Premier and Christian informed me that troops should be brought in at once and should shoot if necessary, a view from which I strongly dissented since the Commissioner of Police had rightly advised the Minister that the resources of the Police were by no means exhausted in fact the Police had managed to get the situation at the Rice Marketing Board under control.

6.Another cause of general unrest has been the Government's introduction of Labour Relations Bill which is substantially in the same form as the 1953 Bill that gave so much concern at the time. The Bill was published in a Gazette Extraordinary on March 25, and was given its first reading on March 27."

(CO 1031/4757)

The flash points are now flowing into each other and combining to form the basis of concerted covert action and racist terrorist insurgency. The presence of Russian ships loading rice at the docks of the Rice Marketing Board (RMB) conjures up a cold war flashpoint but it is expressed and mediated in racist power relations and violence. The Board is managed by a PPP political appointee an Indo Guyanese and the working force is divided on the basis of race. The pro-PPP union doing battle with the BGTUC affiliated union representing workers of different black races and the scab labour bought in to break the strike is predominantly Indo Guyanese. The perception arises that the RMB is in the process of racial cleansing as Afro Guyanese workers and their union are to be flushed from the RMB. Cold War flashpoint becomes black on black race war engagement and the PPP and its supporters are not victims but active participants in a battle for racist hegemony. The reality is that the RMB docks are in Georgetown where Indo Guyanese are a besieged minority. The racist backlash is inevitable and the PPP feeds on the discourse of Indian victimhood that is a paltry attempt at masking the strategic incompetence of PPP leadership commencing with Cheddi Jagan.

This is clearly indicated in his repeated requests for colonial troops to shoot down his perceived race enemies in Georgetown and Mackenzie but never making said calls for the same to be done in the cane belt. Jagan actually complained bitterly to the colonial office that the Governor and the expatriate white Commissioner of Police refused to call in the colonial military on repeated occasions to shoot down rioting civilians in Georgetown, Mackenzie, Wismar and Christianburg, and of police violence against Indo Guyanese in the cane belt all in an attempt to mask Indo Guyanese involvement in racist terrorism. What Jagan wanted therefore was to pressure the colonial military into solving his race problem and assuring Indo racist hegemony via the barrel of the white colonial gun. Denial to the point of needing medication. What Jagan failed to understand was that in 1963 the British colonial was willing to give him racist hegemony in return for him walking away from his dogmatic Stalinist rhetoric and his embrace of Fidel Castro since 1959 at least until after independence. This was attainable as Jagan's legislative measures and budgets since 1953 were all within the boundaries of capitalist modernism. His rhetoric and embrace of Fidel Castro were then at odds with his governance since 1953 in fact it was schizophrenic even showing signs of multiple personalities. Moreover his race base did not want a Stalinist utopia or Castro's revolution premised on the socialising of poverty. Jagan failed to do what was necessary to ensure his racist hegemony because he believed as the maximum leader of the majority race in the colony a race that was inherently superior to the other major black race, power was an entitlement to his race. It was his to wield as he so desired and for this racist denial he sat in opposition from 1964 to 1992 and Guyana the nation was stillborn.

The intelligence report for 14th June 1963 states:

> "4. Unfortunately as reported in the Secret Report there were regrettable scenes of mob violence at the Minister's funeral followed by some looting and damage to the property and persons of East Indians when the hooligan element again broke out.
>
> 5. As is indicated in the Secret and Personal Report, the Premier still has not faced up to the country's serious financial position and does not appear to have realised that, without considerable financial help from outside, the Government is unlikely to be able to make its commitments as the end of the month..."

At the funeral of Claude Christian the racist violence flowed. The message to the PPP was clear that they had no hegemony over Georgetown, this was hostile territory and in response the PPP would now launch its offensive in its race domain, the cane and rice belt of the coastal plains.

The Governor in his overview of the intelligence committee's May 1963 report states:

"I agree generally with the last two paragraphs of the Committee's assessment-there is no doubt that the TUC leaders lost control of the situation that resulted from their misconceived 'passive resistance' campaign. Whether or not their followers behaved, others took advantage of the atmosphere and created havoc. And it is certainly true that the longer the strike continues (and there seems no sense of urgency in either Government or TUC to end it), the greater the danger of widespread disorders. I doubt, however, whether racial animosity should be attributed to discrimination in the distribution of essential supplies. In this field, as regrettably in so many aspects of local life now, each racial group (while loudly disclaiming any racial bias) attributes evil doing to the other. I doubt if the roots go deep but the plant of racial antipathy has unhappily sprouted enormously in the present political climate."

(CO 1031/4757)

The general strike called by the TUC was then the basis of the second flashpoint for 1963. A general strike that was again played out on the basis of race and which intensified the race hate creating the spiral to race cleansing. One perception that drove this race hate was the discrimination against and the exploitation of Afro Guyanese economic weakness by Indo Guyanese business people in the sale and distribution of food in the colony in the aftermath of the general strike. Looting became then a weapon in the race war.

The report of the intelligence committee for May 1963 states:

"There has been an overall deterioration in the general situation as a result of the shortage of foodstuffs and lack of the means to purchase supplies at steadily increasing prices.

Racial animosity has increased and could be attributed in part, to the alleged discrimination in the distribution of essential supplies.

Everyday the strike continues, the greater the danger of incidents and racial clashes occurring on a wider scale simultaneously in Georgetown and in the rural areas, with the resulting strain on the forces of Law and Order.

With the deterioration in the situation and increasing shortages of food and other essential supplies, there is danger of the leaders of the Trade Union Council losing control of their followers. If this happens, there is likelihood of disturbances over a wide area."

(CO 1031/4757)

The Governor in his overview thrashes the position of the intelligence committee but both essentially miss the mark for alas they are not of us they were all expatriate white. Thanks to the colonial social order the black on black racism in the colony was organic, necessary to preserving white hegemony. The shortage of food and the profiteering and speculation that drove the prices of available items out of the reach of the urban Afro Guyanese working poor and underclass stoked race anger for survival was now an intensely pressing issue even more than the normal daily grind. Flashpoints then became opportunities to shop without paying, to shop till you drop. Then there was the deliberate policy to use Afro Guyanese comparative economic weakness to the advantage of the drive for racist hegemony. In this scenario Indo Guyanese businesses were targeted but so were those of the Portuguese and the Chinese. It was then equal opportunity expropriation by looting. A state of emergency was declared on 8th May 1963 to ensure the maintenance of essential services.

The intelligence report dated 18th July 1963 states:

> "12.Cuban Trade: During the strike the Government managed to arrange for the supply of certain essential commodities such as flour, petrol, kerosene, etc., from Cuba, and these supplies arrived in mid June by two Cuban ships. As passengers on the two ships were Osvaldo Cardenas Junguera and Clinton Lloyd Adlum, both Cuban citizens, who have since applied for British Guiana residence permits for a period of three months.
>
> 14. Clinton Lloyd Adlum, mentioned above, was one of the members of the original mission to whom visas were refused last year. At that time nothing was known about him from a security point of view but he has since been identified as a senior Cuban intelligence officer. A watch is being kept on his activities."

(CO 1031/4757)

The Minister of Home Affairs granted the residency permits of both Cuban applicants. Jagan and the PPP had now crossed the line finally empowering the US covert and overt agenda to destroy his relevance to governance to the colony and independence. The arrival of Adlum meant that the CIA station in the colony was no longer involved in monitoring the presence of low level Communists as they moved within and out of the colony. There was now red meat on the table to feed the Washington elites calling for Jagan's demise. Adlum's presence in the colony raises the question of a KGB presence also for

Cuban Intelligence was the hand maiden of the KGB during the Cold War. The Cold War was then heating up in the colony.

> "One fact that has emerged from the strike is the success of the campaign conducted by the PPP sponsored Guiana Agricultural Workers' Union to recruit new members at the expense of the MPCA."

(CO 1031/4757)

The PPP strategy to blunt the assault of the TUC is then clear but the assault on the MPCA in the cane belt would in fact launch the third flashpoint of 1963 that becomes the major theatre of operation of the race war of 1964: cane and rice regions of the coastal belt. Having lost hegemony over Georgetown as a government the next move was to race cleanse the cane and rice belts in a strategy that targeted the operations of Booker. The PPP driven racist hegemonists were then calling out the colonial Massa but yet not making war on the military of the colonial Massa, a product of faulty logic that cost the PPP state power from 1964 to 1992.

The intelligence report dated 14th August 1963 by the Governor states:

> "12.Of the acts of sabotage during July, the dynamiting of the Rice Marketing Board when the Russian ship 'Mitchurinsk' was at the wharf, appears to have been an extension of the activities of those responsible for the dynamiting of Government buildings in June. Although there have not yet been any convictions of those believed to be responsible, a Police assessment based on such information as is available, concludes that elements in the PNC, with at least the connivance of the TUC, have been responsible for these attacks, which have occurred after office hours. The object of the perpetrators appears to have been nuisance and publicity value, an attempt to frighten civil servants not out on strike and to encourage strikers to remain out. In one attempt at sabotage of an aqueduct on a sugar estate, the timing device used revealed an unpleasant degree of sophistication in sabotage techniques. If this, as is possible, was a PPP supporter attempting to strike a blow for the GAWU, it reveals an unhealthy potential which the PPP may use in future. The military-type grenades that have been used in a few incidents have almost certainly been acquired by PPP followers. The home-made incendiary bottle-bomb is unfortunately a technique which has been adopted by both sides in the struggle."

(CO 1031/4757)

The Governor reports on the escalating terrorist acts and the increasing sophistication of the technology being utilised in the devices uncovered. The covert response of the colonial overlord has not been declassified to date and may never be.

The report of the intelligence committee for August 1963 states:

> "14.Mackenzie. Between 3rd July and 18th August 1963 there were over forty incidents in the Mackenzie/Wismar area directed almost exclusively against Indians or Indian owned property. The incidents consisted of arson, attempted arson, looting, assault, and missile throwing, and fell into four broad time groups: about the 4/5 July, 29/30 July, 10/11 August and 18 August. It was noted that the MCA for Mackenzie, Robert Jordan, PNC, visited Mackenzie shortly before each of these outbreaks: on the 3rd and 27th July and 10th and 17th August. On the 27th July Jordan spoke at a public meeting, suggesting in his speech that the PNC was strong enough in the Mackenzie/ Wismar area to retaliate for any attacks by the PPP on the PNC in other areas. Probably as a result of these incidents there has been a movement of Indians from the area, a recent survey shows that 27 complete families have left, some of the heads of families resigning from Demba, and 25 other heads of families have sent their wives and children out of the area.

(CO 1031/4757)

The race cleansing in Mackenzie/ Wismar was duly noted in the report of the intelligence committee. The Governor in his overview does not list this hot spot but the Colonial Office official in London marked the left margin of the said report. It is then apparent that what exploded in Wismar in 1964 was in the eyes of the colonial Massa collateral damage.

The report of the intelligence committee for September 1963 states:

> "41.An explosion took place at the home of Dr. Ptolemy Reid in Georgetown while rubbish was being burned on 27 September 1963. A search of the debris indicated that approximately 200 detonators had been buried near the site of the fire. Dr. Reid's name has been mentioned in connection with the PNC Defence Organisation. He claims to have no knowledge of the detonators."

(CO 1031/4757)

In the overview of the Governor for September 1963 no reference is made to this incident involving Reid of the PNC. In fact the Governor in the declassified files read never spoke in detail of a PNC militia involved in acts of racist terrorism. The reports of the intelligence committee were presented to the PPP Minister of Home Affairs. The Governor would speak in his reports of PYO racist terrorist acts in the declassified files.

The intelligence report of the Governor dated 14th November 1963 states:

> "8.Ten Cubans arrived on board the Cuban vessel, Las Villas, to attend the Congress as delegates and were given temporary permits to cover this period. Applications were however made for an extension to enable then 'to see something of the country'. The leader of the delegation, Francisco Valdes, was described in a press release as a national leader (executive member) of the 100,000 strong Communist Youth League, the youth arm of the ruling United Party of the Socialist Revolution of Cuba."

(CO 1031/4757)

In the aftermath of the October 1963 body blow by the Secretary of State the PPP makes public its ties to Fidel Castro.

> "9.In addition to the report of arms training included in the Secret and Personal report for October 1963, a further report in late October, as yet unconfirmed, was received about arms being unloaded from ships in the Essequibo River and then transported to Georgetown in vehicles owned by Toolsie Persaud. According to the report they are then stored in the grocery store of Latchman and Sons, Georgetown. No arms have yet been found, but a certain amount of support for this report has been received from Trinidad Special Branch in a mention of the activities in British Guiana of Henry Lee Sing, who visited this country in September and again in October this year. Lee Sing also claimed that the PPP are obtaining arms through the 'Cuban Commissioner' (the Cuban Commissioner is based in the colony)."

(CO 1031/4757)

The delicate source has to be covert and if the source was MI5 a report would have been lodged in London then sanitised for the Colonial Office such was the operational reality. Governors simply did not have the capacity to run assets within the PPP, PNC and UF and this was deliberate for this was the preserve of the Security Service (MI5) and this organisation reported directly to the British Prime Minister. In the absence of the declassified MI5 files it is quite possible that the Governor's delicate source was playing him, the Special Branch in the colony and that of Trinidad and Tobago, but the Governor has put the source in play forcing the Colonial Office to verify the accuracy of the information. For that they had to literally solicit the information from MI5 for the Colonial Office was on a need to know basis with MI5.

The report of the intelligence committee for October 1963 states:

> "For some time isolated reports told of military training by the PYO; none was verified although three times in the last six months US military hand-grenades appeared in the hands of PPP and PYO supporters, together with one machine-carbine. These reports have lately increased in frequency, and two inter- connected patterns of information indicate that a PYO member, Bhola Persaud, an ex-Cuban student, recently conducted arms training in Berbice and is now doing the same in Wakenaam (6 Nov 63)."

(CO 1031/4757)

The reports of the intelligence committee with details of PPP/ PYO subversion were handed to a PPP Minister of Home Affairs. Was then the Special Branch of the colony intent on interdicting said subversives and their terrorist activities? Hence the outright rejection of the Special Branch in the colony by Force BG and the demand for an order in Council for Force BG to arrest and detain the subversives of all types PPP, PNC and UF.

The report of the intelligence committee for October 1963 states:

> "To summarise, it seems probable that defence arrangements made so far by the PNC have been primarily directed at the protection of the party machine in Georgetown; its headquarters, its officials and their property. In the rural areas security has been a matter of pure self defence by African gangs armed with clubs and cutlasses. It may now appear necessary that in predominantly Indian areas some more instructed form of defence organisation should be formed as in Canje. If any political ideas need emphasis it will probably be provided by the Georgetown mob, as in the past, and ultimately by the dynamiting group which appears to be at the party's disposal.

(CO 1031/4757)

The PNC mob rules Georgetown but it is a mob that is devoid of firearms in effective numbers if at all. The rural PNC army predominantly Afro Guyanese is also largely devoid of firearms they therefore depend on mob attacks utilising cutlasses, clubs and firebombs. The dynamiting group is remote from the mob, clandestine and has its own agenda, all the signals of a covert agenda.

The intelligence report of the Governor dated December 13th 1963 states:

> "2.I have been disquieted that the non-Personal Report which goes to the Premier and to the Minister of Home Affairs, should have so much material about the two opposition parties, a great deal of which is purely political and in no way relates to the security of the country. It is contrary to accepted convention to give the party in power information about the political dealings of its opponents that is not of security importance. The Commissioner of Police has discussed this with me and has pointed out the difficulty in which the Head of Special Branch finds himself if he does not demonstrate to the Minister of Home Affairs (who is herself one of the principal targets for an intelligence gathering organization concerned with the security of the country and its freedom from Communist subversion) that his organization is able to acquire at least as much information about the Opposition as can the Government Party. I sympathize with this difficulty, but even greater difficulty may arise from giving Ministers reports that are disproportionally full about the Opposition but that have comparatively little about the PPP."

(CO 1031/4757)

The Head of Special Branch is jeopardising the covert/overt operation to banish the PPP to the opposition benches of Guyana's electoral politics. This is a covert operation being managed by MI5 and the Minister of Home Affairs is under surveillance for being a Communist subversive. The protest of the Governor was simply the overt protest the effect was the purging of the leadership of Special Branch at the height of the race war in 1964.

> "8.The PPP are working hard to ensure that Trade Unions sponsored by them are recognized by employers in place of non-PPP Unions. They are helped in this by foolish public disputes between Andrew Jackson and his FUGE and affiliated Unions on the one hand, and Richard Ishmael and the NUPSE on the other. The strength of the TUC built up by its opposition to the Labour Relations Bill, will be eroded unless the leaders forget their feuds and unite against the struggle of PPP-backed Unions for recognition."

(CO 1031/4757)

The Governor is now outwardly political and is calling for action to discipline the anti PPP Trade Unions. The battle between the GAWU and the MPCA led by Richard Ishmael for representation of the cane workers of the colony would be the cover for the launch of the PPP racist terrorist campaign in the cane belt that peaked in 1964.

De- classified file CO 1031/4758 contains intelligence reports on the political situation in British Guiana as CO 1031/ 4757.

The intelligence report of the Governor dated 19th February 1964 states:

> "14. The 'Freedom March' and the widespread cane fires, both initiated in the absence of the Premier and Mrs. Jagan, are indications that the PPP leaders next in line are anxious to demonstrate the party's intimidation potential in a last-ditch attempt to avert the implementation of the solution announced at the end of the 1963 London Conference. The fear of elections under proportional representation is also evident in recent attempts to win over the PNC and the invitation to the Ghana Mission."

(CO 1031/4758)

The report of the intelligence committee for January 1964 states:

> "3.Another fresh development was the start of a series of arson incidents in the sugar industry apparently aimless but causing considerable damage."

(CO 1031/4758)

The appendix to the report above would show that for the period 11th January 1964 to 3rd February 1964 war was in fact declared on Booker plantations. The geography of the attacks was as follows: Skeldon, Felicity, Mon Repos, La Bonne Intention, Mon Repos-Lusignan, Vrgheidlust, Rose Hall, Albion, Providence, Port Mourant, Uitvlugt, Enmore- Strathspey, Enmore- Enterprise, Enterprise, Blairmont. For the period of the report the west wing of the Leonora factory was torched and some 433 acres of cane were burnt. It was then a strategy of the PPP that called out the British colonial overlord by destroying British property but it did not engage the British military. It was then flawed and destined to fail which it did as general elections under the new electoral system were held on 7th December 1964.

The Governor's intelligence report dated 26th March 1964 states:

> "The partial failure of the strike has led to acts of terrorism by GAWU and PPP activists. The most recent and tragic of these occurred on the evening of March 23 when a grenade was thrown into a bus taking children of senior employees at Enmore from school. One child has died from his injuries while two of the other ten who were injured are in a serious condition. Cuban trained PYO extremists appear to be taking matters into their own hands."

(CO 1031/4758)

The children of managers of the Booker Estate were now under attack demanding a British response.

> "13. The Cuban, Ginez Gorriz Castroman, who arrived in British Guiana for two days on the 17 and 18 March has visited British Guiana on two previous occasions, in July and September 1963. He has been identified as Cuban Intelligence Service agent. Gorriz was in touch with Clinton Adlum and PPP and GIMPEX personalities visited the ship while it was in port."

(CO 1031/4758)

The Cubans are now moving in and out of the colony raising the temperature of the cold war engagement.

The report of the intelligence committee for February 1964 states:

> "On 4 March an incendiary bottle was thrown into the back of a truck carrying workers into Albion Estate and an African and an Indian, both non strikers, died from their injuries. On 6 March an African drove his tractor into a GAWU organised group of squatters on a bridge at Leonora Estate, injuring several; Alice Kowsilla, an Indian huckster who had no real connection with the strike died from her injuries. The GAWU had found its martyr."

(CO 1031/4758)

The opening acts of violence against persons resulting in a loss of life were all interpreted as race cleansing and were in fact acts of race war. The path to race war was now being etched on the landscape of the cane belt.

> "the strikers were practically all Indian and many of the workers African: any confrontation of the two elements had in it the seeds of racial conflict. On 9 March an Indian was killed in Berbice in an argument involving men of both races; on 13 March there were three cases of Africans being attacked by Indian strikers in East Coast Demerara, and on the same evening there was a disturbance at Springlands involving 400 Africans and Indians which necessitated police intervention."

(CO 1031/4758)

The attempts to enforce the strike were in fact interpreted as race attacks and involved race attacks which became the basis for race war.

The Governor's intelligence report dated 31st July 1964 states:

"2.The Secret and Personal Report covers approximately three month of mounting racial tension and increasing inter communal violence. During the first month (March 19-April 20) 4 persons lost their lives and 75 others were injured; between April 20 and May 21 8 people were killed and 139 injured; while during the last month ending June 22, 36 persons died as a result of disturbances and a further 263 were wounded.

3.Indicated that Cuban trained PYO trained extremists were largely responsible for carrying out the acts of violence and organising terror in support of the GAWU's quest for recognition. These same activists were equally prominent in terrorist activities during the period covered by this report, but their aims became more far reaching.

6.Reports received about the end of May from several secret sources indicated that the PPP was planning to carry out attacks on the persons and property of prominent members of the United Force, members of the Portuguese community and expatriates. Fires which were set in the houses of four well known UF families early in June were almost certainly the first fruits of this plan.

10.Since the establishment of a fairly frequent shipping service between British Guiana and Cuba, British Guiana has become one of the recognised ways for Communists from the Western Hemisphere to enter and leave Cuba.

The detention on June 13 of 36 persons connected with the organisation of violence brought about an immediate but only temporary improvement in the security situation. Terrorist activities were recommenced about a week later and after Mrs. Jagan had been observed on several occasions late at night at points on the East Bank and East Coast Demerara. With the possible exception of the attack on East Indians at Wismar, none of the incidents attributable to non East Indians shows any sign of organisation by the opposition parties whose interests are seen to lie in the holding of elections as soon as possible.

Much of the determination to segregate into racial communities along the coast may well spring from the desire of the PPP to be in a better position to influence East Indians prior to the general elections."

(CO 1031/4758)

The Governor's report fingers Mrs. Jagan as a major player in the terrorist agenda of the PPP and he indicates that roundups of functionaries did not remove the head of the PPP snake. The political leadership of the PPP was then leading the terrorist agenda utilising their offices in the government to cover their terrorist activities. The Governor attributes race cleansing as a means to political dominance failing to understand that racist hegemony drives the politics not the other way around and race cleansing is an instrument in the quest for racist hegemony. In the midst of the race war the colony has become a portal for travel to and from Cuba, a threat to US security that must be neutralised.

The report of the intelligence committee for the period 17th March 22nd June 1964 states:

> "6.Violence. The campaign of intimidation and terrorism attending the GAWU strike, and the recovery of a small armoury of automatic weapons, underlined the PPP's growing capacity for violence, and it was discovered that the party had at its disposal a cadre terrorist organisation with some training and experience, with arms and the ability to produce sabotage, and terrorist equipment, and with ambitions of insurgency.
>
> The worst phase of communal disturbance and terrorism on the West Coast Demerara was at a Negro family who were removing their household to another area; later in the same area, two other Negroes were wounded by gunfire probably by the same assailant. This led to a spiral of radical racial fighting which was only suppressed by massive employment of security forces and which continued sporadically until the end of May. Incidents during this phase, although by no means one sided, suggested that deliberate attempts were being made by Indians to provoke racial antagonism by selective attacks and the use in many cases of sophisticated weapons, not characteristic of normal spontaneous racial fighting. On 21 June three separate shooting attacks were made on a total of twelve negroes and Portuguese, killing one and wounding eight, on the East Coast Demerara; on 22 June, in the neighbouring Albany area, two Indians shot and killed a negro cattleman; in the night 22/23 June a gang of Indians raided the village of Perth-Mahaicony, setting fire to nine houses and opening fire with a machine- carbine on people coming to extinguish the fires- two negroes were killed and two others wounded. These incidents have clearly created the conditions for racial fighting in the area; the fact that they are premeditated, lacked justification, and were so close in time and location suggests the existence of a common plan.

b.Intimidation. Other incidents point to the use of terrorism as a means of lowering the morale of people who might have some influence on decisions about the colony's future: the bombing of a school bus at Enmore on 23 March resulting in one death and several wounded; the attempted murder of an anti PPP European newspaper proprietor near Georgetown on 1 April, the murder of an European at Springlands on 23 April; the attempted murder of a European estate manager near Leonora on 13 May, and the arson attack on the house of a senior civil servant in Georgetown in 12 June, resulting in the loss of eight lives."

(CO 1031/4758)

The Governor in his intelligence report dated 31ˢᵗ July 1964 reported on the PPP militia as follows:

"5.There have been a number of secret reports on the establishment of units of a PPP irregular army in widely separated parts of the country. The members of this organisation, known variously as the Guyana Liberation Army or the Guyana National Army, are required to take an oath of secrecy. About nine groups of an average strength of about ten members have been mentioned. None has so far been reported as fully trained and armed. Most members are selected from the ranks of the PYO but others who have no political affiliation are recruited on the basis of their reputations as thugs who will not hesitate to carry out acts of violence and brutality. This 'army' capacity for violence is covered in paragraph 7 of the Secret and Personal Report."

(CO 1031/4758)

On the attacks of the PPP militia on members of the UF, Portuguese Guyanese and expatriates the Governor in the said report states:

"It was almost certainly one of these fires that resulted in the death of Mr. Abraham and seven of his children."

(CO 1031/4758)

Mr. Abraham was a senior Guyanese civil servant at the time of the attack on his residence.

The report of the intelligence committee for the period 17ᵗʰ March to 22ⁿᵈ June 1964 states:

"7. Capacity for violence. The period showed an increase in the sophistication and complexity of terrorist weapons. The use of pipe bombs became commonplace, and there were joined by another simple bomb, made of a press top milk tin filled with a mixture of gelignite and scrap metals, fused with a five or ten second fuse and a commercial detonator. On 31 March a tin bomb was found at Uitvlugt, fitted with an electric detonator and batteries, fired through a timing device made from a cheap watch. On 9 May, near Leonora, an attack was attempted on a police land rover with a locally constructed electrically fired landmine. In mid June a bomb was found at the house of a detainee at La Jalousie, it consisted of a piece of large bore pipe, closed at both ends with welded caps, filled with home made powder with a high carbon content and fired by short length of fuse and a commercial detonator; the fuse ran through a delay chamber in the top of the bomb, presumably to prevent pre ignition."

(CO 1031/4758)

The said report of the intelligence committee continues:

"16. The PNC and violence. The party was concerned avoid any action which would cause delay in the election process. It was reported that in many areas party canvassers urged restraint on the African population to limit outbreaks of racial fighting, but such advice was not always popular, and it appeared that Burnham was having increasing difficulty in maintaining his authority; it was suspected that his advisers-Claude Graham and Hugh Cholmondeley-were counselling some kind of violent response. A round of incidents which started on the East Coast about 20 May probably owed something to African initiative and on 24 May, responding as in the past to events in the coastal strip, the African population in Wismar fell upon the Indian minority; before the disturbances came to an end a hundred and sixty houses and seventeen shops, mainly Indian and Chinese property, had been destroyed, four people lost their lives, and approximately fifteen hundred Indians were evacuated to Georgetown. Political inspiration in the Wismar incident has not been established and it is likely that the development was inevitable, but there is some reason to believe that some impetus was given to it by the PNC. Reports were received of a local PNC member, previously named as a supplier of explosives to the PNC, visiting Georgetown shortly before the disturbances to ask for help; he was also named in connection with the storage of incendiary material at Wismar."

(CO 1031/4758)

The report of the intelligence committee for March 1964 states:

"One of the worst episodes was the clearly premeditated bombing of a bus carrying children of the senior staff of Enmore Estate on 23 March 64. A number of children sustained injuries, some of them serious and permanent, and one child died. The choice of weapon-a service hand grenade-and the conduct of the attack left little doubt that it had been directed specifically at that target-a bus load of children."

(CO 1031/4758)

The bombing of the school bus on the 23rd March 1964 was carried out at Annandale. On the 15th April 1964 in the course of a bomb attack on the house of Victor Downer a known criminal, an Indo Guyanese, and PPP/GAWU activist was killed in the explosion.

The report of the intelligence committee for the month of April 1964 states:

"4.Incidents. Violence changed its aspect from arson and sabotage to intimidation and terrorism, and persistent attacks by strikers against workers and would be workers produced the expected deterioration into racial fighting. This development was concentrated mainly on West Demerara, but spread at times to other parts of the colony; in West Demerara it led to Indian and African minorities taking their own measures of segregation and removing to villages of their own race."

(CO 1031/4758)

By April 1964 the strategy was no longer to cripple the operations of the Booker Estates hence the cane belt but to now race cleanse the cane belt. In March 1964 there was a change of Governor Richard Luyt replaced Ralph Grey on the 7 March 1964. The nature of the intelligence reports changed dramatically becoming politically driven. Clearly Luyt was the player briefed and sent in to attain the British exit strategy as he so did in 1966. The reporting of the intelligence committee also changed dramatically as the activities of the PPP/PYO were detailed whereas before the Head of Special Branch played political games with the Minister of Home Affairs, with his departure the move to breaking political bones was apparent. Clearly this was the end time for the PPP.

The report of the intelligence committee for April 1964 states:

"21.The development of racial violence out of the sugar labour dispute has been discussed above. This was to some extent predictable; each of the unions has its own racial appeal, and it was inevitable that Africans would be brought in to redress the absence of part of the Indian labour force. The ferocity of the attacks by strikers on workers, however, and the sophisticated nature of some of the weapons involved is a departure from the normal conduct of an inter union dispute, whatever its degree of acrimony.

The use of firearms in the dispute commenced on 14th April, when a shotgun was fired at an estate land rover at Uitvlugt, and on 19th April five Africans were wounded by shotgun fire at Uitvlugt and Meten-Meer-Zong. Between 16-19th April there was a total of twenty-eight racial incidents in the Leonora- Uitvlugt area resulting in six Africans and seven Indians being admitted to hospital; one Indian subsequently died, and in the following days there were more racial incidents and attacks on the property of workers, both Indian and African, involving the use of home made bombs, and incendiary devices; one tactic was to set fire to a house and shoot at the people coming to fight the fire; among the victims of this were a police inspector and a sergeant of rural constabulary-both wounded. In many cases the races segregated themselves into larger racial groups. On the morning of 10th May, at Meten-Meer-Zong a negro was shot dead while on his usual morning walk to work, for no apparent reason."

(CO 1031/4758)

The report indicates that for April 1964 there were thirty incidents involving the use of firearms in the coastal strip with one death and seven wounded. For the same period there were thirty one incidents involving the use of explosives with one death and two persons injured on the coastal strip. There were sixty four incidents of racial attacks where firearms and explosives were not used, thirty three by Indo Guyanese on Afro Guyanese and thirty one by Afro Guyanese on Indo Guyanese. The Afro Guyanese population were outgunned with a technological and population deficit in the coastal strip as a result they were being cleansed from the coastal strip. Both black races were then intent on confirming the worst fears of life in Guyana under Indo or Afro racist hegemony hence the nation of Guyana was still born on 26th May 1966.

At this juncture of the text the nature of British covert operations in specific areas of their anorexic empire on the road to independence must be placed in context. Covert operations were not at the behest of any specific exit strategy in a specific colony. Covert work served the wide political interests of Britain and the major concern was the creation of neo-colonial power relations in the post independence period that served British interests. MI5 assiduously monitored Kwame Nkrumah determining his intimate relations with members of the Communist Party of Britain and the Soviet Bloc whilst at the same time the British handed Ghana to Nkrumah on a silver platter. Nkrumah's dance with Communist operatives was irrelevant because he was the only candidate to hand Ghana to in the eyes of the British. The surveillance of Nkrumah would be of supreme strategic importance when the time came to remove Nkrumah from power in a post colonial Ghana. Surveillance is for the express need to create leverage over post colonial politicians.

The secret sources in British Guiana that the Governor speaks of are assets of MI5 within the political militias they are there not there to build prosecutable cases against these militias. Most likely the secret sources themselves are involved in the bombings, the arson, the murders and the racial attacks. MI5 does not care about law, order and morality as the target is access, influence and information that serve British interests after independence. The MI5 penetration of the PPP militia in 1964 means that MI5 wields influence in the PPP in 2009. Delicate sources do not swear to affidavits or testify in a court of law. They rise to the top by being cold and efficient at the roles they are given to serve the organisations they have penetrated. Those who died, those were maimed, injured and had their lives destroyed were all collateral damage to put Jagan and the PPP down in the general elections of 1964. And Jagan In his Incompetence as a strategist played into the British hands and in fact made the attainment of their exit strategy easier. In general elections under proportional representation the PPP did not need a race based voting bloc they now needed a multi racial voting bloc. Its response to the urban race terrorism of the PNC in 1962 and 1963 was to launch its brand of race terrorism in the coastal strip and elsewhere destroying the basis of a multi racial voter base large enough to dominate a general election based on proportional representation. The British both covertly/ overtly facilitated Jagan and the PPP's futile dance of self destruction for in the face of racist hegemony that drove all race groups and race based political parties in the colony a coalition to form a government between the PNC and the UF after the 1964 general elections was the key to the removal of the PPP. In this the American political elites delivered the knock out blow to the PPP.

The reader must also understand that the intelligence reports of the Governor are going to the Colonial Office and ultimately the Secretary of State for the colonies and eventually to the Prime Minister. The Governor's intelligence reports were constantly under scrutiny to verify its accuracy for the Governor was the arm of the British political elite in the colony and you do not lie to your personal overlord and survive within the structures of colonial governance. In the case of British Guiana from 1953-1964 MI5 reports directly to the Prime Minister and the Garrison Commander reports to the

Ministry of Defence and the Chiefs of Staff. Furthermore the Governor is the literal dictator of the empire presiding over the colony who is charged with ensuring the hegemony of the empire. The Governor who lies to the Secretary of State is removed as is the Governor that embellishes reality to persuade the Secretary of State to adopt a specific strategic path is eventually censored when failure to attain a given end is apparent. Governors were committed agents of empire at the frontline of the battle to exit the empire on British terms and conditions. The intelligence reports on the terrorist agenda of the PPP, PNC and UF in the colony are then accurate reports of reality for the British, a reality that the colonial overlord acted on and manipulated to their benefit enabled and empowered by the politicians and citizens of the colony trapped in a world premised on realities constructed by the ever pressing desire for racist hegemony and a social order derived from. Duly constituted by the white man's racist hegemony we have embraced racist hegemony as the greatest legacy bequeathed to us by the colonial overlord to this day.

The report of the intelligence committee for May 1964 states:

> "20.Incidents. During the period under review the sugar industry strike has lost its significance in the general situation. The state of unrest has now taken on the form of a fierce racial conflict between Africans and East Indians determined on both sides to bring about distinct racial communities.

> The methods used to achieve this are savage and brutal and in many instances fatal. The cause of this bitterness and attacks on each other have come about at first from Indian workers who resented the influx of Africans to take up employment at the various sugar estates. The Indians saw this as a means to defeat them from winning support for GAWU, and began to deter African workers by threats and other forms of intimidation at first, then later by acts of violence to person and property and terrorism. From 11 to 15 May, the WCD continued to be most turbulent area with the occurrence of incidents along the established pattern-arson, sabotage to communications, sudden clashes and shooting at the police."

(CO 1031/4758)

The assault on the Booker owned sugar industry in the colony revealed the non-existence of the possibility of mass action against the colonial overlord. In response to the strike Booker played its card replacing striking labour predominantly Indo Guyanese with Afro Guyanese. The PPP/PYO responded with terror and the British military was there to ensure that the action remained at the level of racist terrorism and race cleansing. The Indo Guyanese of the cane belt responded in a manner constituted by the colonial overlord that power was an entitlement and the enemy was the other black race, a position reinforced by racist terrorism unleashed by the PNC in 1962 and 1963 in Georgetown. The Booker strategy meant the end of the Booker presence in Guyana as it was inevitable that Burnham would move to end the Booker presence in Guyana given the power Booker wielded in stoking the race war of the 1960's.

The report of the intelligence committee for May 1964 presents descriptions of the race cleansing of specific villages as follows:

> "22. At 2230 hours on 16 May an African of Bachelor's Adventure East Coast Demerara who was employed as a watchman was shot at and seriously injured aback of Enterprise, ECD. The reaction at Bachelor's Adventure was almost immediate. On the morning of 17 May, groups of Africans moved about the area and assaulted several East Indians. This developed rapidly with clashes in the days following. The result was an East Indian woman was killed, several persons injured and complete destruction to the houses of several East Indians in the area. Tension remained high at the Bachelor's Adventure/ Enterprise areas and as is the pattern in other affected areas, East Indians, the minority group at Bachelor's Adventure, were constantly attacked by the Africans and forced to evacuate from there to Enterprise, a predominant Indian area, while Africans suffered a similar fate at Enterprise, as a minority.
>
> 23. On the night of 20/21 May two Africans, man and wife, were murdered at the back of Friendship on their farm. When the bodies were discovered on the morning of 22 May, tension rose immediately in Buxton and news spread rapidly to Georgetown. The Rosignol/Georgetown train was attacked soon afterwards and East Indian passengers were severely beaten. African vendors at the Stabroek and Buxton Markets whose homes are at Buxton assaulted some East Indians in the markets and then returned to Buxton. Racial disturbances then occurred in Georgetown where groups of Africans roamed the city attacking Indians. The attacks seemed in many cases to be linked with robbery."

(CO 1031/4758)

Two instances of race cleansing that created an entirely new landscape of settlements and race relations that have impacted the Guyanese social order to this day. This new landscape was the product of racist hegemony that was the foundation of colonial domination by the white Massa and it was racist hegemony embraced by the inmates of Massa's plantation and the desire of Massa to maintain hegemony in the post independence era that ripped asunder the old colonial racist order creating a post independence racist hegemony and its attendant racist social order. The apprentices of Massa proving that they were in the tradition of Massa ever clinging to his racist legacy.

The report of the intelligence committee for June 1964 states:

> "Acts of violence and the use of firearms became an established pattern and the present time there seems little likelihood of racial harmony, unless the leaders of the PPP and the PNC take much stronger action to control their extremist elements who are obviously prepared to bring about a state of anarchy."

(CO 1031/4758)

The Governors' intelligence report for the months July to November 1964 dated 22nd December 1964 states:

> "2. The period covered by the above mentioned reports has been eventful, encompassing as it does the culmination of the GAWU/PYO terrorist campaign, the retaliatory action by the PNC thugs, the gradual return of law and order and the pre election political campaign. Finally, since no reports were written, the election itself on December 7 which resulted in victory of the combined PNC and UF parties (22 seats and 7 seats respectively) over the PPP (24 seats) and the complete elimination of the four minor parties.
>
> 3. The progressive decline in lawlessness in the country can be ascribed to several factors. The two mentioned in the first paragraph of the 'Personal' report i.e. the end of the GAWU strike and the decision of the PPP to contest the election, albeit under protest, played a large part, but also a particular importance were the detention of 34 PYO and 2 PNC members in August. This action deprived the two major parties of the leaders of their 'strong arm' groups and other active political subversives.
>
> The withdrawal in July of firearms, other than revolvers, from the civilian population in all the disturbed areas and the largely spontaneous formation of Home Guards throughout the country were other factors which helped stop acts of violence.
>
> 4. The months of violence caused a marked degree of segregation along the coastal areas as members of the Indian and African communities sought refuge among their own kind. While this in itself helped to lessen interracial strife, it has caused other problems,

one of the most important being the creation of separate Indian and African schools in a number of areas."

(CO 1031/4758)

The Governor has to posit that colonial might won out over the terrorist actions of inferior races but there are realities that show otherwise. The violence in the cane belt married to a strike meant that whilst the terrorist violence was being unleashed on race enemies the workers were on the breadline and cane workers were the poorest in the colony. There was then extreme hardship over an issue that in the long run became trivial to daily survival. The early onslaught on workers who refused to strike and on labour brought in to break the strike was a lesson to keep the striking workers in line with the PPP/ PYO strategy. The racist terrorist attacks served PPP/PYO interests as it became apparent that there was now an African threat and this kept the PPP/PYO hegemony intact.

The racist terrorists did not attack the British military which meant that no energy was expended by the British military on self defence and assaults in their defence. This was not then an insurgency as the colonial state was never challenged. The Force BG simply bided its time to unleash the offensive premised on detentions which broke the back of the organised terrorist groups. This offensive was effective because the racist terror was aimed at race minorities in specific settlements in the coastal belt. The forced migration of race minorities to their kind then created less and less targets to attack which blunted the effectiveness of racist terror attacks. African and Indian dominated settlements were not viable targets for the racist terrorists indicating the fact that the racist terrorists were not committed to race cleansing as is the case of Bosnia/Herzegovina and genocide as in the case of Rwanda.

What the racist terrorists of British Guyana wanted to achieve remains a mystery as it is apparent from the study that hate rather than grand political strategy drove the actions. The PNC led by Burnham were the victors but the PNC was to pressure the colonial overlord to change the electoral system hence the PNC assaults on Georgetown. In the aftermath of October 1963 the PNC task was accomplished and the political agenda becomes paramount which was to form a coalition thereby defeating the PPP in the aftermath of the December 1964 election which Burnham and his American handlers did. The PPP on the other hand took the decision to force by terror the British to rescind the decision declared in October 1963. This was a stupid position to adopt as it lacked strategic clarity. The PPP did not have the means, the leadership and the international support to take on the British military and win.

The reality is that the PPP did not take on the Force BG as it first unleashed strikes in the cane belt, then sabotage of the Booker infrastructure, then terrorist acts on workers, then terrorist acts on managers, then blatantly racist terrorist attacks, but in all this in the coastal belt Force BG was left unscathed. In response Booker unleashed the race weapon hiring African labour to replace striking Indo labour and racist hegemony and its locomotive of hate gained momentum and ran riot. The racist terrorism was from the outset perpetuated on race minorities in the coastal belt forever changing the settlement landscape of the belt and in turn defeating the racist terrorist agenda. As the minorities fled to join single race settlements race garrisons were created in the midst of an Indo Guyanese dominated coastal belt. Race minorities became garrisoned and protected themselves upping the cost of terrorist assaults on newly formed garrisons. Force BG simply monitored and waited knowing fully well that the race garrisons had forever changed the terrain of engagement and then Force BG took control of the coastal belt from the police and moved to unleash search, seizure and detention and that was the end of the PPP/PYO terrorist agenda.

In response to this reality the PPP then entered the general elections race after mortally wounding its chances to win more than 24 seats under a proportional representation election system out of a total of 53 seats. The PPP racist terrorist strategy then backfired, failed miserably and left the PPP in opposition until 1992. To respond to PNC racist terrorism with PPP racist terrorism meant in effect that you threw away the ability to appeal to a multi racial voter base in an attempt to win enough votes to be allocated 29 seats. Race based voting only assured the PPP of 24 seats to win 5 extra seats meant a multi racial voting base and multi racial appeal. Jagan was totally myopic unable to foresee that the assaults on the MPCA and Booker were sterile, futile acts that cost the PPP the 1964 general elections. In addition there was no benefit derived from embracing Fidel Castro since he was using Jagan and the colony to create a proxy in his war with the Americans. Jagan heightened American resolve to remove him and placed the government of the Conservative Party of Britain in a very difficult position for their adamant position that Jagan and the PPP was the Party to hand an independent Guyana to. Jagan failed to see that changing the electoral system was the final play of the Conservative Government to keep the Cold War crusader President Kennedy at bay.

By November 1963 President Kennedy was dead and President Johnson was distracted. At this strategic juncture Jagan did everything in his power to prove to Johnson that he was a Cold War outpost for Cuban subversion of Latin America. Jagan worked under the mistaken assumption that he had powerful friends in the upper hierarchy of the British Labour Party in fact Jagan would be sold on the auction block to the Johnson Administration before the Labour Party assumed office. He failed to understand that it was the Labour Party that had a tract record of being unrepentant colonial imperialists as they did their best to keep the empire intact in the post 1945 era. Having failed to do so they were now offering British Guiana to the Americans as they wanted an effortless exit from the colony another miserable failure of perception by Jagan that cost Guyana. It was then incumbent upon Jagan to do what was necessary to win 29 seats in December 1964 and that meant dropping the Stalinist rhetoric, never embracing Fidel Castro but embracing Booker and DEMBA and leaving the TUC alone.

The PNC agenda would have sputtered as they became the party of violence and hate led by the supreme anarchist Burnham. It is my position that given the strategy outlined above that Burnham would not have resorted to racist terrorism but sought a coalition with the PPP. British interests would have ensured that the TUC toe the line and with victory at the general elections under proportional representation it was then incumbent upon the Americans to now invade Guyana to remove a government in which Jagan and Burnham were in leadership positions. The desire was for racist hegemony on all sides not for power/hegemony for the sake of domination. As a result the Guyanese nation was stillborn in 1966 and in 2009 it is a failed state. There was then no other path possible than the path adopted by the PPP, the PNC and the UF, the British and the Americans for the desire for racist hegemony drove the environment in which the strategies were applied. Race hate and terror then determined the path to independence and produced a stillborn Guyana on 26th May 1966.

The abiding lesson of this exercise is the intensity of the violence that flooded the colony in the period under study. The reports studied do not tally the number of murders in the period, injuries, the losses to property damaged and destroyed and the number of internally displaced persons forced to build and live in refugee housing. The social and economic order paid a high price and this was the basis for the strangulation of newly independent Guyana, Burnham's policies after 1966 simply finished off a mortally wounded economic order. What is most disturbing is the hate unleashed, the hate made manifest that is driving race relations in Guyana to this day as it continues to push politics in Guyana in racist hegemonist terms. From 1992 to today it is clearly apparent that successive PPP Presidencies are trapped in a 1960's time warp where they are bent on implementing the PPP strategy of governance from 1953 to 1964. Governance for the PPP is settling old scores with adversaries that exist only within the collective mind of the PPP and this has enabled the PPP to form coalitions with their drug trafficking financiers in the execution of 21st century PPP racist hegemony. Is PPP time now!! The PPP is then the lapdog of illicit drug traffickers and Guyana is now a narco trafficking state tottering on narco trafficking failed state status.

I end with this quotation from the report of the intelligence committee for August 1964 as it expresses poignantly hate, race hate. The report states:

> "Between 21-29 August, East Indian gunmen in ambush killed seven Africans, one on the West Coast of Berbice, and six Africans in Mahaicony/Abary Area. The incidents caused a mounting tension in the areas especially at Mahaicony. Later there were rumours about groups of Indians in the Mahaicony planning to attack Africans and this may have some connection with the incident at Branch Road, Mahaicony on the night of 23 August, where Africans shot and killed seven East Indians in their homes. A feature in this attack with the general pattern of violence, is that it is directed against families and Indians suspected to be implicated in murders committed previously on Africans."

(CO 1031/4758)

With this level of terror and race hate made manifest how do you live together and interact to build an independent Guyana?

BIBLIOGRAPHY

Trinidad and Tobago

"Report of the British Caribbean Federal Capital Commission" Colonial Office London 1956

"HANSARD of the Legislative Council of Trinidad and Tobago"

Hylton Edwards, S (1982): Lengthening Shadows Birth and Revolt of the Trinidad Army" Trinidad Inprint Caribbean Limited

Solomon, Patrick (1981): "Solomon: an Autobiography." Trinidad Inprint Caribbean Ltd

Williams, Eric (1969): "Inward Hunger" UK Andre Deutsch

British Declassified Files

CO1031/127, CO 1031/1804, CO 1031/1805, CO 1031/1972, CO 1031/1548, CO 1031/2490, CO 1031/2491, CO 1031/2594, CO 1031/3718, CO 1031/3719, CO 1031/3720, CO 1031/3774, CO 1031/3775, CO 1031/3555, CO 1031/1301, CO 1031/2595, CO 1031/2154, CO 1031/2209, CO 1031/4078, CO 1042/404, DO 200/84, FCO 63/603, FCO 63/858, FCO 63/859.

Guyana

Birbalsingh, Frank (2007): "The People's Progressive Party of Guyana 1950-1992: An Oral History" UK Hansib Publications

Reports

"Report of the British Guiana Constitutional Commission 1954 (The Robertson Commission Report)" Editor: Dr. Odeen Ishmael 2004

"Report of the Commission of Inquiry into the Disturbances in British Guiana in February 1962 (The Wynn Parry Report)" Edited by Dr. Odeen Ishmael 2003

"Report of the Wismar, Christianburg and Mackenzie Commission 1965 (The Wismar Report)" Edited by Dr. Odeen Ishmael 2004

American Declassified Files

"Foreign Relations 1961-1963 Volume 12"
Office of the Historian, US Department of State
"Foreign Relations 1964-1968 Volume 32"
Office of the Historian, US Department of State
CIA Declassified Files
"Special Report Cross Currents in British Guiana 6 December 1963"
"Special Report British Guiana Approaches a Critical Election 20 November 1964"
British Declassified Files
"The Suspension of the British Guiana Constitution-1953 (Declassified British Documents)" Edited by Dr. Odeen Ishmael 2004
"The British Declassified Files on British Guiana-1958-1963" Edited by Dr. Odeen Ishmael 2004
CO 968/750, CO 968/751, CO 968/752, CO 1031/4495, CO 1031/4757, CO 1031/4758, CO 1035/173, CO 1035/194, CO 1035/195.